16LIVES
JOHN MACBRIDE

The 16LIVES Series

JAMES CONNOLLY Lorcan Collins

MICHAEL MALLIN Brian Hughes

JOSEPH PLUNKETT Honor O Brolchain

EDWARD DALY Helen Litton

SEÁN HEUSTON John Gibney

ROGER CASEMENT Angus Mitchell

SEÁN MACDIARMADA Brian Feeney

THOMAS CLARKE Helen Litton

ÉAMONN CEANNT Mary Gallagher

THOMAS MACDONAGH Shane Kenna

WILLIE PEARSE Roisín Ní Ghairbhí

CON COLBERT John O'Callaghan

JOHN MACBRIDE Donal Fallon

MICHAEL O'HANRAHAN Conor Kostick

THOMAS KENT Meda Ryan

PATRICK PEARSE Ruán O'Donnell

DONAL FALLON – AUTHOR OF 16LIVES: JOHN MACBRIDE

Donal Fallon is a lecturer and historian based in Dublin. Co-founder of the popular social history website 'Come Here To Me', his previous publications include *The Pillar: The Life and Afterlife of the Nelson Pillar* (New Island, 2014). He is currently completing a PhD on republican commemoration and memory in 1930s Ireland.

LORCAN COLLINS – SERIES EDITOR

Lorcan Collins was born and raised in Dublin. A lifelong interest in Irish history led to the foundation of his hugely-popular 1916 Walking Tour in 1996. He co-authored *The Easter Rising: A Guide to Dublin in 1916* (O'Brien Press, 2000) with Conor Kostick. His biography of James Connolly was published in the *16 Lives* series in 2012. He is also a regular contributor to radio, television and historical journals. *16 Lives* is Lorcan's concept and he is co-editor of the series.

DR RUÁN O'DONNELL – SERIES EDITOR

Dr Ruán O'Donnell is a senior lecturer at the University of Limerick. A graduate of University College Dublin and the Australian National University, O'Donnell has published extensively on Irish Republicanism. Titles include *Robert Emmet and the Rising of 1803*, *The Impact of 1916* (editor), *Special Category, The IRA in English prisons 1968–1978* and *The O'Brien Pocket History of the Irish Famine*. He is a director of the Irish Manuscript Commission and a frequent contributor to the national and international media on the subject of Irish revolutionary history.

16 LIVES

[illegible]CBRIDE

Donal Fallon

THE O'BRIEN PRESS
DUBLIN

First published 2015 by
The O'Brien Press Ltd,
12 Terenure Road East, Rathgar,
Dublin 6, D06 HD27, Ireland.
Tel: +353 1 4923333; Fax: +353 1 4922777
E-mail: books@obrien.ie.
Website: www.obrien.ie

ISBN: 978-1-84717-270-9

Series concept: Lorcan Collins

8 7 6 5 4 3 2 1
18 17 16 15

All quotations, in English and Irish, have been reproduced with original spelling and punctuation.

Printed and bound by CPI Group (UK) Ltd, Croydon, CR0 4YY
The paper used in this book is produced using pulp from managed forests.

PICTURE CREDITS

The author and publisher thank the following for permission to use photographs and illustrative material: front-cover portrait of John MacBride and back-cover image of Boer group courtesy of the Kilmainham Gaol Collection; inside-front Boer War illustration © The Image Works/TopFoto.
Photo section one: p1 (top) courtesy of Dublin City Library and Archive; p1 (bottom), p5 (bottom right), p7 (top) and p8 (bottom) courtesy of the Kilmainham Gaol Collection; p3 (top) © The Image Works/TopFoto; p7 (bottom) courtesy of the MacBride family, p8 (top) courtesy of the National Library of Ireland.
Photo section two: p1 courtesy of the MacBride family; p2 and p3 (top and bottom) courtesy of the National Library of Ireland; p4 (top left) courtesy of Shay Brady; p4 (top right) courtesy of Lorcan Collins; p4 (bottom left) and p6 (top) courtesy of the Kilmainham Gaol Collection; p5 (top) © 2000 Topham Picturepoint; p5 (bottom) courtesy of Luke Fallon; p6 (bottom) and p7 (top) courtesy of the Irish Capuchin Provincial Archives, Dublin; p7 (bottom) courtesy of the National Museum, Collins Barracks.

DEDICATION

To my parents, Las and Maria. I owe so much to you both

ACKNOWLEDGEMENTS

As the *16 Lives* series nears its conclusion, I want to thank Lorcan Collins and Ruan O'Donnell for inviting me to participate in this exciting project. The series of books is a very meaningful contribution, and indeed a lasting one, to the centenary of the 1916 rebellion.

Historians can only hope to add to the existing body of work on any subject, and in the case of Major John MacBride, a few researchers deserve particular praise for the works from which this study drew upon. Firstly, Donal P. McCracken has done hugely important work on the Irish and the Second Boer War, and indeed on the history of the Irish Diaspora in South Africa. Anthony J. Jordan has brought important primary source materials on MacBride to the public awareness, and has drawn attention to the presence of the MacBride papers in the National Library of Ireland, when they were discovered hidden away in the papers of veteran Fenian Fred Allan. The *Cathair na Mart* journal, which celebrates the local history of Westport and its environs, has also played an important role in telling the story of the MacBride family.

I owe enormous gratitude to all at The O'Brien Press, and to Aoife Barrett of Barrett Editing. Her insights and hard work played no small part in shaping this book. My family have been very helpful and supportive throughout, as they always are, and the encouragement of my parents has always driven me forward.

The staff at various archival institutions and libraries, in particular the Dublin City Library and Archive, the National Library of Ireland and the National Archives of Ireland, continue to do great work in the face of endless cutbacks to their services. It is a joy to research history in Ireland when these institutions, and others like them, are in the hands of people who are passionate about the collections they hold. Long may that stay the case.

My co-workers (or co-walkers) at Historical Walking Tours of Dublin deserve mention. It is a joy to work alongside people who are passionate about history. I am eternally grateful to Tommy Graham for taking me on. Likewise, Trevor White and all in The Little Museum of Dublin deserve thanks for the great support they have shown to me. Ciarán Murray and Sam McGrath of the 'Come Here To Me' website, which I co-founded, are two of the best friends anyone could ask for and keepers of Dublin's history in their own way.

Lastly, my partner Aoife deserves a special mention. She has listened to me talk of nothing but Boers, Fenians, poets and rebellion for quite some time now. She is my anchor, and brings me great joy in life.

Go raibh maith agaibh go léir.

16LIVES Timeline

1845–51. The Great Hunger in Ireland. One million people die and over the next decades millions more emigrate.

1858, March 17. The Irish Republican Brotherhood, or Fenians, are formed with the express intention of overthrowing British rule in Ireland by whatever means necessary.

1867, February and March. Fenian Uprising.

1870, May. Home Rule movement founded by Isaac Butt, who had previously campaigned for amnesty for Fenian prisoners.

1879–81. The Land War. Violent agrarian agitation against English landlords.

1884, November 1. The Gaelic Athletic Association founded – immediately infiltrated by the Irish Republican Brotherhood (IRB).

1893, July 31. Gaelic League founded by Douglas Hyde and Eoin MacNeill. The *Gaelic Revival*, a period of Irish Nationalism, pride in the language, history, culture and sport.

1900, September. *Cumann na nGaedheal* (Irish Council) founded by Arthur Griffith.

1905–07. *Cumann na nGaedheal*, the Dungannon Clubs and the National Council are amalgamated to form *Sinn Féin* (We Ourselves).

1909, August. Countess Markievicz and Bulmer Hobson organise nationalist youths into *Na Fianna Éireann* (Warriors of Ireland) a kind of boy scout brigade.

1912, April. Asquith introduces the Third Home Rule Bill to the British Parliament. Passed by the Commons and rejected by the Lords, the Bill would have to become law due to the Parliament Act. Home Rule expected to be introduced for Ireland by autumn 1914.

1913, January. Sir Edward Carson and James Craig set up Ulster Volunteer Force (UVF) with the intention of defending Ulster against Home Rule.

1913. Jim Larkin, founder of the Irish Transport and General Workers' Union (ITGWU) calls for a workers' strike for better pay and conditions.

1913, August 31. Jim Larkin speaks at a banned rally on Sackville (O'Connell) Street; Bloody Sunday.

1913, November 23. James Connolly, Jack White and Jim Larkin establish the Irish Citizen Army (ICA) in order to protect strikers.

1913, November 25. The Irish Volunteers founded in Dublin to 'secure the rights and liberties common to all the people of Ireland'.

1914, March 20. Resignations of British officers force British government not to use British army to enforce Home Rule, an event known as the 'Curragh Mutiny'.

1914, April 2. In Dublin, Agnes O'Farrelly, Mary MacSwiney, Countess Markievicz and others establish Cumann na mBan as a women's volunteer force dedicated to establishing Irish freedom and assisting the Irish Volunteers.

1914, April 24. A shipment of 25,000 rifles and three million rounds of ammunition is landed at Larne for the UVF.

1914, July 26. Irish Volunteers unload a shipment of 900 rifles and 45,000 rounds of ammunition shipped from Germany aboard Erskine Childers' yacht, the *Asgard*. British troops fire on crowd on Bachelors Walk, Dublin. Three citizens are killed.

1914, August 4. Britain declares war on Germany. Home Rule for Ireland shelved for the duration of the First World War.

1914, September 9. Meeting held at Gaelic League headquarters between IRB and other extreme republicans. Initial decision made to stage an uprising while Britain is at war.

1914, September. 170,000 leave the Volunteers and form the National Volunteers or Redmondites. Only 11,000 remain as the Irish Volunteers under Eóin MacNeill.

1915, May–September. Military Council of the IRB is formed.

1915, August 1. Pearse gives fiery oration at the funeral of Jeremiah O'Donovan Rossa.

1916, January 19–22. James Connolly joins the IRB Military Council, thus ensuring that the ICA shall be involved in the Rising. Rising date confirmed for Easter.

1916, April 20, 4.15pm. *The Aud* arrives at Tralee Bay, laden with 20,000 German rifles for the Rising. Captain Karl Spindler waits in vain for a signal from shore.

1916, April 21, 2.15am. Roger Casement and his two companions go ashore from U-19 and land on Banna Strand. Casement is arrested at McKenna's Fort.

6.30pm. *The Aud* is captured by the British navy and forced to sail towards Cork Harbour.

22 April, 9.30am. *The Aud* is scuttled by her captain off Daunt's Rock.

10pm. Eóin MacNeill as chief-of-staff of the Irish Volunteers issues the countermanding order in Dublin to try to stop the Rising.

1916, April 23, 9am, Easter Sunday. The Military Council meets to discuss the situation, considering MacNeill has placed an advertisement in a Sunday newspaper halting all Volunteer operations. The Rising is put on hold for twenty-four hours. Hundreds of copies of *The Proclamation of the Republic* are printed in Liberty Hall.

1916, April 24, 12 noon, Easter Monday. The Rising begins in Dublin.

16 LIVES MAP

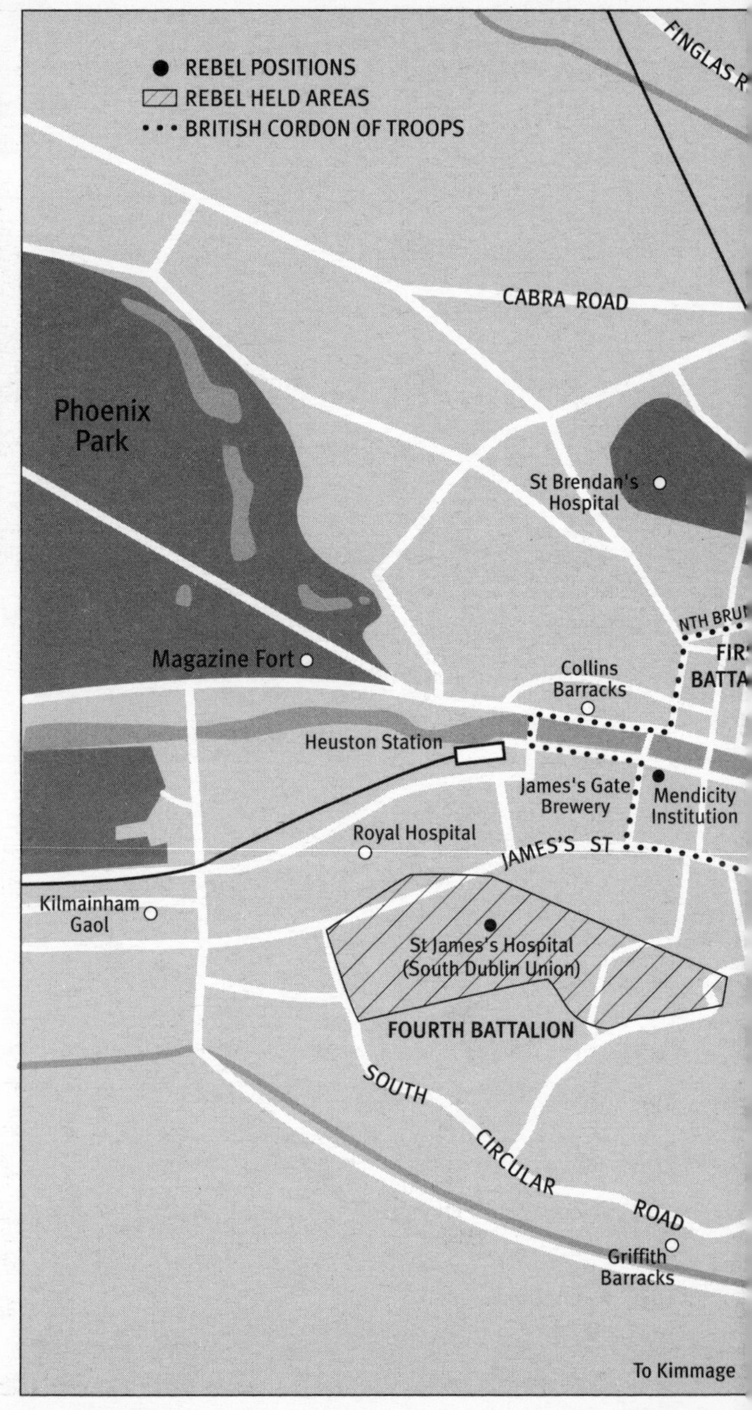

REBEL POSITIONS
REBEL HELD AREAS
BRITISH CORDON OF TROOPS
CABRA ROAD
Phoenix Park
St Brendan's Hospital
Magazine Fort
Collins Barracks
Heuston Station
James's Gate Brewery
Mendicity Institution
Royal Hospital
JAMES'S ST
Kilmainham Gaol
St James's Hospital (South Dublin Union)
FOURTH BATTALION
SOUTH CIRCULAR ROAD
Griffith Barracks
To Kimmage

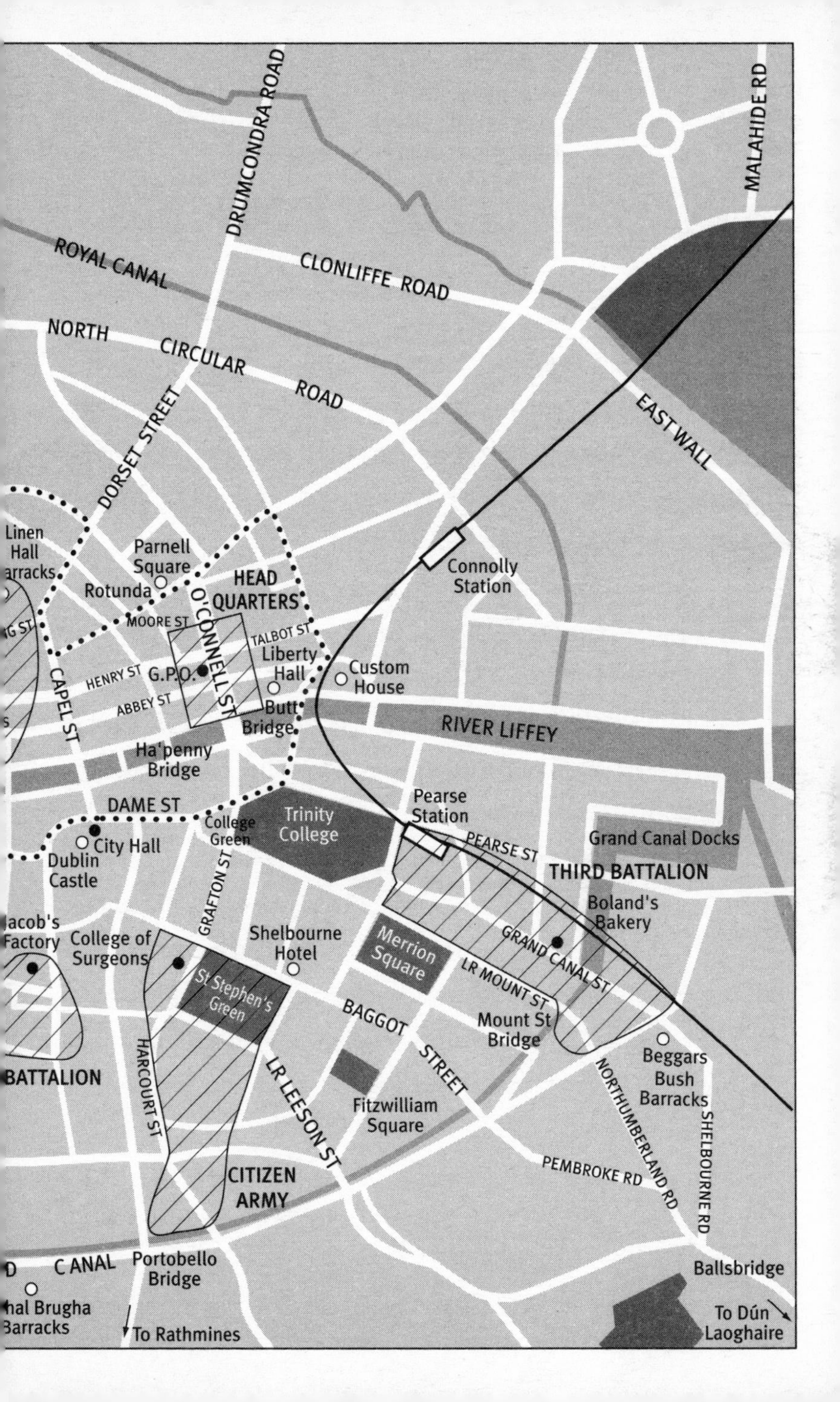
DRUMCONDRA ROAD
MALAHIDE RD
ROYAL CANAL
CLONLIFFE ROAD
NORTH
CIRCULAR
ROAD
DORSET STREET
EAST WALL
Linen
Hall
Barracks
Parnell
Square
Rotunda
HEAD
QUARTERS
O'CONNELL ST
MOORE ST
TALBOT ST
Liberty
Hall
Custom
House
Connolly
Station
HENRY ST
G.P.O.
ABBEY ST
CAPEL ST
Butt
Bridge
RIVER LIFFEY
Ha'penny
Bridge
DAME ST
College
Green
Trinity
College
Pearse
Station
PEARSE ST
City Hall
Dublin
Castle
Grand Canal Docks
THIRD BATTALION
Boland's
Bakery
GRAFTON ST
Jacob's
Factory
College of
Surgeons
Shelbourne
Hotel
Merrion
Square
GRAND CANAL ST
St Stephen's
Green
LR MOUNT ST
BAGGOT
STREET
Mount St
Bridge
Beggars
Bush
Barracks
BATTALION
HARCOURT ST
LR LEESON ST
Fitzwilliam
Square
NORTHUMBERLAND RD
SHELBOURNE RD
PEMBROKE RD
CITIZEN
ARMY
CANAL
Portobello
Bridge
Ballsbridge
Barracks
To Rathmines
To Dún
Laoghaire

16LIVES – Series Introduction

This book is part of a series called *16 LIVES*, conceived with the objective of recording for posterity the lives of the sixteen men who were executed after the 1916 Easter Rising. Who were these people and what drove them to commit themselves to violent revolution?

The rank and file as well as the leadership were all from diverse backgrounds. Some were privileged and some had no material wealth. Some were highly educated writers, poets or teachers and others had little formal schooling. Their common desire, to set Ireland on the road to national freedom, united them under the one banner of the army of the Irish Republic. They occupied key buildings in Dublin and around Ireland for one week before they were forced to surrender. The leaders were singled out for harsh treatment and all sixteen men were executed for their role in the Rising.

Meticulously researched yet written in an accessible fashion, the *16 LIVES* biographies can be read as individual volumes but together they make a highly collectible series.

Lorcan Collins & Dr Ruán O'Donnell,
16 Lives *Series Editors*

CONTENTS

Introduction

At the beginning of the twentieth century, when many of the leaders of the Easter Rising were still relatively unknown figures on the peripheries of Irish political and cultural life, the name Major John MacBride was already becoming familiar in Ireland, and indeed to the Irish nationalist Diaspora.

MacBride was part of a small band of armed men known as the 'Irish Brigade', *uitlanders* (or foreigners) in the Transvaal. During the Second Boer War (1899–1902) they had taken up arms to fight against what they saw as British imperial aggression in South Africa. Transvaal flags flew in the breeze in Dublin and tens of thousands demonstrated across the island in sympathy with the Boer cause. It was a war that sparked something in nationalist Ireland, and moved W. B. Yeats to write, 'the war has made the air electrical just now.'[1]

W. B. Yeats plays a significant part in the story of John MacBride. Though the two knew little of one another in person, they moved in the same nationalist circles, were both disciples of the veteran Fenian John O'Leary and, most crucially, both fell in love with the nationalist campaigner Maud Gonne. The popular image of John MacBride today has been derived from Yeats and his poem 'Easter 1916', in which

MacBride assumes the role of a 'drunken, vainglorious lout'. Gonne would write that the poem was 'not worthy of Willie's genius, and still less of the subject.'[2]

The marriage of John MacBride and Maud Gonne was, in a single word, disastrous. Relatives of each, and indeed influential Irish nationalists, had urged the two not to marry. During their divorce case, allegations of violence, drunkenness and sexual impropriety were levelled against MacBride, though of these only drunkenness was found against him in court. The bitter separation that followed left MacBride estranged from his wife and distant from his young son Seán. They remained in France while MacBride returned to Ireland. In recent years the discovery of John MacBride's papers in the collections of Fenian leader Fred Allan has enabled historians and biographers to re-examine the disastrous marriage and the controversial separation that followed. Deposited in the National Library of Ireland (NLI), the papers give crucial new insights into a traumatic chapter in the lives of both Gonne and MacBride.

John MacBride had little doubt that he would be executed for his role in the Easter Rising, even though he was not a member of the Irish Volunteers, and most likely stumbled across the insurrection by a degree of chance on 24 April 1916. Having taken up arms in the conflict in South Africa, he knew his past would stand against him. He was proved correct.

General Sir John Maxwell, the British general sent to Dublin to suppress the insurrection, wrote to Prime Minister Herbert Asquith in the aftermath of the Rising. He began the justification for MacBride's execution by stating, 'This man fought on the side of the Boers in the South African war of 1899 and held the rank of Major in that Army, being in command of a body known as the Irish Brigade.'[3] Maxwell was himself a veteran of the same Boer War in which MacBride had fought.

John MacBride was duly executed on 5 May 1916, when he was placed in front of a firing squad in the stone-breakers' yard of Kilmainham Gaol. This biography sets out to demonstrate that MacBride was an altogether more complex figure than the caricature of the man depicted in both the poetry and studies of the period has allowed him to be. It seeks to look at the context in which MacBride emigrated to South Africa, showing the emergence of a separatist Irish nationalist community there, even before the outbreak of the Second Boer War in 1899. It examines the separation of MacBride and Gonne in detail and also examines MacBride's return and readjustment to Ireland in the aftermath of that sad affair, in a period when great change was underway. Lastly, it draws on the testimony of the men and women who were there in 1916 and who fought alongside MacBride, to demonstrate that the leadership skills he developed in South Africa were apparent during that very eventful week on the streets of Dublin.

Chapter 1

The Development of a Young Fenian

> His great-grandfather took part in the insurrection of 1798; his grandfather followed the fortunes of the Young Irelanders who first struggled for the establishment of an Irish parliament and ultimately drifted into revolution; his father and uncles were members of the Irish Revolutionary Brotherhood of 1867 … Irish patriotism was therefore, so to say, in his blood.[4]

While preparing for his bitter and public separation from Maud Gonne, John MacBride penned the above words in a brief autobiography for his legal team. While the blood of Fenianism certainly flowed in MacBride's veins, it came not from his father but rather from his mother, Honoria Gill's, side. John MacBride's father, Patrick, was in fact the captain of a merchant schooner. He was of Ulster-Scots Protestant heritage and hailed from Glenshesk in Antrim. Patrick had settled in Westport and married into the respected Gill family in the mid-nineteenth century. They were the years when the Quay of Westport was alive with ships and commerce, bringing men like Patrick to the town. In the 1960s John Davis O'Dowd, a relative of John MacBride, would recall the Quay's former glory:

> If you ever go down the Quay Hill to the Custom House and look down that half-mile, or more, of desolation, you will have some conception of the sadness it brings to one who saw it over seventy years ago, when the tall ships lined the Quay.[5]

Though earlier than O'Dowd's recollections, the Quay was bustling too in the time of John MacBride's arrival. Born on 7 May 1868, John was the youngest of five children. Blessed with a head of red hair, 'Foxy Jack', as John would become known, was the 'child' of the family. MacBride's elder siblings were all boys, and the brothers would lead interesting and varied lives, though they shared one thing in common – all held strong nationalist convictions. Joseph, the eldest of John's brothers, was eight years his senior. He would find work with the Harbour Commissioners, later becoming a Sinn Féin TD in 1918 and remaining active in Irish politics throughout his life. Anthony would become an important figure in the Irish republican movement in London, establishing himself as a Doctor there before later returning to Ireland where he continued his medical pursuits. His achievement in passing the Royal University Degree Examination in Medicine in 1889 was reported in the *Connaught Telegraph*, indicating the standing of the family locally. It congratulated the son of the respected Honoria MacBride of Westport Quay 'on his successful collegiate course, which is highly creditable to a genial man so young.'[6] John's third brother, Francis, emigrated to Australia, while Patrick eventually assumed control of the family business in Westport.

MacBride's mother Honoria was a woman who was of strong Mayo stock, and one of nine children herself. Two of her cousins had taken part in the doomed Fenian rebellion of 1867. Éamon de Valera would praise her while speaking in the town at the unveiling of a plaque to John MacBride in 1963:

> It is said that there is an island in Clew Bay for every day of the year. That may be so, but for John MacBride there was one island in particular: Island More. His mother's people came from Island More. She was Honoria Gill: a truly remarkable woman, forceful, kind, but always masterful. There was a strong Fenian tradition in the Gill family. James Stephens, the Fenian, was a friend. Martin Gallagher who married a Gill was the Head Centre of the Fenians in Mayo; he made a spectacular escape to America and later took part in the Fenian invasion of Canada in 1870.[7]

At only thirty-five-years of age, John MacBride's father Patrick died of typhus in 1868, leaving Honoria with both the raising of the family and the maintenance of the family business. To lose her husband in the same year as the birth of her youngest son left Honoria in a difficult position but the family operated as a wholesale grocer, described also as a 'tea, wine and spirit merchant' and she managed to keep the business going. It remained a commercially successful enterprise that allowed Honoria to educate her children well and to give her sons a degree of comfort in life.

Honoria would ultimately outlive her youngest son, passing away in 1919, having taken the news of his execution with great dignity. She also lived to see Joseph, elected as the first Sinn Féin TD for the constituency in the 1918 elections. At the time of her death, the high regard in which she and her family were held was evident from the outpouring of local grief. The Castlebar Board of Guardians passed a resolution of sympathy, and one member of the board noted that 'I have known the MacBride family for many years and I can say that there is not a more respected family in Mayo.'[8]

The MacBride's business thrived in John's early years as Westport in the nineteenth century stood in stark contrast to more impoverished areas of Mayo. It had once been the seat of the Marquis of Sligo, who owned an extraordinary estate of 114,881 acres, making it the largest estate in Mayo and one of the largest on the island. The county was devastated by the famine of the 1840s and poverty remained a fact of life for many in Mayo in subsequent decades.

In 1879 *The Freeman's Journal* reported that in a summer of intense weather and misery 'the two props of the Mayo farmer's homestead have collapsed miserably upon his head. The potatoes are bad – the turf is worse.'[9] Westport itself became the staging ground for significant agitation from the poor and landless, with thousands gathering on the edge of the town to hear Charles Stewart Parnell speak in June of that same year. Despite the meeting being condemned in no uncertain terms by the Catholic Archbishop of Tuam, John MacHale, there was much anger among the Mayo poor that day, enough to ignore clerical denunciation and attend the rally. The people listened as Parnell urged them that 'you must show the landlords that you intend to keep a firm grip on your homesteads and lands. You must not allow yourselves to be dispossessed as you were dispossessed in 1847.'[10] Also addressing the meeting was Michael Davitt, a native of Mayo, who would become synonymous with the 'Land War' in Ireland and the battle of the rural peasantry and landless for better rights as tenants. The crowd also listened to militant speakers such as the Fenian Michael M. O'Sullivan, who informed them that 'moral force' had to be backed up by 'the power of the sword'[11].

While the messages of class discontent resonated with the poor of the county and province on that June day, the

MacBride family were of a different stock, as small business owners in the town. John was educated firstly by the Christian Brothers in Westport, before attending St Malachy's College in Belfast. The oldest Catholic grammar school in Ulster, St Malachy's was established in the 1830s in the wake of Catholic Emancipation. Former graduates included Sir Charles Gavan Duffy, a founding member of the radical newspaper *The Nation* in the 1840s, while Eoin MacNeill, one of the founders of the Gaelic League and a man who would come to play no small part in the story of the 1916 Rising, was a contemporary of MacBride's. The school, it has been noted, 'was long regarded as the jewel in the crown of Catholic education in the town, producing future clerics and professional men alike.'[12] While St Malachy's College was a Catholic institution in a predominantly Protestant city, there does not appear to have been much nationalistic feeling among the student body. Patrick McCartan, later a member of the Supreme Council of the IRB, attended the school in the 1890s and remembered:

> I wouldn't say there was much nationalism there. I did not see any signs of nationalism amongst the students. There was one professor who started a branch of the Gaelic League there, named O'Cleary. He was not much good as a teacher, as a matter of fact, very bad, because he used to do more talking than teaching during class hours.[13]

Work opportunities for the young John, as a teenage graduate of St Malachy's, came firstly via his family connections. They helped arrange an apprenticeship for him with John Fitzgibbon, a draper based in Castlerea, County Roscommon. MacBride claimed in his brief autobiographical sketch that it was as a young man of fifteen that he 'took an oath to do my best to establish a free and independent Irish nation', and that by the time he had arrived in the capital he was 'associated with the party known as 'Advanced Nationalists', a term used to describe those whose nationalism favoured a republican approach, which stood in contrast with the constitutional nationalism of the Home Rule movement. [14]

The oath to which MacBride referred to taking at this point in his life was, of course, the Fenian oath of the Irish Republican Brotherhood (IRB), a secret, oath-bound society which strove to bring about an independent Irish republic. Variations of this oath had been in place since the establishment of the IRB in March 1858, and it was a pledge MacBride would prove faithful to, a promise to do all in his power to establish the independence of his country:

> I, John MacBride, in the presence of Almighty God, do solemnly swear allegiance to the Irish Republic, now virtually established; and that I will do my very utmost, at every risk, while life lasts, to defend its independence and integrity; and, finally, that I will yield implicit obedience in all things, not contrary to the laws of God, to the commands of my

superior officers. So help me God. Amen'.[15]

There is evidence that MacBride did involve himself in radical nationalist activities during his time in Castlerea, despite being only in his mid-teens. Michael J. Cassidy, a native of Castlerea and a contemporary of MacBride, would comment decades later:

> I remember the late Mr Fitzgibbon telling me during the Boer War that MacBride was an extreme nationalist when he worked as an apprentice in his shop. When I went to serve my time in Castlerea I met from time to time a number of the old Fenians and heard from them that MacBride, during his apprenticeship years, was very active organising the Brotherhood. During the Boer War his name was constantly mentioned in Castlerea.[16]

Fitzgibbon himself had nationalist political sympathies. He was active in his lifetime within the Gaelic League and the Land League movement, and became a United Irish League MP for South Mayo in 1910. MacBride spent some time working for Fitzgibbon in Castlerea, though by the apprentice draper's own admission, 'not finding that occupation congenial I left it and went back to St. Malachy's for another year. After leaving St. Malachy's I entered into the employment of Hugh Moore.'[17]

In Dublin, Hugh Moore maintained a wholesale druggists and grocer, and MacBride would spend several years with the firm, on and off. Years after his time in the Dublin chemist, a rather dismissive account of MacBride's work there appeared in the magazine *The Chemist and Druggist*, essentially an in-house publication for those in the industry. When MacBride secured a degree of notoriety by fighting alongside the Boers in South Africa, a March 1900 edition of the magazine gloated:

> When our correspondent was in Messrs. Hugh Moore & Co. drug-department MacBride came to the house from his mother's shop in Westport (co. Mayo), which is a grocers, and he was put into the sundry-department, the stock there consisting only of grocery goods, such as coffee, biscuits, confectionery tinned meats etc. He never served an hour to the drug-trade, and in our correspondent's opinion he would not know 'the difference between Epsom salts and powdered opium'.[18]

The presence of a young, sixteen-year-old John MacBride is noted in the minute books of the Young Ireland Society (YIS), Dublin. Young Ireland was an organisation which troubled Dublin Castle authorities greatly as they believed it to be little more than a front for the Irish Republican Brotherhood (IRB). On paper it was a nationalist literary and debating society, which publicly stated its goals as being to promote an interest in Irish literature, culture, history and debate. The premises of the YIS were raided by the Dublin

Metropolitan Police on the day following its opening, indicating that the authorities were deeply troubled by the organisation's very being.[19]

Participation in the Young Ireland Society and the cultural nationalist movement around it brought John MacBride into contact with a wide variety of nationalists, with differing opinions, including John O'Leary, Arthur Griffith and William Butler Yeats.

O'Leary was a veteran of the struggle and would become an important figure in MacBride's life. The Tipperary native had certainly played his part in the Fenian movement, having spent years in English prisons and later in exile in the 1860s and 1870s. An unapologetic defender of armed separatism for much of his life, O'Leary would recall in his memoirs of the Fenian movement that:

> Nations, any more than individuals, live not by bread alone. It was a proud and not undeserved boast of the Young Irelanders that they 'brought back a soul into Éire', but before Fenianism arouse that soul had fled. Fenianism brought it back again, teaching men to sacrifice themselves for Ireland instead of selling themselves and Ireland to England.[20]

If O'Leary was something of an elder statesman to the separatist movement, and an important inspiration to young activists such as John MacBride, it is important to note that O'Leary's politics had evolved and changed with time. Indeed, even as he recalled his own political sentiments above, his political ideology had long since moved to a more comfortable centre. It has even been argued that he had become a 'conservative … who favoured a constitutional monarchy.'[21] O'Leary has perhaps best been defined as 'a monument to an antique style of nationalism'.[22] The veteran nationalist John Devoy recalled that 'he thought there was so little difference between a moderate Republic and a liberal limited Monarchy.'[23]

O'Leary as a symbol and O'Leary as a contemporary political voice appear to have been two very different things. It was telling that John MacBride and Maud Gonne would later ask him to be the godfather of their son, indicating their respect for the aging figure and that they viewed his approval and indeed association with him as important. To a detective of Dublin Castle, O'Leary was 'an old crank full of whims and honesty'[24], but Irish historian and academic Roy Foster has suggested that for many O'Leary represented 'a voice from the heroic past', and that to William Butler Yeats he was an introduction to 'the acceptable face of the extremist Fenian tradition'.[25] In his autobiography, Yeats recalled of O'Leary that 'he had the moral genius that moves all young people and moves them the more if they are repelled by those who have strict opinions and yet have lived commonplace lives'.[26] O'Leary's influence over individuals such as MacBride and Yeats would prove hugely significant, and it was the elder statesman who would later introduce MacBride to the important US Fenian leader John Devoy.

Aside from the Young Ireland Society, another organisation John MacBride was active within when he moved to Dublin was the Gaelic Athletic Association (GAA). He had involved himself in it with vigour during his youth in Mayo, and there was a real commitment to the organisation from the MacBride family. Joseph later served with the Connaught Council of the GAA and was elected as its President at its inaugural meeting in Claremorris in November 1902. In many ways the GAA served as both a sporting outlet and a social one for its membership, with very clear political undertones. Founded in 1884 by Michael Cusack, the organisation had approached Charles Stewart Parnell, Michael Davitt and Archbishop Croke of Cashel to serve as patrons. As W. F. Mandle has noted, this was a cunning move, as:

> Virtually the whole spectrum of Irish nationalist politics was covered by the three, none of whom, apart possibly from Croke, who professed an admiration for handball, could be accounted sporting identities or having sporting interests. The political role and the political implications of the GAA were set from the start.[27]

To Archbishop Croke, the GAA would serve as a boulder against the increasing Anglicisation of Irish society. He warned that:

> We are daily importing from England, not only her manufactured goods ... but together with her fashions, her accents, her vicious literature, her music, her dances and her manifold mannerisms, her games also and her pastimes, to the utter discredit of our own grand national sports ... as though we are ashamed of them.[28]

British authorities closely monitored this new organisation from its infancy. A Dublin Castle report from 1888 noted that 'the question was not whether the association was a political one, but only to what particular section of Irish national politics it could be annexed.'[29]

If the GAA was as much about political ideology as it was sporting endeavour, then this was clearly reflected from the very beginning, and indeed in the prehistory of the body. As Eoghan Corry has suggested, there were also strong class dimensions to the formation of this new body, as historically athletic sports in rural Ireland tended to fall under the patronage of local landowning elites and aristocrats.[30] In 1879, five years before the formation of the GAA, class tensions became clear in Mayo when the nationalist Patrick Nally organised an athletics programme at Balla which stood in stark contrast to the traditional athletics events held in the town, where Sir Robert L. Blosse served as patron. At these new games, Charles Stewart Parnell was a listed patron, and the games were attended by up to 2,000 people, with banners reading 'God Save Ireland' and 'Pay Not' in the crowd.

Nally's experiment at Balla was repeated the following year, with the MacBride brothers in attendance.[31] Nally would be central to the formation of the GAA a few years later, meeting Michael Cusack in 1881. In addition to his sporting interests, Nally was a nationalist firebrand. He was a leading figure in both the Land League and the Irish Republican Brotherhood in Mayo and spent three months in Manchester in the winter of 1880, making arrangements to import 300 rifles into Mayo.[32]

Nally became Connaught IRB leader and he was a familiar figure to nationalist families in Mayo like the MacBride household. His activism saw him and six other IRB men arrested in May 1883. He was charged with membership of a criminal secret society, leading to his imprisonment for a period of ten years. Nally had also been charged with conspiracy to murder, based on the evidence of a man named Andrew Coleman, who claimed that he was also a member of the IRB. Coleman insisted that Nally had been planning the assassination of a landlord agent in Mayo. Owing to a fear of public outrage, Nally's trial occurred not in Castlebar but rather in Cork, and as Owen McGee has noted 'the belief that Nally was completely innocent was widespread', and his sentencing to ten years imprisonment created great resentment among the nationalist people of Mayo.[33]

Nally's family, and the nationalist community of Mayo, believed that he suffered ill-treatment during his incarnation.

Only days before his release in November 1891 Nally died in Mountjoy Prison, reportedly of typhoid fever, though many blamed the conditions in which he had been held. Owen McGee has noted 'there was a large attendance at his funeral, including eleven members of parliament as well as leaders of the GAA and the IRB. As a symbolic gesture, his coffin was covered with the same green flag that had covered Parnell's coffin the previous month.'[34]

Among those to march in Nally's funeral procession was John MacBride. He had also taken part in the funeral of Parnell in October 1891, on that occasion as a member of the GAA. During that incredible show of nationalist strength, the men of the GAA each carried a hurley draped in black, held in reverse as if to resemble a rifle, and marched through the streets of the capital to Glasnevin Cemetery, Dublin. There, not far from the round tower of Daniel O'Connell, Parnell was laid to rest. One contemporary account noted that 'stout burley fellows all ... they marched six abreast with splendid military precision ... the Gaels raised their camáns aloft and a wail rose from the people.'[35]

Involvement in a range of nationalist organisations provided the young John MacBride with a social and political purpose. By the mid-1890s MacBride was serving on the executive committee of the Young Ireland League which had emerged out of the Young Ireland Society and was in many ways an umbrella organisation for such bodies. The

Young Ireland movement of cultural and literary societies was sizeable, with about 2,000 men affiliated to around a dozen branches of the body nationwide.[36]

MacBride also attended meetings of the Celtic Literary Society. Established in 1893, it was an organisation which included many of the individuals who were active in the Young Ireland Society. It was largely driven by the passion of Willie Rooney, a prominent journalist and nationalist who had been born in a Mabbot Street tenement in the heart of inner-city Dublin. The area around Mabbot Street is infamous in Irish history and Dublin folklore as the Monto, a red-light district which existed in the crumbling shells of eighteenth-century splendour, with the Georgian buildings of old becoming the decayed brothels and slums of the late nineteenth century. Rooney's humble tenement beginnings contrast greatly with the middle class youth of MacBride. While Mabbot Street was certainly a world away from the family business on The Quay of Westport and MacBride's years in a Belfast boarding school, the two young nationalists shared a devotion to such literary societies, even though some republican activists questioned if such societies could truly impact politically.

The Celtic Literary Society met at 32 Lower Abbey Street, and placed great emphasis on Irish cultural expression and the native language. Rooney edited *An Seanachuidhe,* the journal of the society, and his influence over it is clear from the memories of J. J. O'Kelly. Known as the writer *Sceilg,* Kelly penned several important nationalist historical articles, and recalled:

> Willie Rooney was the backbone of the Celtic Literary Society .... He had a wonderful aptitude for poetry and, in the matter of general information, was a regular encyclopaedia. I often heard him say: 'If anyone has any doubt about that, he will find it on page so-and-so of such-and-such a book.' In his zeal for a thorough mastery of Ireland's history, he burned himself out: of that, there can be no doubt. There was hardly a weekly meeting of the Society at which he did not lecture brilliantly or speak at some length.[37]

Rooney's name is largely forgotten today but protagonists of the period recall him as an immensely important figure. Augustine Ingoldsby, secretary of Cumann na nGaedheal from 1898, remembered that 'great credit is due to Rooney, Griffith and their followers for keeping up the opposition to the shoneenism and Union Jackery of the vast majority of the population.'[38] While it was certainly a severe exaggeration to claim that the 'vast majority' of the populace in Dublin engaged in pro-British rituals, Ingoldsby's recollections show how those active in the period recalled Rooney and Griffith.

The Celtic Literary Society had emerged from the earlier Leinster Literary Society, but it has been noted that 'both were small and marginal. Their membership was young and lacked the political connections, especially with the Irish Parliamentary Party, characteristic of organisations with similar concerns, such as the Fenian Young Ireland Societies of the 1880s or the Gaelic League.'[39] If these emerging movements did lack political connections or influence, they were still significant as they brought like-minded people into contact with one another. With people such as Arthur Griffith, John O'Leary and others moving throughout these various cultural nationalist movements, it is clear that in MacBride's case organisations such as The Celtic Literary Society helped to forge political unions and personal friendships which would remain in place for years to come, and prove influential in the development of advanced nationalism.

As Irish republican politics evolved throughout the 1890s, various individuals sought to guide what was a broad movement. MacBride found himself joining the Irish National Alliance (INA) in 1895, a body sometimes referred to as the Irish National Brotherhood (INB). It has been described as 'a radical organisation comprised of old Clan na Gael renegades, traditionalist Fenians, a resurrected cabal of Invincibles, and a London-centered association of regular IRB dissidents.'[40] Essentially, the INA was a short-lived offshoot of the Irish Republican Brotherhood (IRB), with Dr Mark Ryan of London the central figure in the emergence of the new body on this side of the Atlantic. The split had its origins in power struggles within the American Fenian movement, which would ultimately produce the Irish National Brotherhood, claiming the lineage and role of the Irish Republican Brotherhood.

Dr Ryan is an important figure in the life of MacBride. It was allegedly with Ryan that MacBride would re-take his Fenian oath in his mid-twenties, years after first taking it as a teenager in the west of Ireland. Ryan recalled the event in his memoir *Fenian Memories*, a wonderfully colourful and vivid account of a life devoted to Irish nationalism. Twenty years after John MacBride's execution, his brother, Dr Anthony MacBride was present at a ceremony in honour of Dr Ryan at the Mansion House in Dublin. Also present were Éamon de Valera, Seán T. O'Kelly, ITGWU Secretary William O'Brien and W. T. Cosgrave. The audience was indicative of the broad respect for Ryan across the political spectrum, reflecting both sides of the Civil War divide of 1920s Irish politics.

Anthony MacBride claimed that he first met Dr Ryan when he went to the Fenian leader as a young medical assistant in London and that the two had never lost contact. Anthony noted that John 'did not think his initiation by him [Anthony] into the Fenian movement was enough', indicating that it was from his elder brother that John first took the Fenian oath as a fifteen-year-old. According to Anthony his brother 'insisted on going to London' to take the Fenian oath from Dr Ryan and that this 'was an instance of the influence Dr Ryan exercised on Irishmen with whom he was brought into association.'[41]

From his autobiographical notes John MacBride appears to have been a significant figure in the short-lived Irish National Alliance in Dublin. He recalled that he travelled as a delegate from Ireland to the Irish National Alliance Convention held in Chicago in 1895. The American media reported on events at the convention in detail, with the *Los Angeles Herald* noting that the following motion was 'submitted and met with instantaneous approval at the hands of the convention':

> That this convention recommends the formation of military companies wherever practicable, in order to foster and preserve the military spirit of the Irish race and to be prepared for action in the hour of England's difficulty.[42]

In the aftermath of the convention, a representative of the Irish National Alliance informed the press that:

> The new organisation will concentrate the efforts of the Irish race and unite the Irish people all over the world for one object – Irish independence. It will become the ally of any power with which England may become involved, and will aid any such power with men and money in order to weaken England's prestige and curb her arrogance.[43]

While the Alliance would ultimately prove a short-lived split from the IRB, the organisation's ideological approach, of supporting those beyond Ireland's shores who were at war with England, is certainly something which would later influence John MacBride to go to South Africa to take up arms against the British state.

Joseph MacBride, still residing in the west of Ireland, also appears to have involved himself in the activities of the Irish National Alliance. An 1896 police report on him noted that his mother 'is a grocer and publican in the town of Westport, and also deals in dynamite detonators. Until recently MacBride never took an active part in Secret Society work. He is now believed to be actively engaged in furthering the Irish National Alliance.'[44]

Travelling to the United States and participating in the INA conference brought unwanted attention however. John claimed that 'on my return from the United States to Dublin I resumed my position in Hugh Moore's and I was regarded as the best protected man in Ireland at the time as I would not be able to go about anywhere without having a brace of detectives on my heels.'[45]

Despite the intense surveillance from the Dublin Metropolitan Police (DMP) and Castle authorities, MacBride remained politically active, and involved himself with the Amnesty Association. Dr Ryan claimed that 'before leaving for South Africa he had been a member of the Irish Executive of the Association.'[46]

The Amnesty Association campaigned for the rights of Irish political prisoners, and Dr Ryan recalled:

> As a result of steady agitation, we succeeded in securing visits to the prisoners, of whom there were eighteen when we started our branch of the Amnesty Association ... With John Redmond, M.P., I visited Portland, and saw some of the prisoners, including Tom Clarke and John Daly. Some of our members also saw other political prisoners, whose treatment we brought before the public through questions and debates in Parliament and reports of our meetings in the press.[47]

When political prisoners were released from prison, they were often greatly traumatised by their experiences. Dr Mark Ryan recalled that when for example Dr Thomas Gallagher was released from Portland Prison, having been arrested alongside Thomas Clarke in relation to the Dynamite Plot, he was in poor health, both physically and with regards his mental health. The Dynamite Plot, which was an intensive campaign of bombings that brought carnage and terror to the streets of London and other British cities between 1881 and 1885, had led to the imprisonment of leading Fenian activists in British prisons. Of Gallagher, Ryan remembered:

> On their release in 1896, Dr. Gallagher was found to be insane .... Owing to the serious condition of Dr. Gallagher,

> we sent Dr. Anthony MacBride from the Amnesty Association in London to accompany him to America, where the unfortunate man was committed to an asylum.[48]

While the authorities may have been closely monitoring John MacBride and his activities with the Amnesty Association, and thus regarded him as a person of significant threat, he was not destined to remain in Ireland at this point. Perhaps the unwanted attention of intelligence police officers was a contributing factor in the young man's decision to leave Ireland. J. J. O'Kelly, who knew the young MacBride, would recall that 'my feeling now is that John was a young chemist, and that the reason he went to Africa was that he did not care about Dublin and thought he would like to go abroad. I feel sure he told me more than once, but it made no lodgement in my memory.'[49] It is, however, important to acknowledge that MacBride's enthusiasm for political activism in Dublin stands in stark contrast with O'Kelly's claims.

J. J. O'Kelly may have believed it was a sense of wanderlust that led the young man towards South Africa, but MacBride himself would later claim it was political aspirations. Certainly, MacBride was not the only young Irishman of his generation to set sail for South Africa, and he would waste little time in establishing himself there as an important figure in Irish nationalist circles.

Chapter 2

The Irish and South Africa: Migration and Agitation

Walking up Dublin's Grafton Street, a visitor will see the impressive commemorative arch at St Stephen's Green coming into view. Known in local lingo as 'Traitor's Gate', the monument is often mistakenly believed to be a memorial to Irishmen who fought in the ranks of the British armed forces in the First World War. In reality, it commemorates an earlier conflict, largely forgotten in the city today. Funded by public subscription, the arch serves to remember Irishmen who gave their lives fighting in the uniform of the Royal Dublin Fusiliers during the Second Boer War. Unveiled in 1907, and modelled on the Arch of Titus in Rome, Fusilier's Arch cuts an imposing shape in a city that has few remaining imperial monuments on any grand scale. One side of the monument bears the marks of another dramatic event in Irish history, as during the Easter Rising the Arch was peppered with machine-gun fire from the guns mounted on the rooftops of neighbouring buildings. Traitor's Gate is a permanent reminder of the intersections of Irish and South African history in the early twentieth century.

Whatever his motivation, John MacBride left Dublin in 1896 and travelled to South Africa to join the Boers in their fight against the British in the Second Boer War. Much of the folk memory and historical discourse around MacBride has centered on this period of his life, and in particular on his involvement in military activities there. To understand just what may have drawn him, and other young Irishmen, to a country which was not traditionally associated with mass Irish emigration it is necessary to review the South African political situation MacBride emigrated into in the 1890s.

It is important to note that the Boer Wars were two separate armed conflicts: the First Boer War was fought during 1880–1881; and the Second Boer War took place from 1899–1902. The motivating source of the conflicts can be essentially attributed to colonial tensions in the region between Britain and the Boer population of South Africa. The word 'Boer' is Afrikaans for farmer, and the origins of the later conflicts can be traced right back to the beginning of the Cape Colony in 1652 when it was established by the Dutch East India Company. The first Europeans to settle at the Cape were the forefathers of a people who became known as the Afrikaners. The historian Gregory Fremont-

Barnes has noted:

> By the early 18th century these farmers, or Boers, had developed a dialect of Dutch which, over time, developed into Afrikaans, and a new race of people – Afrikaners – came into being. Some of them populated the area around Cape Town, but most lived in isolated farmsteads on the veld, living hard, frugal lives based on Dutch Calvinism and a fierce individualism. The land was, in their view, theirs by the grace of God.[50]

The colony was seized by Britain in 1806, during the Napoleonic wars. It was formally annexed in 1815, creating a very real tension between the Afrikaners and their new British authorities. This ultimately led to what became known as the 'Great Trek', a period of mass-migration beginning in the mid-1830s which saw many people of Boer origin leaving the Cape Colony in favour of the establishment of independently ruled Boer Republics. 'The Trek' brought about new tensions, as it 'constituted a deliberate and organised migration and settlement, not in open or unoccupied land, but in an area that had long known settlement by a variety of Nguni and Sotho-Tswana peoples.'[51] While the Boers were escaping a colonial power, they would find that in the land they seized the native people would come to see them in much the same light as the Afrikaners viewed the British, as the Boers in their turn became a colonising force.

It has been estimated that between 1836 and 1840, 4,000 'Voortrekkers' set out north from the Cape Colony on the 'Great Trek'. They were divided between those who would settle in the Transvaal and those who would attempt settlement in Natal, leading to violent confrontations with Zulu tribespeople. The Orange Free State, or *Oranje-Vrystaat*, was formally founded in 1854, while the South African Republic was established in 1856.

The First Boer War was fought from 1880–1881 and has also been named the Transvaal Rebellion, as the Boers of the Transvaal revolted against a British annexation of 1877, which was deeply resented. In Afrikaans, the war is known as the *Eerste Vryheidsoorlog*, meaning the 'First Freedom War'. The conflict ultimately resulted in the British agreeing to complete Boer self-government in the Transvaal, though under British suzerainty. It was a significant blow to British imperial efforts, and the war received great media attention in Ireland, not least in the nationalist press. *The Nation* reported with glee that 'British arms do not seem to be making any great headway in the Transvaal. The sturdy Boers are more than holding their own.'[52] *The Irish World* proclaimed that the Irish should give thanks to God, as 'the Boers … are fighting the battle of Ireland, although they don't know it.'[53]

Yet despite the sympathetic coverage in Irish nationalist media, much of what was written about the Boers in the newspapers of the Britain and Ireland was far from complimentary, with the Boers often presented as an uncivilised and unruly people. One popular account of the First Boer War in Britain noted that the Afrikaners were filled with a 'land hunger, to which that of the Irish peasant is a weak and colourless sentiment', and went on to boldly state about the typical Boer:

> Perhaps, however, the most striking of all his oddities is his abhorrence of all government, more especially if that government be carried out according to English principles. The Boers have always been more or less in rebellion; they rebelled against the rule of the Company when the Cape belonged to Holland, they rebelled against the English Government in the Cape, they were always in a state of semi-rebellion against their own Government in the Transvaal, and now they have for the second time, with the most complete success, rebelled against the English Government.[54]

The period leading up to the Second Boer War, between 1880 and 1900, was defined by the clash of two men, Cecil Rhodes and Paul Kruger, and their bitter struggle for control of southern Africa. Kruger, elected President of the Transvaal Republic in December 1880, stood in great contrast to Cecil Rhodes, a British mining magnate and Prime Minister of the British Cape with imperial ambitions. In 1895, Rhodes launched a disastrous invasion of the Transvaal, known as the Jameson Raid (named after a lieutenant of Rhodes). Rhodes had confidently predicted: 'I will win and South Africa will belong to England.'[55] In secret correspondence, Cecil Rhodes claimed that the Jameson Raid would be the 'big idea which makes England dominant in Africa, in fact gives England the African continent.'[56] Ultimately, the doomed raid, which saw several hundred armed men spill into the Transvaal with the intention of beginning an insurrection, served only to heighten tensions in the region, and destroyed any lingering hope of Boer-British harmony. It was a colossal military failure from a British perspective and Kruger used the heightened political climate created by the raid as a rationale for the importation of arms and munitions for self-defence.

A significant factor in the tensions of the region, and in the decision to launch the doomed Jameson Raid, was the issue of gold. It was something that was at the forefront of public discourse on South Africa, and which would remain there, particularly following the Witwatersrand Gold Rush of 1896, a year on from the Jameson Raid. It has been argued that after the British defeat in the First Boer War 'Transvaal affairs might have continued without British interference indefinitely had gold not been discovered in extraordinary quantities at the Witwatersrand.'[57] This gold rush 'led to a flood of foreign prospectors – known to the Boers as *Uitlanders* (outsiders) – arriving into Kruger's territory and to the birth of the boom-town of Johannesburg.'[58] It was undoubtedly the gold rushes of the region which attracted migrant labourers in significant numbers, including Irish labourers, whose absence had been noted in earlier decades. In 1876, *The Cape Town Daily News* had commented:

> We are afraid we could not induce the Irish labouring classes to come to this colony in anything like sufficient numbers. They know nothing of it beyond having a dim idea that it is associated with Kaffir wars; but they know all about America and Australia, or think they do, having heard them talked about from their infancy by those who had friends there.[59]

The *Uitlanders* who arrived in 1896 to work in the new territory had many restrictions placed on them by the Boers, for example with regards voting rights. There was a belief among Rhodes and other authorities that with these *Uitlanders* constituting about half the population of the Transvaal, dissatisfaction with Boer rule would be rife among them. Rhodes believed this was something which, given time, could create a coup situation, allowing the British to seize control.

Certainly, there were very real tensions between the Boers and the foreign outsiders based in the mining communities. Writing in 1900, Arthur Conan Doyle, a writer undoubtedly best remembered for his creation Sherlock Holmes, described how the discovery of gold had a dramatic impact on the population of the region:

> It was a field for elaborate machinery, which could only be provided by capital. Managers, engineers, miners, technical experts, and the tradesmen and middlemen who live upon them, these were the *Uitlanders,* drawn from all races under the sun, but with the Anglo-Celtic vastly predominant. The best engineers were American, the best miners were Cornish, the best managers were English, the money to run the mines was largely subscribed in England.... Soon the population of the mining centres became greater than that of the whole Boer community, and consisted mainly of men in the prime of life – men, too, of exceptional intelligence and energy.[60]

Doyle later remarked that the Boers proved 'the most formidable antagonist who ever crossed the path of Imperial Britain. Our military history has largely consisted in our conflicts with France, but Napoleon and all his veterans have never treated us so roughly as these hard-bitten farmers.'[61]

Perhaps it was Britain's defeat in the early 1880s, or the 1895 Jameson Raid fiasco, that motivated Joseph Chamberlain, speaking to the British House of Commons in May 1896, to warn:

> A war in South Africa would be one of the most serious wars that could possibly be waged. It would be in the nature

> of a civil war. It would be a long war, a bitter war, and a costly war .... It would leave behind it the embers of a strife which I believe generations would hardly be long enough to extinguish.[62]

Donal P. McCracken has noted that while there was no mass Irish migration to South Africa even during the gold rush, Dublin Castle was aware from the mid-1890s that some 'advanced Irish nationalists', a term frequently used to describe those who believed in the physical force tradition, were making for the Transvaal Republic. According to his research, 'by 1896 there were about 1,000 Irish living in the mining settlement of Johannesburg as well as others in Pretoria and in more far-flung corps, such as Middelburg.'[63]

While English mining settlers were more likely to be hostile to Kruger and the Boers, there is evidence of Irish sympathies resting with their cause and sharing a belief of opposition to British colonialism. In Johannesburg, a noticeable increase in political activity among Irish migrants, coupled with the emergence of haunts and meeting places favoured by the Irish, was evidence of a growing and vocal community.

In September 1896 South Africa had representation at the Irish Race Convention in Dublin. It was a convention which drew 2000 delegates to hear speakers at Leinster Hall, with organisations from Glasgow Celtic Football Club to Catholic bodies in North America represented. While the South

African representation was drawn from moderate nationalist opinion, and not the 'advanced nationalist' elements, there was considerable Irish interest in the delegates. The official report of proceedings noted:

> Among those in whom the greatest interest was centered at the great Convention in Dublin was Mr Moses Cornwall, Kimberley, South Africa. Coming as he did from that distant land, whose name is not very familiar in Irish homes, and which sounds to Irish ears more distant than in reality it is, his every word was listened to with rapt attention.[64]

Recalling the reasons for his own migration to South Africa, MacBride would claim that 'shortly after the Jameson Raid, I resolved to go to the South African Republic as I knew that England had her mind made up to take the country, and I wanted to organise my countrymen there, so as to be in a position to strike a blow at England's power abroad when we could not, unfortunately, do so at home.'[65]

On his arrival in South Africa in 1896, MacBride aligned himself with a body known as the Irish National Foresters. A branch had been established in Johannesburg that same year and named in honour of Theobald Wolfe Tone. This body had begun life as one broadly sympathetic to the cause of Home Rule for Ireland, though it ultimately drifted towards radical separatism.

The departure of well-known 'advanced nationalists' for

South Africa was noted by Dublin Castle authorities. An internal report of 14 January 1897 noted the departure of John R. Whelan, a well-known member of the Irish National Alliance:

> Departure of John R. Whelan for South Africa.
>
> Under Secretary
>
> The above named who is a B.A. of the Royal University is a prominent member of the INA. He held a lucrative appointment here and his departure for South Africa this time is very suspicious. He is the fifth INA man who has gone to South Africa within a recent very short period.[66]

John R. Whelan wrote to *The Freeman's Journal* in January 1906, describing the course of events following his own arrival in South Africa in 1897, and talking about the leading role MacBride had taken among the Irish community there. Whelan claimed that 'his [MacBride's] first public act in Johannesburg when he was unknown and a stranger, was to attend a public meeting of the Amnesty Association, and there denounce the pro-British and Jingo speeches of some of the orators.'

In 1899 the nationalist newspaper the *United Irishman* reported on the same event:

> Nearly four years ago, a young Irishman – a stranger in the land – wandered in one night to an Irish meeting in Johan-

> nesburg. In the chair he saw an Irish millionaire – on the platform an Irish peer – around the hall 500 Irish working men. He listened to the orators in evening dress preaching whiggery and West Britonism … he heard them praise the vampire empire that was sucking away the life-blood of his country and he marked how the men of the race he loved – for the love of which that night he was in exile – listened to the genteel dastards. Then he sprang to the platform and faced the men of his nation. Amongst them all there was not one whom he know. He was no cunning orator with art to sway the hearts and minds of men; he was simply a fearless Irishman whose soul revolted at falsehood he heard being preached to his brethren, yet never an orator won men's hearts as he did that night.[67]

For Whelan, MacBride was a leading figure in the Irish community, and 'no man ever looked to Mac in vain, either for advice or assistance'. He was adamant too that MacBride was the central figure in bringing about the Irish Brigade during the Second Boer War writing that:

> Now, as to the organisation of the Transvaal Irish Brigade, to Major MacBride unquestionably belongs all the credit. In his brain the project had been maturing until the time would come to create it into a reality. Those who knew Major MacBride before the war know that his voice was unceasingly raised imploring his countrymen to prepare

> themselves to wipe out the disgrace on our race and character caused by the raising of a pro-British 'Irish Corps' in Johannesburg during the Jameson Raid.[68]

Not alone were Irish nationalist viewpoints represented in political societies in South Africa, but there were also active Irish unionist societies and organisations established there around the turn off the century. In their 1903 end of year report, the County Down Loyal Orange Order noted that an application had been received from 'members of the Institution residing in Johannesburg, South Africa, praying for a Warrant to open an Orange Lodge in Johannesburg, to be called 'The William Johnston Memorial'.'[69]

Young Irish nationalists arriving in the Transvaal in the late 1890s, like the nineteen-year-old Thomas Byrne, continued to enlist in the Irish National Foresters, seeing it as the only active Irish organisation on offer. Byrne also went to South Africa in 1896, and recalled the importance of MacBride to the small community of advanced nationalists there. The nineteen-year-old claimed that despite the failure of the Jameson Raid, English influence in the region was growing:

> In 1896, when I was 19 years of age, I went to Johannesburg in South Africa. This was 10 months after the Jameson Raid. Johannesburg at this time was practically an English city. The country around this town for an area of thirty miles on each side is studded with mines. The people working these

> mines were practically all British. There were very few Irish people there. Curiously enough, the only Irish organisation in Johannesburg when I was there was a branch of the Irish National Foresters. John MacBride belonged to this Branch and I also became a member. MacBride was the only outstanding Irishman in the Transvaal at this time.[70]

MacBride's name began to appear in nationalist newspapers in Ireland, not long after he first arrived in the country. In *The Nation*, it was reported in October 1896 that the Irish National Amnesty Association learned with 'extreme pleasure' that John MacBride, 'until lately an energetic member of the Central Executive', was working hard for the Association in his new homeland.[71]

Arthur Griffith, a friend from MacBride's Celtic Literary Society days, arrived in the Transvaal in late January 1897. The Dubliner landed in Pretoria, where there existed a small but active Irish separatist community. Many young Irishmen like Griffith would turn up in South Africa, unmarried and without commitments, and would spend only a short period in the country. In many cases they also arrived without arranged work placements. Griffith first attempted his hand as a journalist, his profession at home. In Middleburg, he started to edit a weekly newspaper entitled *The Courant*. The popular account of this story is that Griffith's anti-British sentiment led to him losing this job. In his statement to the Bureau of Military History, Richard Walsh told the tale:

> The anti-Boer group in Johannesburg wanted a newspaper to carry on propaganda on their behalf. They discovered that Griffith was a newspaperman by profession and he was offered the job of editing the paper without being informed of what the editorial policy of the paper was to be, with the result that the first issue produced by Griffith was violently anti-British and pro-Boer. The second issue was even more so, with the result that the body running the paper raided Griffith's office with guns in their hands and he only escaped with his life, through a skylight.[72]

Griffith himself would recall that 'there were some drawbacks to journalism in Middleburg, but on the whole it was exhilarating.'[73] Exhilarating it may have been, though financially rewarding it was not. It was the mines which were to provide employment to both Griffith and MacBride, as they had for many Irish migrants. Griffith found work at the Robinson mine at Langlaagte, in a particularly dangerous role, working with machines which put him in close contact with lethal cyanide. A first-hand account of work at the Langlaagte mines comes from Thomas Richard Adlam who visited there as a young boy and was in awe of what he saw:

> Here the shaft went down vertically. An engineer showed Duncan and me over the surface works, and did his best to explain the chemical processes for extracting the gold from the finely powdered rock with quicksilver and a

> deadly poisonous cyanide. The winding engines, with their huge, bright steel crankshafts and connecting rods and massive flywheels impressed me most. Indeed, I afterwards had nightmares involving me and that awe-inspiring machinery.[74]

The mines were dangerous, and workers' lives were lost. On the 13 April 1897 it was a particularly grim day at the Langlaagte mines, when over thirty lives were lost in minutes owing to the deadly nature of the nitro-glycerine fumes workers were exposed too. While South Africa may have been an adventure for many young Irishmen, it was an adventure not without risk.

For the young Westport man, however, his focus was elsewhere. He devoted himself to attempting to bring together those among the Irish community who shared nationalist sentiment. John MacBride later wrote a detailed collection of articles for *The Freeman's Journal* on his time in South Africa. He recalled 'working on the Robinson Gold Mine outside Johannesburg and during my spare hours devoting my time, energy and money to organising my countrymen.' One of the first challenges, and indeed one of the first opportunities to publicly show the growing confidence of the Irish nationalist community there, would be the centenary of the 1798 insurrection.[75]

For the Irish Diaspora, the centenary of the United Irish rebellion of 1798 provided a focal point for community and commemoration. MacBride himself recalled that immediately after his arrival in South Africa, he involved himself in the preparations for the centenary of 1798, and that 'I and my associates in South Africa held our celebration in conjunction with the celebration at home and also sent a delegate to Ireland to represent us'.[76] To MacBride, 1898 was a chance to 'worthily honour the names and memories of Wolfe Tone and his gallant associates in the great movement of the United Irishmen.'[77]

In Dublin, it was the Irish Republican Brotherhood and John O'Leary who were central to organising an executive committee for the purpose of commemorating the insurrection, though, as is a recurring feature in commemorative practice, it was contemporary political agendas which shaped the discourse of events. This ranged from the leadership of the United Irishmen being proclaimed near proto-socialist in the *Workers' Republic*, the newspaper of Scottish radical James Connolly, to a more conservative narrative from defiant priests in parts of rural Ireland where the clergy told congregations, the men of 1798 were 'hanged, drawn and quartered for Faith and Fatherland'.[78] There was also much tussling for influence on centenary committees. Constitutional nationalist leaders such as John Redmond and John Dillon succeeded in obtaining positions of influence in commemorative bodies and speaking at major events. Indeed, historian Dr Senia Paseta has argued that 'once constitutional nationalists flexed their political muscle and influence, they could not be prevented from all but dominating '98 events.'[79]

The centenary year threw up several peculiar moments. In Ulster, the province from which John MacBride's father hailed, a commemorative parade in Belfast was attacked by a hostile mob in June. As Peter Collins has noted, 'the 1798 rising in Ulster had been mainly a Presbyterian affair. Ironically, in 1898 it was being commemorated primarily by Catholics, in areas with little or no connection with the events of 1798.'[80] In Belfast the media complained that the 'scourge of rowdy Orangemen has been thoroughly roused, and the slightest pretext only is needed to let slip the dogs of riot.'[81]

The work of organising for the centenary year had begun long before 1898. Maud Gonne, a well-known nationalist firebrand, recalled:

> The centenary commemoration, for which such great preparation had been made, seemed to me a little disappointing, as public ceremonies so often are. The preparations for it had been the really important part, for it had given an opportunity to bring the hope of complete independence and of the means of its attainment – Wolfe Tone's means – slumbering in the hearts of the whole Irish race, to the surface consciousness of the people.[82]

In MacBride's home county, the year was met with enthusiasm by local nationalists. In January 1898 the *Western People* reported:

> On Sunday last one of the largest and finest demonstrations ever held in Mayo, even going back to the monster gatherings of O'Connell, took place at French Hill, about three miles outside Castlebar, to make preparations for celebrating in a fitting manner during the summer months the centenary of the Irish rebellion of 1798.[83]

It was MacBride's future wife who addressed the huge crowd on that occasion, and it was Maud Gonne again who would unveil the foundation stone of a monument at Ballina later in 1898, to commemorate the assistance of the French Republic to Ireland in 1798.

In London, Anthony MacBride was on the platform at a commemorative meeting in January 1898 which was addressed by W. B. Yeats and Dr Mark Ryan. Anthony also became Treasurer of a branch of the Centenary Association there.

From South Africa, John MacBride contributed to the fund for the construction of another monument in Mayo, to the memory of those who had died in the rebellion. The following letter, from Johannesburg, appeared under his name in the *Western People* of 7 May 1898:

> I have much pleasure in sending you my subscription, £1 1s, for the Mayo Monument Fund. It would be a very sad

> thing, indeed, if we should forget to pay honour to the memory of the illustrious men who died in the effort to set our native land free. Trusting the monument will be worthy of Mayo men, and worthy of the times and the men it is intended to commemorate.[84]

MacBride maintained contact with the Westport '98 Centenary Committee too, and also sent money to the Mayo Centenary Association. He was adamant in that correspondence that elected representatives and political parties generally should not be allowed to seize control of the Monument fund, noting that 'it would be a fatal mistake to allow such a hallowed undertaking as this to fall into the hands of a few to be perverted to party purposes.' MacBride told the Mayo Centenary Association that 'my one regret is that I cannot be with you, but I promise that though 7000 miles away ... the exiles will not fear to speak of '98, and in spirit will tread the hillsides of Antrim, Wexford and Mayo, where the soil has drunk deep of the blood of Martyrs.'[85]

Perhaps the highlight of the centenary year at home occurred in the capital, with the laying of a foundation stone for a Wolfe Tone memorial at Stephen's Green, on 15 August 1898. John O'Leary presided over events and personally laid the foundation stone. He told the huge crowd assembled that 'Tone's failure is grander than many a success, for he fell gloriously in a great attempt.'[86] John Redmond, John Dillon and W. B. Yeats were among the other speakers. The poet informed the gathering that 'England has persuaded herself that she could settle the Irish question by a handful of arms. We have answered England by this great demonstration. She is no longer deceived. She now knows that Ireland cherishes the same spirit still.'[87] Symbolically, the foundation stone for the Wolfe Tone memorial had come from Cave Hill in Belfast, the birthplace of the United Irish movement.

One publication which was important to the centenary commemorations in Ireland, and with which MacBride was in contact, was *The Shan Van Vocht*. This was a monthly literary magazine founded in Belfast in 1896 by the poet and cultural nationalist Alice Milligan. Despite being born into a Methodist and unionist background, Milligan had become an outspoken nationalist activist, who was particularly influenced by the ideals of the United Irishmen. Milligan was among those who had brought the Wolfe Tone memorial foundation stone to Dublin, and as Catharine Morris has noted, to Milligan 'the United Irishmen activated the first coherent struggle against English colonial rule that was in part led by an enlightened Protestant input.'[88] MacBride forwarded a list of subscriptions to *The Shan Van Vocht* from Irish people in Johannesburg which included many names from the ranks of the Irish National Foresters and the broad Irish advanced nationalist community.[89]

Although far away in Johannesburg, MacBride and the body of men around him were determined to fittingly commemorate the United Irish rebellion. A sizeable commemorative march through the centre of Johannesburg was attended not only by Irish exiles but by a number of Boer leaders, and by *Uitlanders* from Germany, America and other nations. A banquet in commemoration of the uprising was attended by Ben Viljoen, a general in the Boer army who would famously tell his people to put their faith 'in God and the Mauser'. There was also representation of the Irish community in South Africa at commemorative events in Dublin. At an August banquet in the Frascati restaurant in Dublin, Solomon Gillingham represented the Irish community of the Transvaal. MacBride had started working closely with Gillingham on his arrival in South Africa.

Solomon Gillingham is a mysterious figure in the history of the Irish in the Transvaal, but an important one nonetheless. Dismissed in one pro-British account of life in the Transvaal (published in 1901) as the 'notorious Solomon Gillingham, a Colonial of Irish extraction, who carries on a lucrative business in Pretoria as a baker and confectioner', it was claimed there that Gillingham was part of a 'powerful and unscrupulous body' of businessmen in cahoots with Boer leaders.[90] Dr Mark Ryan, John MacBride's Fenian mentor, recalled Solomon as 'the Irish Boer' noting:

> Solomon Gillingham and myself became close friends when he first came to London from Pretoria in 1896. We were photographed together, and he presented me with a pair

> of gold cuff links, with President Kruger's head engraved on them, and a scarf pin which I still wear. He was a big businessman in Pretoria, and, when trouble was developing between the Boer Republic and England, he acted as agent for Kruger in London.[91]

Gillingham was not the only Irish representative to travel from South Africa. A commemorative event in Dublin at Newgate Prison, site of the execution of some of the most important figures in the United Irishmen, such as the Brothers Sheares, was addressed by an unnamed representative from Johannesburg. According to a report in the *Freeman's Journal,* he received loud and enthusiastic cheers each time the name of President Kruger was mentioned. The visiting speaker informed the gathering that 'Irishmen had enemies out there – not the Boers – but they had enemies who tried to undermine everything Irish.'[92] That there was such enthusiasm from the crowd gathered in 1898 for every mention of Kruger and the Boer cause, before the outbreak of the Second Boer War, is an interesting insight into the views of nationalist Ireland at the time.

The centenary of 1798 was arguably a greater success for those in the Transvaal than for those attending the commemorations in Ireland, where events were largely lacklustre despite moments of great symbolism. Separatist political ideology, which promoted an armed response to the British presence in Ireland, was gaining influence in the South African Irish community, 'dividing it along contemporary South African political lines'.[93] In a sense, radicals like MacBride had succeeded in melding Irish radical ideology and the commemoration with a sympathetic line of solidarity to the Boers. They had used the centenary of the United Irishmen to unite sections of Irishmen in the Transvaal.

1898 would also be the year of Arthur Griffith's departure from South Africa. He was drawn back to Ireland primarily by the encouragement of his friend and ally, journalist Willie Rooney, and by the proposition of editing *The United Irishmen*, a new nationalist newspaper. This paper would come to provide Griffith with a public platform for his developing political ideas. It would also provide important coverage of John MacBride's escapades in the Second Boer War, proving central in creating MacBride's public persona in Ireland. When its first edition appeared in March 1899, Griffith used his editorial to proclaim: 'Lest there might be a doubt in any mind, we will say that we accept the nationalism of '98, '48 and '67 as the true nationalism'.[94]

Police intelligence officers were fearful of the potential influence of this new paper, noting that it had been endorsed by Dr Mark Ryan during a visit to Dublin in June 1899.[95] James Joyce would come to describe the *United Irishman* as 'the only paper in Dublin worth reading'.[96]

Chapter 3

• • • • •

Ireland's Boer War

The Second Boer War, which made a household name of John MacBride in Ireland, clearly captivated nationalist Ireland. The war led to mass protests of opposition and to popular expressions of support for the Boer people, in a way that was most unusual for a war fought on foreign shores. It was also a conflict in which some 28,000 Irishmen would fight, from within the ranks of the British Army. For some, like the working-class Dublin playwright and socialist Sean O'Casey, this created a dilemma as his brother fought in South Africa with the Royal Dublin Fusiliers. For others, like John MacBride, it was a black and white issue, and England's difficulty was merely Ireland's opportunity. What has often been described as an 'anti-war' movement in Ireland during the conflict is perhaps better described as an 'anti-British' movement.

Prominent nationalist voices in Irish society offered support to those fighting the British Empire in a wide variety of forms. Seamus Robinson, a participant in the Easter Rising and one of the men who would begin the War of Independence with the Soloheadbeg Ambush in rural Tipperary in 1919, recalled:

> Heavens! What thrills we got out of that great struggle. Bonfires in the streets on the news of a Boer victory, complete disbelief in Boer reverses! The Irish Boer Brigade! How we wished we were old enough to be with them.[97]

The conflict formally broke out on 11 October 1899, following an ultimatum issued two days earlier to the British government by Paul Kruger, President of the South African Republic. President Kruger gave the British 48-hours to withdraw from the borders of both Boer Republics, stating that failure to comply with the ultimatum would result in a declaration of war.

In Ireland, passionate demonstrations followed on from these events. There had been sizeable protests in the days before the ultimatum was issued, as people denounced what was seen as British aggression in the region. On 1 October 1899, a crowd numbering more than 20,000 had gathered at Beresford Place, where the Transvaal flag flew proudly and Irish nationalists made speeches condemning Britain. A letter was read from the Mayor of Kilkenny, who proposed that two maxim guns be sent to the Boers by the people of Ireland with which they could defend themselves. One could be called 'Parnell', and the other 'Wolfe Tone'.[98] Among those who had gathered at Beresford Place were numerous elected Members of Parliament such as T. D. Sullivan, author of *God Save Ireland*, and other public personalities such as W. B. Yeats.

The movement that emerged in Ireland in opposition to Britain's actions in South Africa was broad. It spanned all organisations, from the radical socialist left to veteran Fenians and from emerging women's organisations to cultural and literary societies. Among the bodies central to promoting protest of the conflict was the fledging Irish Socialist Republican Party (ISRP), the small political party of Edinburgh-radical James Connolly. When British MP Joseph Chamberlain, who had worried about the effect of another Boer War, appeared in Dublin in December 1889 to accept an honorary doctorate at Trinity College, the ISRP held a vocal picket at the front gates, denouncing his support of the British war effort.[99] There was much protest and confrontation in the city that day. The fictional Leopold Bloom would recall in James Joyce's *Ulysses* 'That horsepoliceman the day Joe Chamberlain was given his degree in Trinity, he got a run for his money. My word he did!'

Reporting on a meeting of 'Socialist Nationalists' held at Foster Place in late October 1889, *The Irish Times* had noted that 'a person with a strongly marked North of Ireland or Scotch accent' chaired proceedings, most likely a reference to Connolly, and that 'a resolution was proposed congratulating the Boers on their plucky fight.'[100] That same month, *The Irish Times* had run a report that indicated just how strong feelings were in relation to the far-off conflict:

> Last evening there were scenes of disorder in the vicinity of College Green and Dame Street, arising out of demonstrations, which are now a nightly occurrence, in front of the office of the *Irish Daily Independent* newspaper. It is the custom of the management of this paper to keep the people in the street posted in the doings in the Transvaal ... The intelligence as to the Boer War invariably evokes demonstrations of pro-Boer sentiment on the part of the crowd. Last evening, however, a large party of Trinity College students made a counter demonstration, and scenes of considerable excitement and disorder were enacted in front of the College during the evening.[101]

The paper noted that over 100 students, singing the British national anthem with gusto, had confronted pro-Boer sympathisers at the offices of the newspaper, and that later there was a stand-off on College Green. 'God Save Ireland' and 'Who Fears to Speak of '98' were sung in response to 'Rule Britannia' and 'God Save The Queen'. It was clear that both sides were utilising a war in a far-off field to further domestic political agendas. In his Bureau of Military History witness statement Kevin O'Shiel, a Judicial Commissioner in the Dáil Éireann Land Courts during the War of Independence period, recalled this being his interpretation of public feeling at the time of the Boer War:

> In the last years of the last century the Boer War dominated every other topic. Outside town and country politics, the Boer War provided the only other excitement that then stirred citizens in any degree. In that issue the populace was divided into pro-Boer and anti-Boer, the divisions, of course, corresponding to those on either side of the traditional gulf – Catholic and Nationalist, and Protestant and Unionist.[102]

At home, no newspaper was more significant in promoting the message of the Boers than Arthur Griffith's *United Irishman*. This paper frequently carried articles by political activists such as Maud Gonne, as well as publishing a series of letters from John MacBride himself.

Maud Gonne's articles on the war showed little understanding of its complexities, and as Karen Steele has noted 'she showed little awareness of Dutch colonialism and even less concern for natives in Southern Africa, hoping only to humiliate Britain.'[103] Gonne also wrote of the 'thrill of fraternal sympathy' among the French 'at the sight of those peasant armies of the Republics striking down imperial tyranny'. This failed to take into account that at this stage France was guilty of imperialist crimes against African people, a reality far removed from the romantic republican vision Gonne and others had of French society, which perhaps owed more to Theobald Wolfe Tone's time than her own. Gonne's articles were wrapped up in Irish nationalist, political sentiment. For example in a January 1900 edition of the *United Irishman* she noted:

> The heroes of the South African Republics are showing us that courage counts more than numbers. They are breaking down the falsehood of England's greatness, that falsehood on which the British Empire has been built, and the nations who accepted the legend of England's might look on in wonder, and some in shame, and all in admiration and delight.[104]

Maud Gonne was a central figure in the opposition to the war in Ireland, as President of the Inghinidhe na hÉireann (Daughters of Ireland) organisation. This body was established in 1900, largely out of opposition to an official visit to Ireland by Queen Victoria, who was denounced by Gonne as the 'Famine Queen'. Gonne herself stated that Inghinidhe na hÉireann came about as a women's society directly inspired by the Celtic Literary Society. Maire O'Brolchain, Vice-President of the group, recalled in her statement to the Bureau of Military History that 'during the Boer War, Inghinidhe distributed anti-recruiting leaflets to soldiers and their girlfriends, who usually walked past the G.P.O. every night.'[105] Helena Molony, a veteran of the organisation, who would later join the Irish Citizen Army (ICA), recalled that 'the leading spirit of anti-British activity was Miss Maud Gonne, who became the first President of Inghinidhe na hÉireann.'[106]

Pro-Boer voices found common ground in the Irish Transvaal Committee. It was based in Dublin and also active nationwide. In October and November 1900, the Committee was central to pushing for Dublin Corporation to confer the Freedom of the City upon President Paul Kruger. The presence of John O'Leary, Arthur Griffith, W. B. Yeats and Maud Gonne was recorded at meetings in this period. A motion was put before Dublin Corporation, stating:

> That the Freedom of the Ancient City of Dublin be conferred on His Excellency President Kruger, of the Transvaal Republic, in consideration of his patriotic and gallant efforts to maintain his country's freedom, and as a protest against the characteristic action of the English government, and their sordid and brutal endeavours to enslave the brave and unconquerable Boers.[107]

The motion for President Kruger to be granted the Freedom of the City of Dublin was unsuccessful, though it did succeed in grabbing the public imagination, and in securing widespread media coverage for the Irish pro-Boer movement. Kruger was honoured symbolically with the Freedom of the City of Limerick later that year. John Daly, himself a veteran Fenian leader, was the serving Lord Mayor of Limerick at the time, and honouring Kruger was an act of solidarity on the part of Limerick nationalists with the Boer people.

The Irish Transvaal Committee utilised the war to whip-up anti-recruitment feeling in Ireland. For example in February 1900, 20,000 leaflets were distributed in towns in the south of Ireland where there were British army recruitment centres and military stations. Local Irish Republican Brotherhood activists were central to this process.[108]

While all this agitation and protest was occurring in Ireland, Irish men were physically fighting alongside the Boers, thousands of miles away. In Michael Davitt's account of the Second Boer War, he claimed:

> The Irish Brigade was organised in Johannesburg chiefly by the exertions of Mr John MacBride, a native of Mayo, who was at the time employed as assayer in one of the Rand mines. He was warmly supported by other prominent Irishmen on the Rand. A manifesto was issued appealing to Irishmen to remember England's manifold infamies against their own country, and on this account to volunteer the more readily to fight against a common enemy for the defence of Boer freedom.[109]

By September 1899, a proposal for an Irish Transvaal Brigade, numbering 700, was put to the Boer government and accepted. There had been earlier proposals to assemble such a force, though such offers had been politely declined. Now, with war clearly imminent, the task of assembling such a force began.

John MacBride detailed the experiences of the Irish Brigade in the Boer War in the years that followed, most frequently in his series of articles for the *Freeman's Journal.* In a January 1907 letter to the same paper, MacBride was adamant that while he had played a role in organising the Brigade, 'I never claimed to have done more than one man's part. The fact that Mr Sol Gillingham came first to me with private news of the impending war, and a hint to get the Irish Nationalists together, and that the word, therefore, went around from me, I suppose, gave my name some prominence in the work.' MacBride detailed his belief that if credit was due to anyone for the formation of the Irish Brigade is was to Sol Gillingham, who he claimed carried out all arrangements with the Executive for recognition of this Irish Brigade.[110]

MacBride's account of organising the Brigade, and its exploits in battle, make for fascinating reading. He discussed his 'pain and indignation' at hearing of Irishmen who had fought alongside the British during the Jameson Raid, and commented 'as I afterwards learned in South Africa, the number of those Irish 'heroes' did not exceed 30, and their 'loyalty' to the crown and Constitution had been purchased by the so-called 'Reform Committee' for the gift of a rifle and a pound a day for their valuable services.[111]

Thomas Byrne provided insights into the manner in which men were recruited for the Irish Brigade in his statement to the Bureau of Military History. Like MacBride, Byrne would go on to fight another day in the revolutionary period at home, becoming an active member of the Irish Volunteers and later the Irish Republican Army. In his statement Byrne described a recruitment process that had begun in the Transvaal some time before the commencement of open hostilities:

> One day in Johannesburg I met Dan O'Hare, a Belfast man, and Richard McDonagh from Listowel, Co. Kerry, and the three of us discussed the possibilities of war. Dan O'Hare suggested that, in the event of war, we should have an Irish contingent with the Boer army, to which McDonagh and I agreed. The question then was how to get in touch with all those who were liable to have the same opinions as ourselves, and it was decided that one or two of us; should interview John on the Langlaagte mine. MacBride, of course, agreed.[112]

The men drew upon the support of the Irish community in Johannesburg for their planning meetings, with Byrne recalling that 'a Mr Mitchell from Galway, who had a cleaning and pressing works in Johannesburg, agreed to let us have the use of his place for meetings. We held some meetings;

there on Sundays when the men would have come in from the mines.' Byrne noted that the mines of the region provided fertile recruitment grounds, commenting that himself and McDonagh travelled from mine to mine attempting to enlist sympathetic men:

> McDonagh and I spent the weekdays going from one mine to another, interviewing Irishmen, whose names had been given to us, or whom we happened to know. On Saturdays we returned to Johannesburg to attend the meetings on the following Sunday mornings. This organising went on for about six weeks.[113]

MacBride recalled that while he was 'offered the position of commander right away', he felt it necessary to decline the 'high honour … on account of my lack of military training and experience.'[114] If not MacBride, then who would lead the Irish Brigade? That task fell to John Blake, an Irish American native of Missouri in the United States. Blake was a veteran of conflict, who had served in the American armed forces during the Apache Wars until his resignation in 1889. He had arrived in South Africa shortly before the Jameson Raid, and Michael Davitt noted that he had 'a slight suggestion of Buffalo Bill in his general appearances and bearing.'[115]

Blake later wrote his own memoir of his time in South Africa, entitled *A West Pointer with the Boers,* published in 1903. His account of his time in South Africa is colourful and in it he proves himself a capable propagandist. Writing about the build-up to the Second Boer War, Blake alleged that the British media presented the Boers as deeply anti-Catholic, to drum up Irish recruitment for the war effort. To him:

> All this infamous lying was for the sole purpose of inducing the Irish to enlist in the British army, and I regret to say that the Irish fell into the trap. Thousands of them joined the British army, and today thousands of them are buried in South Africa. Few English are buried in South Africa, but the graves of the Irish and Scotch can be counted by the thousand.[116]

Blake noted that the formal offer of leading the Irish Brigade was made to him on 1 October 1899, when it was clear war was inevitable. This, coincidentally, was the same day that 20,000 protesters mobilised on the streets of Dublin in sympathy with the Boer cause. The newly-appointed Colonel Blake was willing to lead the Irish Brigade, which he describes as being Irish and Irish American in composition, on the condition that 'not one of them would expect or accept one cent of money for his services, and that all would fight purely for their love and liberty and for down-trodden Ireland.'[117]

Of the 300 men who formed the backbone of the Irish Brigade, it has been written that they included 'a Catholic chaplain, some Gaelic speakers and about forty Protestants. There were two sets of fathers and sons. Only a few men, however, had fighting experience.'[118] MacBride, now a Major, would recall that 'the bulk of the men were of pure Irish blood; but we had several Irish-Americans and about a dozen Frenchmen with us. A few gallant Americans who had never seen Ireland also accompanied us.'[119]

In his subsequent articles for the *Freeman's Journal* MacBride described the men setting off to join the Boers on 6 October 1899, marching behind a green flag proudly carried by a Balbriggan man, Sergeant Joe Wade. As the men prepared to board trains, 'groups of Boer ladies came to the station to wish us God speed and to bestow lavish gifts of flowery fruits, and cigars on the men who were going to help their country in its fight against a foreign aggressor.'[120]

The Irish Brigade joined Boer fighters at the Natal border, where they awaited the commencement of hostilities. The men found themselves guarding Boer guns, alongside Commandant Trichardt, an artillery commander.

Within days the soldiers of the Irish Brigade had experienced active military combat in South Africa, sometimes in direct opposition to Irish regiments of the British armed forces. Ireland can often feel a small place, but it's remarkable to think that in the Boer War men who knew each other, or indeed who were related to one another, were fighting on opposite sides of the conflict. The 28,000 Irishmen within the British army in South Africa formed a significant force in the British war effort. One song, printed in a 1902 collection from the South African War, satirised the manner in which Irishmen found themselves fighting on both sides of the war:

> On the mountain side the battle raged, there was no stop or stay;
> Mackin captured Private Burke and Ensign Michael Shea,
> Fitzgerald got Fitzpatrick, Brannigan found O'Rourke;
> Finnigan took a man named Fay and a couple of lads from Cork.
> Sudden they heard McManus shout 'Hands up or I'll run you through'
> He thought he had a Yorkshire 'Tyke' – twas Corporal Donoghue
> McGarry took O'Leary, O'Brien got McNamee
> That's how the English fought the Dutch at the Battle of Dundee.[121]

MacBride later wrote that the Brigade's 'baptism of fire' came on the morning of 20 October 1899. They marched to Dundee in the company of the Boer Commandant Trichardt and MacBride recalled:

> There was no shrinking or shirking of duty. Every man was alert, active, and determined, the one thing being uppermost in their minds being that of upholding the honour

> and dignity of their beloved country. The marksmanship of the English gunners was wretchedly poor, and their shells of very defective quality, many of them sinking into the Veldt with a heavy thud without exploding.[122]

At the Battle of Dundee, the men of the Irish Brigade encountered the Royal Dublin Fusiliers and the Irish Fusiliers. MacBride claimed that soldiers from these Irish regiments 'were driven into a cattle-kraal and compelled to surrender. A number of the prisoners had been in school in Ireland with members of the Brigade, who naturally could not help feeling sad and humiliated at seeing their own countrymen and former schoolmates in such a humiliating position.'[123] Blake stated in his memoir that 'of the 196 Irishmen captured, eighty-five begged to join the Irish Brigade and fight with the Boers .... When first captured, all were half scared to death and the first thing they wished to know was whether the Boers would shoot them or not.'[124]

If MacBride found that his men could not help but feel mixed emotion on capturing fellow Irishmen, there were sometimes mixed emotions at home too, for those waving-off Irishmen who were destined to fight for the British army in South Africa. Sean O'Casey vividly recalled his brother Tom going to war, and the effect it had on him. Writing of his youth, and of a time when he was still identified as Johnny, Sean O'Casey recalled:

> Johnny's whole world was divided against itself. England was at war with the Boer Republics. His brother Tom [...] had been called up; had been dressed in khaki, helmet and all; had marched, with a contingent of his regiment, the Dublin Fusiliers, through the city, Johnny by his side, carrying his rifle [...] Thousands of Irishmen were out there on the veldt, risking all for England; for her honour, and, Johnny thought bitterly, for the gold and diamond mines of Johannesburg.[125]

In contrast, after the Battle of Dundee the men of the Irish Brigade continued onwards in their war against the British, and, in many cases, against their fellow countrymen serving in British Army uniforms. The Brigade pressed on towards Ladysmith and shortly afterwards encountered fierce fighting near the town.

Ladysmith had become something of a garrison town, occupied by over 12,000 British soldiers under the command of Field Marshall Sir George Stuart White. White, ironically, was the father of Jack White, who helped establish the Irish Citizen Army which would fight, albeit without him, on the streets of Dublin in 1916. Jack White was also serving as a member of the British armed forces in South Africa. From the hills around Ladysmith, Boer guerrilla fighters caused great difficulty for the British. Blake recalled that 'General Sir George White, with his 13,000 trained soldiers and fifty cannon, held and occupied all the mountains, but ignored

Pepworth Hill, lying to the north-east at a distance of about 6,000 yards from the town.'[126]

On 30 October, MacBride would recall 'the whiz of shell passing over the camp gave warning that the English were about to make an effort to drive us from our positions.'[127] Field Marshall White had made the decision to attack the Boers. The men of the Irish Brigade, still guarding the guns of the Boer forces, found themselves right in the heart of the action. MacBride commented that 'we, naturally, felt very proud at being placed in so prominent a position in the big fight. The duty imposed on the Brigade that day was of the most difficult and trying character.'[128]

In his definitive history of the Boer War, Thomas Pakenham has noted that White's plan to attack the Boers was very much 'of the old field-day formula.' Firstly, there would be an artillery barrage against the Boers, secondly a flank attack on Pepworth to capture the Boer guns and lastly his cavalry would be called upon to pursue the fleeing Boers.[129] In addition to attacking the Boers at Pepworth Hill, Field Marshall White also sent a sizeable detachment, including the First Battalion of the Royal Irish Fusiliers, to capture what was known as Nicholson's Nek, about 3 miles from Pepworth Hill. He was hoping that this would prevent Boer reinforcements from coming to the assistance of those at Pepworth Hill. War, however, rarely goes to plan.

The attack upon Pepworth Hill was intense. MacBride

wrote that during lulls in the fighting the men would joke among themselves as if it were the most ordinary of days: 'One of the boys voiced a very general feeling when he said that he wished that their friends at home could see them'.[130] Blake described the madness during the attack:

> Shells were bursting over our heads on the ground, among us, and great chunks of iron were whizzing about from stone to stone. At times the uproar was so great that we could scarcely hear each other speak, yet the Irish boys, who had not the least protecting, never once showed any inclination to waver.[131]

The first fatality of the Irish Brigade was Tommy Oates. He was an eighteen-year-old who MacBride described as being 'as brave as a young lion', and was the Brigade's standard bearer. Also killed in action early in the conflict was Hugh Carberry, who had played in the All-Ireland football semi-final for Armagh in 1890 against Cork.[132] Carberry's death became the focal point for much nationalist commemoration at home. In 1902 a huge crowd attended the unveiling of a memorial cross to him in Armagh Cemetery, with Michael Davitt addressing those in attendance.

The men of the Irish Brigade proved themselves willing to risk life and limb on Pepworth Hill. In dangerous circumstances volunteers from the Brigade were carrying ammunition to the 'Long Tom' guns used to return fire on

British artillery. When the guns went quiet, it was Irishmen who carried ammunition to them once again, and MacBride noted that the shells carried by Irish volunteers succeeded in 'scattering an English infantry regiment like chaff before the wind.'[133]

There are interesting accounts of the engagement from the other side of the divide too. For example H. H. S. Pearse, an embedded war journalist from *The Daily News,* published his book, *Four Months Besieged: The Story of Ladysmith*, in 1900. Pearse wrote of the presence of 'renegade Irishmen' in the Boer ranks, and commented on the presence of a 'foreign legion' and claimed that the men carried a red flag:

> One contingent, apparently some foreign legion, showing traces of elementary discipline and evidently not numbering in its ranks many Boers of the old school, advanced boldly across ground that afforded them little cover, and there began to "front form" in fairly good order. They were well within range of Lee-Enfield rifles, and a few volleys well directed sent them to the right-about in anything but good order. Soon after, a second column advanced with even more bravado, headed by a standard-bearer, who carried a red flag. These were said to be Irishmen, who, having elected to serve a republic, and being debarred from fighting under the green banner of their own country, yet not quite ready to acknowledge the supremacy of another race, may have flaunted the emblem of liberty by way of com-

> promise. More probably, however, they were a mixed lot owning no common country, but willing or unwilling to serve under any colours with equal impartiality.[134]

Reference to the Irish pro-Boers fighters also appeared in Winston Churchill's recollections of the war. Like Pearse, the future Prime Minister was an embedded war journalist at the time of the conflict. Churchill was captured when an armoured car in which he was travelling was wrecked by Boer forces. He recalled that he and members of the Royal Dublin Fusiliers were marched to a prison camp by their Boer captors, becoming a spectacle of great interest to curious civilians:

> I do not know how many men I saw, but certainly during this one march not less than 5,000. Of this great number two only offered insults to the gang of prisoners. One was a dirty, mean-looking little Hollander. He said, "Well, Tommy, you've got your franchise, anyhow." The other was an Irishman. He addressed himself to Frankland, whose badges proclaimed his regiment. What he said when disentangled from obscenity amounted to this: "I am glad to see you Dublin fellows in trouble."[135]

While the Irish Brigade was engaged at Pepworth Hill, there was disaster for the British regiments at Nicholson's Nek. The men Field Marshall White had sent to seize the hill and to prevent Boer reinforcements from joining the men at Pepworth Hill were confronted by a Boer force under the stewardship of General De Wet, of the Orange Free State. De Wet and a force of only 300 men besieged White's men, ultimately taking more than 800 of them prisoner. In his memoir of the struggle, General De Wet recalled that 'our losses amounted to four killed and five wounded. As to the losses of the English, I myself counted 203 dead and wounded and there must have been many whom I did not see. In regard to our prisoners, as they marched past me four deep I counted 817.'[136]

Colonel Blake was wounded during the British assault on Pepworth Hill on 30 October, an injury that would leave him out of action until December. Major MacBride recalled that 'the command of the Brigade then devolved on myself, and I felt the responsibilities of the position keenly at all times.' The Brigade proved itself at this fight in the view of MacBride, as 'up to this battle … the less educated burghers [Boers] had regarded our men with suspicion, because hearing them speak nothing but English, they considered that they must also be English in sympathy … the Brigade's work at Modderspruit [Ladysmith], however, definitely settled the minds of these not unreasoning doubters.'[137]

MacBride would recall that following this decisive military success, the Brigade advanced in the direction of Ladysmith. They halted within easy distance of the town and waited 'for the expected order to storm the town along with the other commandos – an order that unfortunately never came.'

Tensions began to emerge between Major MacBride and General Joubert, the Boer General to whom the Brigade now answered. MacBride detailed this hostility in his recollections of the war, noting that General Joubert ordered MacBride and half a dozen men of the Brigade to 'go to Colenso to blow up the bridge there'. The order 'rather astonished' him, as with Blake being wounded 'I did not think it right that I should be asked to leave the men in order to superintend the blowing-up of a bridge.' Colenso was still firmly occupied by English soldiers, and MacBride recalled, 'I must confess that I was not much impressed with the wisdom of sending a half-dozen men on a mission that seemed to have such a slender chance of being successful.' MacBride believed that he had been sent on this mission as 'General Joubert, I knew, did not like me. I had spoken rather hotly and impatiently to him after the Battle of Modderspruit … and I fear he never forgave me my hastiness.'[138]

For the task, MacBride selected Sergeant MacCallum, Jim O'Keefe, Joe Tully, Joe Wade and Tom Balfour, all 'well-known dynamiters on the Rand'. He recalled being 'convinced that it meant almost certain death for all of us', but still he followed orders. Ultimately, the highly dangerous order was countermanded. Upon returning to camp MacBride found that General Joubert 'seemed to have arrived at the conclusion that the mission on which he had dispatched us was an impossible one under the circumstances.'[139]

On 28 November 1899, word was received of another attack on Ladysmith, and MacBride received orders to take 100 men to a position situated about a mile in front of Lombard's Kop. He noted that the expected attack did not take place, but that instead he was ordered to make a reconnaissance to ascertain the strength of British forces. MacBride divided his force into two bands of men. Among his own fifty men, he noted that the men came from Counties Kilkenny, Down and Cork among other places, and that 'with characteristic impetuosity, the brave fellows dashed at the English positions, two of which were captured, one right after the other, before the English had begun to realise what was happening.' MacBride claimed that his men advanced up to within 1200 yards of Ladysmith, 'and if our numbers had been five hundred instead of fifty, we could unquestionably have pushed right into the town.' MacBride mocked the ability of the British soldiers who the Irish Brigade engaged in close-range fire-fights. He claimed that 'my soft white shirt and green sash afforded a good mark for the English – if they had been able to hit even a haystack except by pure accident.'[140]

In a series of raids from Ladysmith, British forces attempted to incapacitate the Boer artillery. For example on the night of 8 December, MacBride claimed 'six hundred Britishers moved silently out of Ladysmith … and put a charge of dynamite in Long Tom's muzzle.' This led to the Boers and Irish Brigade members hauling the gun from the hill it was placed upon and sending it via train to Pretoria for repairs. In MacBride's elegant words, 'in a fortnight [it] was once more vomiting shells into Ladysmith.'

In the aftermath of these raids on the Boer artillery, it was necessary for the important weapons of war to be closely guarded, with the Irish Brigade central to the task. MacBride acknowledged the courageous nature of the British raids against the guns, noting that they were 'undoubtedly characterised by much pluck and daring, and were the only redeeming features in the whole conduct of the English troops during the siege of Ladysmith.'[141]

Boer forces utilised their guns with devastating effect. Sergeant Walter Appleyard of the Royal Dublin Fusiliers would write home that:

> The campaign is likely to last much longer than was at first supposed, as, in point of armament, our enemies are far superior to us; they have some excellent artillery and evidently know how to use it, contrary to the opinion of some newspaper correspondents.[142]

The Battle of Colenso was a violent and brutal affair. It was launched on 15 December 1899, when a sizeable force under British General Sir Redvers Buller attempted to relieve those besieged at Ladysmith. The combat came only days after the return of Colonel Blake to the fold. In his memoir the Irish American rejoiced at the sight of the plain of Colenso 'strewn with dead and wounded Irish Tommies.'[143] Over 140 belligerents on the side of the British forces were lost at the Battle of Colenso, with over 750 wounded, while the Boer forces lost a mere eight combatants.

General Buller's arrival in the British fold had been greeted with jubilation by many troops. He had a reputation as a capable and fearless leader, who had played a significant role in the Anglo-Zulu War. Roy Digby Thomas, in his study of the British General, notes that he was seen as a 'soldier's soldier', and that one soldier wrote: 'Buller's arrival was almost everything. I have never seen troops re-tempered like this by one man.'[144] Thomas has noted though that despite Buller's reputation, former military experience and accolades, he too would learn the immense difficulty of confronting a guerrilla enemy in their own territory:

> Maps on the British side were rudimentary. Attempts to reconnoitre the territory were constantly disrupted by the Boers, who sent out scouting parties to chase the surveyors away....The main map contained large areas of blank paper, where little was known of the terrain.[145]

The savage fighting at Colenso saw MacBride himself almost killed. MacBride's horse was shot from under him and he recalled that 'a big 4.7 inch lyddite shell burst a few yard in front of me killing my horse and sending myself somersaulting in the air. The boys all thought I was dead.'[146] MacBride's life was saved thanks to the heroism of Sergeant-Major Frank O'Reilly, who used his own horse and body to shield Major MacBride, exposing himself to considerable danger and allowing the Mayo man to run to shelter. MacBride remembered that 'Frank O'Reilly accomplished as heroic a deed as the brave soldier could be capable of on the field of battle.'[147]

Members of the Royal Dublin Fusiliers, the Royal Inniskilling Fusiliers and the Connaught Rangers were among the Irishmen engaged in the Battle of Colenso in the ranks of the British armed forces. The official history of the Second Battalion of the Royal Dublin Fusiliers in South Africa acknowledged that 'the regiment had suffered heavily', detailing that two Officers were killed and three wounded. The total casualties suffered by the soldiers of the Royal Dublin Fusiliers were 219, of which 52 were killed.[148] Yet, in contemporary newspapers, readers would form the view that the Boers were being easily brushed aside. On 23 December 1899 for example *The Irish Times,* a resolutely unionist newspaper, reported: 'The Boer prisoners state that their loss is heavy. They wish they had never seen Colenso.'[149] In reality, it was Britain who suffered a humiliating loss, and it would not be their last in South Africa.

On that same December day in 1899, the Irishmen who

were fighting not against the Boers, but rather amongst their ranks, were presented with a flag by Dannie Trichardt, the wife of the Boer Commander under whom the Brigade were serving. The banner, green with a gold fringe and a harp in its centre, was inscribed with the words 'Our Land – Our People – Our Language', in Irish. The flag was a welcome gift from home, sent by activists within the anti-war movement there, including the Irish Transvaal Committee and the Daughters of Ireland. It arrived at a time when 'the thoughts of the lads quite naturally began to dwell more deeply and fondly on the old homeland, and the dear ones there.' MacBride later recalled some of Mrs Trichardt's speech and recounted that she had told the men of her hope that someday the flag would be carried by men fighting for the freedom of Ireland on Irish soil, and that she knew these men would always stand by the flag and even die for it, rather than disgracing it by dishonour or cowardice. As the flag was planted in the midst of the camp, John MacBride remembered that 'there was a tear in many an eye, and a lump in many a throat when we stood around and, having drank the toast of 'Ireland a Nation', sang *The Volkslied* with our guests.'

Transvaalers join the chorus, singing
Of heroes hand in hand,
Where'd our rifle shots are ringing,
There is our Fatherland.

Our Fatherland,
Our Fatherland,
This is our own, our Fatherland.[150]

Christmas Mass was delivered by Father Baudry, the Chaplain of the Irish Brigade a few days later. While the majority of the men in the ranks of the Brigade were Catholic it is significant to note that there were Protestant men there too, something MacBride went to great lengths to make clear in his memoir of the conflict. Of the Protestants in the force, he was adamant 'there were no more bitter haters of English oppression amongst us. I never throughout the whole campaign heard of word of dissension on religion amongst the boys; and let us hope that the day will arrive when, like those men of the Irish Brigade, our countrymen will all unite for Ireland and will know no difference.' There may have been mass and even gifts, but this was no ordinary Christmas, as while 'there was plenty of goodwill amongst our men, peace on earth could not hold much place in our minds when we were always looking out for news of the latest skirmish.'[151]

MacBride remembered a concert, at which Colonel Blake presided, as one of the highlights of this unorthodox Christmas celebration. There was no cheer as loud as that reserved for the Dubliner Tom O'Byrne, who sang 'The Song of the Transvaal Irish Brigade':

Oh mother of the wounded breast!

Oh mother of the tears!
The sons you loved and trusted best
Have grasped their battle-spears
From Shannon, Lagan, Liffey, Lee,
On Africa's soil today,
We strike for Ireland, brave old Ireland
Ireland far away!
We smite for Ireland, brave old Ireland,
Ireland boys, hurrah!

'Who Fears to Speak of '98?', 'The West's Asleep', 'The Boys of Kilkenny' and other songs were sung in the camp that night, and MacBride would remember the day emotionally as one that brought together 'the Brigade of the bravest and most lovable of Irishmen who had gathered together in this generation.'[152]

The *United Irishman* newspaper greatly exaggerated the numbers of the Brigade, claiming at one point that as many as 1700 men were actively involved with the force.153 The newspaper published a new edition of the republican ballad 'The Wearing of the Green', loaded with praise for MacBride:

> From land to land throughout the world the news is going round
> That Ireland's flag triumphant waves on high o'er English ground.
> In far-off Africa today the English fly dismayed

Before the flag of green and gold borne by MacBride's Brigade.
With guns and bayonets in their hands, their Irish flag on high
As down they swept on England's ranks out rang their battle-cry:
Revenge! Remember 98! And how our fathers died!
We'll pay the English back today, cried fearless John MacBride.[154]

The paper also strongly promoted the image of MacBride as the leader of the Irish community in South Africa. It told readers of how he had arrived in South Africa a stranger but had quickly won the Irish community over to his brand of nationalist politics.

In February 1900, a by-election in South Mayo, brought about as a result of Michael Davitt's dramatic resignation from Westminster in protest at the war, was seen as an opportunity by supporters of the Irish Brigade. Born at the height of Famine in Ireland, Davitt's long and varied political career had seen him agitate on many fronts, both national and international. His decision to leave his Westminster seat in 1899 brought huge publicity to the cause of the Boer Republics. He travelled to South Africa in sympathy and solidarity with the Boer cause, and in 1902 he published the work *The Boer Fight for Freedom,* a not entirely unbiased account of the conflict and its causes. To Davitt, it was clear that:

> No one who wanted to be a witness to the truth could travel through the Transvaal, either before war began or during its earlier progress, without seeing evidence everywhere of both careful and enlightened administration in its cities and towns, and of comfort and content in the homes and habits of the people.... Its working classes were better housed than those of London, Manchester or Dublin, while the taxation on wages in the Transvaal was much less than the amount which English working men have to pay annually in their own country.[155]

The idea of putting Major John MacBride forward as a candidate for Davitt's vacant South Mayo seat had popular support among the pro-Boer solidarity movement in Ireland. The election proved disastrous, however, as Griffith and the *United Irishman* had incorrectly anticipated that MacBride would not face opposition from Home Rule nationalists. The newspaper had gone as far as to write:

> We do not anticipate that any opposition will be offered to his return … we expect the news will be flashed round the globe that the men of Mayo have honoured themselves by choosing as their representative the gallant Westport man, whose devoted patriotism and magnificent enthusiasm have led to the formation once again of an Irish Brigade, fighting under the Irish flag against the enemy of the Irish race….

> The effect of John MacBride's election will be widely felt. Its significance will be understood by the people and press of Europe. It will make the attitude of the Irish people to the British Empire plain to everyone.[156]

Not alone did the Irish Parliamentary Party compete in the election against MacBride, their candidate, John O'Donnell, comfortably won the seat. O'Donnell was also of Westport stock. The *United Irishman* claimed that during the election there was intimidation of those canvassing for MacBride, while O'Donnell encountered some abuse too, owing to his application to join the Royal Irish Constabulary in his younger days. Out of an electorate of 7000, less than 3000 took to the polls, with MacBride achieving 427 votes. As O'Donnell was seen very much as a protégé of constitutional nationalist William O'Brien, the election could be seen to represent a head-on collision between the forces of constitutional nationalism and the physical force, armed tradition of MacBride.

After the election MacBride acknowledged those who had voted for him in a letter to the press in Ireland:

> Fellow Nationalists – I have to return you my most sincere thanks for supporting my candidacy in South Mayo. I am satisfied that in recording your votes in my favour you were influenced solely by the consideration that you were not only registering a strong protest against an unjust

Left: Honoria MacBride, Westport shopkeeper and beloved mother of John.

Below: John MacBride posing with the captured sight of a British cannon, seized at Colenso. It became a prized memento of the Boer War.

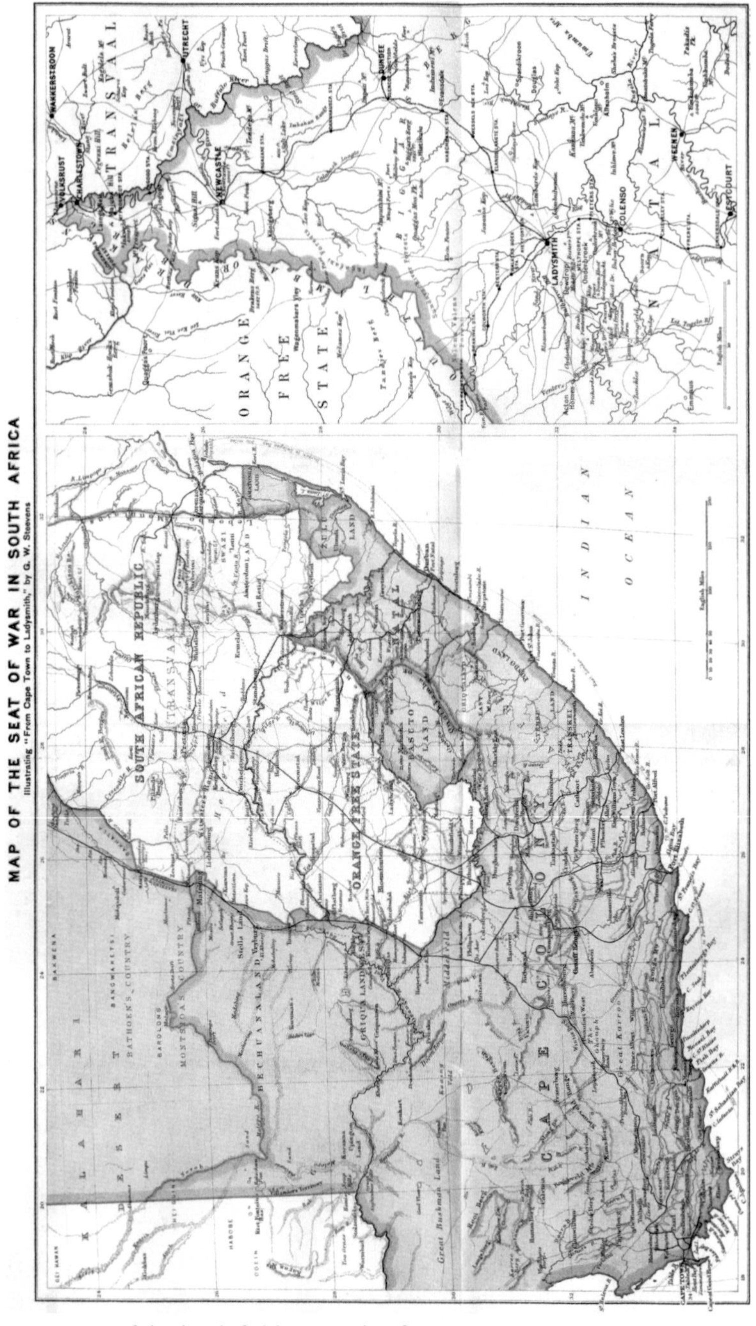

A map of the battlefield in South Africa c. 1900.

Above: Illustrations like this one, depicting a Boer ambush on British forces, were commonly found in the British press during the conflict.

Right: An illustration of Michael Davitt in South Africa. The Mayo radical resigned his Westminster seat in protest at Britain's involvement in the Boer War, with MacBride unsuccessfully contesting the ensuing election.

General Sir John Maxwell. Like MacBride, he was destined to see action in South Africa via the Boer War, albeit for the British Empire. He was central to the suppression of the Easter Rising.

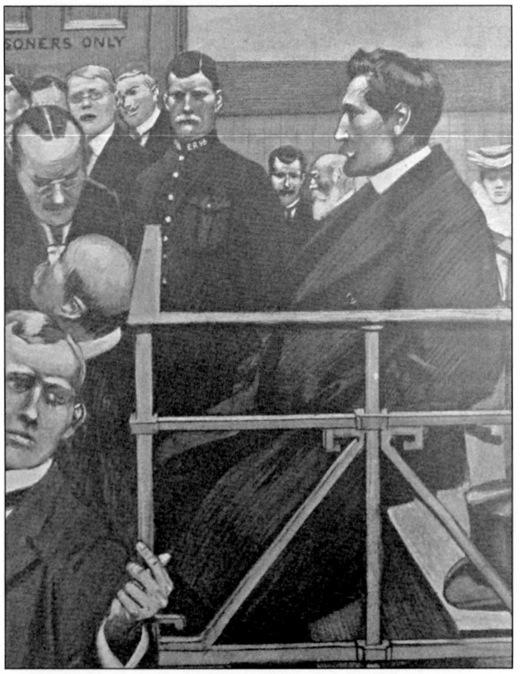

A second Irish Brigade entered the war at a later stage, under the command of Arthur Lynch. He would later stand trial for his actions.

Paul Kruger, the Boer President. Attempts were made by nationalists in Dublin to bestow the Freedom of the City upon him during the war.

Left: Col. John Y. F. Blake, leader of the Irish Brigade. He would later pen a colourful account of his time in South Africa.

Above: Blake is shown alongside some of those who had travelled to partake in the war effort.

Left: Thomas Byrne, a friend to MacBride. He participated in the Irish Brigade in the Boer War, before fighting in the 1916 Rising in Dublin.

Below: A child called Lizzie van Zyl, who died from typhoid fever in the Bloemfontein concentration camp during the Second Boer War.

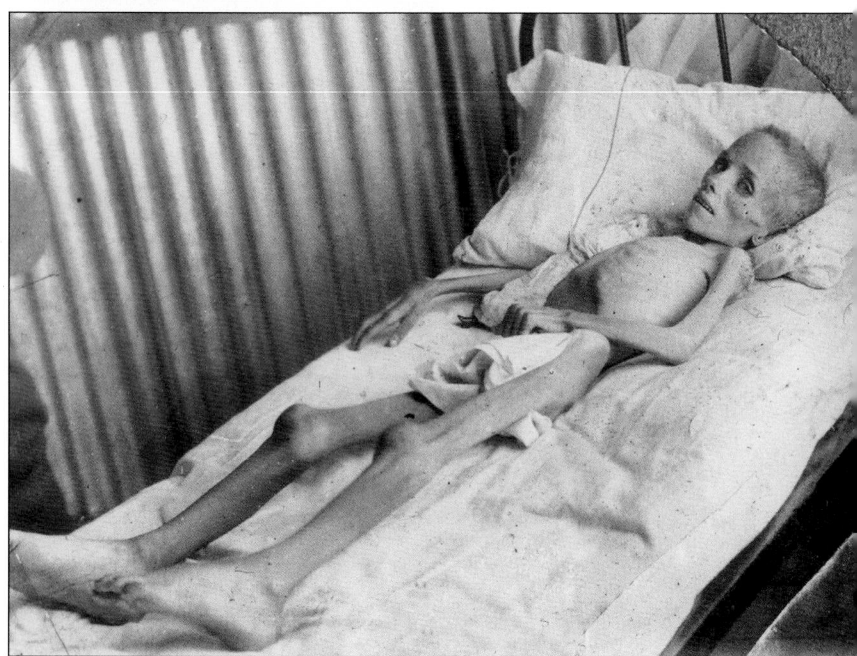

Maud Gonne's Inghinidhe na hÉireann, which was later submerged into the Cumann na mBan movement in 1914.

Maud Gonne, John MacBride and their young son Seán in Paris. Notice the gun upon the table, and the flag beside them.

Above: John O'Leary and John MacBride in Fontenoy, France, in 1905.

Left: In Paris, MacBride mingled in Irish nationalist circles.

> war, but emphasising before the world your sympathy with the burghers of the South African Republics in the gallant stand they are making in a cause which is so closely akin to our own.[157]

That MacBride was defeated by a constitutional nationalist should not give the impression that Irish constitutional nationalism stood in opposition to the Boer resistance. Indeed, John Redmond delivered a blistering attack on British policy in South Africa in the very same month MacBride endured electoral defeat. In a powerful condemnation, Redmond told parliamentarians:

> Someday, not perhaps far off, in that Ireland which you are about to create for yourselves in South Africa, you may find white people rejoicing in the Empire's difficulties and sending messages of sympathy to your foes. I would urge this country, before it is involved more deeply in this ill-fated war, to endeavour to learn something from the history of your own experience in Ireland and the American colonies, and from contrasting the history of other great portions of the Empire, and to beware of pursuing to the bitter end the chapter which, whatever way the military operations may go, whether you succeed in this war, can only be a story of misfortune and disgrace. I admit in the frankest manner, that the feeling of the mass of the Irish people is hostile to the Empire. At this moment it would be hypocrisy for me

> to attempt to deny it, and it would be the utmost folly for you to attempt to minimise it.[158]

Though MacBride may have failed to win the votes of the Mayo electorate, after the by-election he was rather oddly celebrated through the renaming of sporting clubs and institutions in his name. For example, the *Western People* reported in September 1901 on the Annual General Meeting of the Ballinrobe (Major MacBride) association football club, though sadly we do not know what the GAA-aligned MacBride thought about such a soccer club existing![159]

In Ulster, there was little such risk of soccer clubs being named in honour of the Mayoman. Indeed, the Irish Football Association made the decision in January 1900 to donate £20 to the Transvaal War Fund towards the comfort of British soldiers. More controversially, the Association installed Field Marshall Earl Roberts and General Sir George White as Honorary Vice-Presidents at their 1900 AGM! If GAA was the game of nationalists, association football – in the north-east of Ireland at least – was firmly a game controlled by unionists. [160]

Shortly after the by-election, Westport native John M. Coughlan felt compelled to write to the Major from New York, with well wishes for his 'fellow-countryman, school-mate, towns-man and neighbour.' News of the South African escapades of a fellow Westport man had moved Coughlan to express his deep admiration, and his hope that 'it may well be of some pleasure to get a line from an old town-man and well-wisher.' In America, he believed ,'I am safe in saying that 90% of it is with the Boers.'[161]

As the war raged on, Maud Gonne's activities on behalf of those fighting the British ranged from organising to send an ambulance to the Transvaal to more extreme proposals. One such activity involved a plan, which was later described as a 'lunatic scheme', would have involved placing bombs disguised as lumps of coal in the holds of British troopships destined for South Africa. Gonne proposed this to Transvaal representatives who dismissed it as outside the rules of war. Their response led Gonne to remark that 'whether you kill your enemies on land or at sea, it does not seem to me to make any difference.'[162]

Maud Gonne was utilised as a public face for the pro-Boer movement in Ireland, travelling to the US to drum up support for the cause among Irish Americans. On a tour of America in 1900, she spoke in twelve cities. The highlight was a packed meeting at the Academy of Music in New York City. Gonne, the *New York Tribune* reported, told the gathered crowd that 'England's difficulty is Ireland's opportunity, and if you are men, having the freedom of Ireland at heart, now is your time.'[163] The American media took a keen interest in Gonne. The newspaper the *Kentucky Irish American* drew a familiar comparison between her and Joan of Arc writing:

> Her name is Maud Gonne. She is called the Irish Joan of

> Arc, and is proud of the name. Perhaps that has something to do with her offer to ride into battle at the head of a regiment. She hates England because of the wrongs of Ireland – not her own wrongs, for she belongs to the favoured class, and might easily, if her heart would let her, avert her eyes from the sufferings of the lowly.[164]

Press reports of Gonne's 1900 lecture tour give insight into not only the huge crowds who attended demonstrations in support of the Boers, but the manner in which Irish, American and Boer symbols and iconography appeared alongside one another in a strange mix-match of nationalist sentiment. Of one demonstration in Boston, a journalist noted:

> Miss Maud Gonne lectured in the Tremond Theatre, Boston, on Sunday evening, 18 February, on the South African war and was given a most cordial greeting by the big audience, numbering something like 2,000 persons. The theatre was tastefully decorated with red, white and blue bunting on the upper balcony, and green and white bunting around the lower balcony. The stage was one mass of bunting. Large oil portraits of President Kruger and General Joubert were placed at the back of the stage setting and were surrounded with the Boer flag, the Stars and Stripes and the colours of Ireland.[165]

Gonne's fundraising and propaganda efforts were important for the solidarity movement that had sprung up on both sides of the Atlantic and they were also crucial in highlighting the activities of the Irish Brigade as they continued to fight against the British. While John MacBride may have lacked military experience prior to taking his place in the Irish Brigade, in a few short months campaigning in South Africa he was exposed to the full brutality of war. Following the Battle of Spion Kop on 24 January 1900, a battle in which the Irish Brigade played no part, MacBride visited the site with the new chaplain of the Brigade, Father Van Hecke, and others. He remembered 'we were profoundly impressed with the horror of the spectacle presented to our eyes, whilst we almost became physically sick at the abominable stench which arouse from the numberless half-buried corpses, whose positions were firmly indicated by numerous legs and arms protruding up through the soft clay of the Kop.'[166] It was shortly after visiting the horror of Spion Kop that MacBride received word that a 'second Irish Brigade' was in formation.

While in the folklore of the Boer conflict the words 'Irish Brigade' usually bring to mind the small band of men who fought with Blake and MacBride, there was a second so-called Irish Brigade in South Africa, led by Arthur Lynch. Lynch, born in Australia in 1861 and one of fourteen children, was a fascinating character in his own right. His father was originally from County Clare, while his mother hailed from Perth in Scotland. While working in London as a journalist in the 1890s, Lynch involved himself in the Irish National League of Great Britain, and stood unsuccessfully as a Parnellite candidate for Galway in July 1892. Lynch dabbled in various Irish nationalistic societies and movements, as he continued to earn a living as a very capable journalist and columnist. Through the London Young Ireland Society, which was established in 1896, Lynch encountered Maud Gonne, and as the Paris correspondent of the *Daily Mail* he developed links with the Irish nationalist movement in the French capital. Arthur Lynch first encountered the war in South Africa as a journalist. By February 1900 he was instrumental in forming a new fighting Irish force, having made contact with the famed Boer General Louis Botha. E. M. Spiers has noted that 'Blake, a former lieutenant in the US cavalry, had at least fought the Apaches, but Lynch gained the colonelcy of the Second Brigade without any military experience whatsoever.'[167]

MacBride made no secret of his opposition to this second force, recalling that when he received a letter from Sol Gillingham informing him of this second Irish Brigade, he thought the idea of starting such a force 'unnecessary and foolish… as in reality we had not enough of men for the first.'[168] Lynch's force had small numbers of native Irishmen in its ranks, consisting largely of a mix of European fighters. One member of Blake's and MacBride's command described Lynch's force as being 'fifty or sixty soreheads, greasers, half-breeds and dagos.'[169]

Lynch's men saw little action in South Africa, indeed the unit was disbanded by June 1900, but Lynch later travelled to the United States drumming up support for the Boer cause there. He re-entered politics too, successfully contesting the 1901 by-election in Galway North, however he could not take his Westminster seat as he had renounced his British citizenship by aligning himself with the Boer forces in South Africa. Tried for treason and sentenced to be hanged in January 1903, he was granted a pardon by King Edward VII, following the lobbying of Irish nationalist leaders. In a remarkable twist to an extraordinary life, he ultimately served as a Colonel in the British armed forces during the First World War, conducting a significant recruitment programme in Ireland. This led George Bernard Shaw to publish an open letter to Lynch in 1918, denouncing the slaughter of the First World War.

Lynch's lectures detailing his experiences in South Africa provide interesting insights on the conflict, and on how the British had military superiority in some fields. He told an audience in Paris in 1902 that the Boers greatly feared the use of military balloons for example, noting that 'the balloons have been of great utility to the English at various places', and describing how:

> Therefore the Boers took a dislike to the balloons. All the other instruments of war were at their command. They had

> pieces of artillery superior too for the most part, and better served than those of the English; they had all the telegraphic and heliographic apparatus; but the balloons were a symbol of a scientific superiority on the side of the English which seriously disquieted them.[170]

The war in South Africa gradually turned in favour of the British armed forces. Ladysmith was relieved in late February 1900, with General Buller succeeding at last. Among those to die there were Corporal James Flynn and Volunteer Michael Flynn. From the same Longford family, one was a member of the Royal Inniskilling Fusiliers, while his brother fought alongside the Boers. It was in the aftermath of Ladysmith that Queen Victoria ordained that Irish regiments would henceforth wear shamrock on Saint Patrick's Day, in recognition of their gallantry.[171]

To MacBride, this period represented a new phase in the conflict, with the seemingly unconquerable Boers and their Irish allies, seeing 'darker days, bringing test and trial of every man in the splendid volunteer army.'[172] By August 1900 the capitals of the Boer Republics had been seized too, and the British media were heralding what appeared to be an unstoppable victory. In the aftermath of these defeats the Boers wished to switch tactics and move towards a purely guerrilla war – an approach that could not include the Irish Brigade. MacBride himself acknowledged this, later writing that:

> It will be easily understood that, especially at the closing stages of the war, men on foot were useless to the Boer army. The tactics of General Botha and his colleagues at that time were entirely in favour of rapid movements from point to point, harassing the enemy here today, and twenty miles off tomorrow, and in such circumstances we would be less an aid than an encumbrance.[173]

In September 1900, the Boer government provided a steamboat to America for the Brigade's departure. Just prior to leaving South Africa, MacBride received a letter of appreciation from General Louis Botha, expressing his sincere gratitude for the role the Irishmen had played in the conflict. Botha stated:

> Hereby we have much pleasure in expressing our deepest gratitude to you and the Irish Brigade for all the military services rendered to us during the past twelve months, in which we were engaged in a war against Britain. We appreciated very highly the assistance which you have so sincerely rendered us during the war: and we wish you and your men a hearty farewell on your return voyage.[174]

While Britain ultimately succeeded in the annexation of the two Boer Republics, the cost of the conflict was great. In financial terms, a war that was supposedly going to be over by Christmas 1899 had cost the taxpayer in excess of £200 million by 1902. In terms of causalities over 20,000 British soldiers died in South Africa, many as a result of wounds sustained in brutal battle. For the Boers, it has been estimated that anything between 18,000 and 28,000 people were lost in British-run concentration camps, many of them women and children. As Thomas Pakenham noted in *The Boer War*, 'in money and lives, no British war since 1815 has been so prodigal.'[175]

One individual who experienced the war in a very different way from MacBride was British General John Maxwell. In Irish popular memory Maxwell is best remembered for his controversial handling of the Easter Rising and the ultimate execution of the men shot in Dublin's Kilmainham Gaol, including John MacBride. In South Africa Maxwell served under Lord Earl Roberts and was decorated for his role in forming and maintaining concentration camps for surrendered Boers and their families at Bloemfontein and Pretoria. In the British press, the camps became one of the scandals of the conflict, with feminist activists in Britain rallying against the detention of women and children. British authorities feared the effect media coverage of the camps would have on British public feeling. In private correspondence Joseph Chamberlain admitted that 'the mortality in the Concentration Camps has undoubtedly roused deep feeling among people who cannot be classed with the pro Boers. It does not seem to me altogether a complete answer to say that the aggregation of people who are especially liable to infectious disease has produced a state of things which is inevitable.'[176]

Maxwell remained in South Africa until March 1902, and received the prestigious Order of Saint Michael and Saint George as recognition of his work in the region. John MacBride left the Transvaal in 1900 and never returned to South Africa. In the late 1980s, however, a curious story took hold in Ireland concerning one Robert McBride. He was a member of the armed wing of the African National Congress (ANC), *Umkhonto we Sizwe*, who it was claimed was a descendent of John MacBride. It was claimed that Robert was related to Major MacBride through a relationship which allegedly occurred during his time in South Africa between MacBride and a Malaysian woman. David Gordon was Robert McBride's advocate during his trial for involvement in an ANC bombing. Gordon subsequently stated:

> I discovered that there had been a John MacBride who came to South Africa and he fought on the side of the Boers during the Anglo-Boer War ... I knew that he was no relative – I know there was no blood relationship, but I thought that it was just ironic that John MacBride had come to South Africa at the time of the Boer war to fight on the side of the Boers.[177]

Robert McBride has visited Ireland on a number of occasions. In March 1998 the *Irish Independent* reported:

> Robert McBride privately concedes that his alleged descent from Major John MacBride is unproven .... Whatever the connection, MacBride is strongly interested in Irish history and makes no secret of his republican sympathies.[178]

McBride has visited Leinster House as a guest of the Sinn Féin party and even delivered a Bobby Sands' memorial address in Belfast in 2006. The story of John MacBride's African descendent has remained popular, if totally unproven.

The legacy of the Second Boer War, in an Irish radical and nationalist context, was that it became a powerful propaganda tool in the years that followed, with the memory of the crushed Boer Republics often evoked during political debates. James Connolly would write years later of the 'two infant republics' that: 'Britain sent her troops to subjugate them, to wipe them off the map; and although they resisted until the veldt ran red with British and Boer blood, the end of the war saw two small nationalities less in the world.'[179]

Following the Irish Brigade's participation in the Boer War, John MacBride found himself in a perilous position. Returning to Ireland was certainly not an option for any of them. Major John MacBride was fully aware that he would face arrest for treason. The men of the Irish Brigade were now dispersing far and wide in the aftermath of their battle. MacBride would recall:

It was a sad night for myself and the boys of the Brigade the night we bid adieu to the country for whose freedom we had fought against her foe and against Ireland's foe .... The Boer government chartered a steamboat ... paid the passage of the men to America and gave each a present of a small sum of money. I went to Paris to meet my mother, brothers and friends. There I met for the first time Miss Maud Gonne and it would have been far better for me if we had never met for she has brought me nothing but sorrow and shame ever since.[180]

Chapter 4

• • • • •

Paris, Maud Gonne and New Beginnings

At the Gare de Lyon train station in Paris, MacBride would be met by faces old and new. Maud Gonne recalled in her memoirs that this was the first time she set eyes on John MacBride. On that initial glance he appeared 'a wiry, soldierly-looking man with red hair and skin burnt brick-red by the South African sun.' She later wrote that his old friend Arthur Griffith jokingly called him *Rooinek*, a common Boer nickname for the English 'because, while other races burn brown, they burn red'. Gonne remembered that MacBride seemed to be in great spirits, and that members of the Paris Young Ireland Society were among those who had gathered to greet the arrival of this new nationalist icon.

After the welcoming reception in the train station, MacBride was taken to the room that had been secured for him in the *Quartier Latin* of the French capital, but he did not stay there long as he dined with Gonne later that night. She was clearly fascinated by a man who had physically taken the fight to the British Empire, remembering that 'we sat up all night talking. MacBride said he had come back hoping there would be something doing in Ireland.'[181]

Maud Gonne and John MacBride may have shared a deep love of Ireland, but in many ways they were born worlds apart. Gonne, born in Surrey, England, on December 21 1866, was the daughter of a British army officer, Captain Thomas Gonne of the 17th Lancers, and of Edith Cook, whose family had made their fortune in the world of draping. Gonne's biographer Margaret Ward has noted that when Maud's great-grandfather, the founder of the Cook family dynasty, passed away he left an astonishing fortune of over £2,000,000 behind him. Unlike MacBride, Gonne was not born into Irish society, but rather into 'the very heartland of upper-class Victorian England.'[182] Ironically given the course her life took, it was her father's British military career that first brought Maud to Ireland, when he was posted to the Curragh, County Kildare in 1868. The family settled in Donnybrook, but Maud's mother died of tuberculosis a few years later in June 1871. With the loss of her mother, Maud Gonne became the 'Lady of the house', and played an important role in raising her younger sister Kathleen, who had been born three years prior to Edith's death. Maud also spent some of her formative years in a French boarding school which gave her an affinity with the country. Her father Tommy, as he was known to Maud, was a huge influence on her development as a young woman. According to Gonne he was a 'charismatic and doting papa', and was renowned for his 'disregard for social convention'.[183]

To garner a better understanding of the upper-class world Maud inhibited, one needn't look further than her memoir of being presented as a debutante at Dublin Castle:

> I was duly presented at Court and manoeuvred my shimmering dress and water-lily train and huge bouquet of lilies of the valley and ostrich-feather fan quite successfully; and in the shimmering dress, without the train, I danced at the great Court Ball in Saint Patrick's Hall on the following night with the Duke of Clarence, who danced very badly and trod excruciatingly on my satin-slippered toes.[184]

The point at which Gonne rejected her Anglo-Irish upbringing for Irish nationalist sentiment has been disputed, though Gonne herself claimed that it was accounts of the suffering of evicted rural tenants in 1885 that forced her to examine Irish society in new ways. She explained years later that this suffering 'changed the whole course of my life by changing me from a frivolous girl, who thought of little but dancing and race meetings, into a woman of fixed purpose.'[185]

Maud was just a few weeks short of her twentieth birthday

when her father passed away on 30 November 1886 at the Royal Barracks in Dublin. In her memoirs Gonne attempted to present her father as something of a deathbed convert to Irish nationalism. She noted that she had watched a great Land League procession from the Royal Barracks with him, not long before his passing, and that he had informed her that 'the people have a right to the land', and that he intended to resign from the army and stand as a Home Rule candidate for parliament.[186] Undoubtedly, Gonne found it difficult to reconcile her own political beliefs with her father's role as a part of the British state apparatus in Ireland. Her fanciful tale of his eleventh-hour conversion to the Home Rule movement, which seems to be at odds with his career and public persona, can be seen as proof of that; though despite different political outlooks her father was still a significant influence on her life.

Following the death of Colonel Gonne, his daughters moved to London to live with his elder brother William. Maud remembered that 'Uncle William had grown rich, old and crusty, but not as mellow as the port wine in which he traded as his father and grandfather had done before him in the City of London.'[187] If Maud held back her feelings towards William in her autobiography, she certainly unleashed them in her statement to the Bureau of Military History, telling them:

> The shock of his death made me very ill. When I recov-

> ered I found our guardian had sold all our belongings in Ireland.... He was a bitter Unionist and a diehard Tory, we quarrelled violently. I left his house without a penny to earn my living on the stage.[188]

Whilst still residing with William, Maud received some startling news when she was confronted with the existence of Eileen Wilson, her illegitimate half-sister. Eileen, a child of only six weeks old, arrived at William's house in the company of her mother. In her memoirs Maud refers to Eileen's mother as 'Elenaor Robbins', though she was in fact Margaret Wilson. The child is referred to as 'Daphne'. Maud and William were informed by the child's mother than Eileen was the daughter of Colonel Gonne and that he had died before her birth. The arrival of young Eileen into the household undoubtedly came as a great shock.

Within a year of the death of her father, and at a time when John MacBride was in South Africa organising the radicalised Irish community there, Maud had left her uncle's home and travelled to France. She started a relationship with Lucien Millevoye, a married French political figure of right-wing beliefs. She first encountered Lucien at the French spa town of Royat. Maud had gone there on holiday on the advice of her doctor as she was suffering with her lungs. Margaret Ward has noted on Maud's meeting with Lucien:

> She was, she said, convinced they had met before, so famil-

iar did the tall, melancholy looking Frenchman seem to her. Lucien Millevoye also suffered from a lung condition and was at Royat partly for his health, and partly to be close to his idol, General Boulanger, whom the extreme right wing in France was hailing as a new Napoleon.[189]

Georges Ernest Boulanger, who Millevoye idolised, was a French army general who promoted an aggressive and authoritarian nationalism which threatened the overthrow of the Third French Republic. Anti-Semitic and feverishly nationalistic in his political outlook, Millevoye none the less taught Gonne a great deal about French political life and journalism. Though Millevoye was married, he commenced an affair with the twenty-year-old Gonne, who was sixteen years his junior.

This affair was motivated both by sexual and political factors. Gonne claimed in her memoirs that the two formed a political alliance, and that Millevoye told her:

> Why don't you free Ireland as Joan of Arc freed France? You don't understand your own power. To hear a woman like you talking of going on the stage is infamous. Yes, you might become a great *actrice,* bur if you became as great an *actrice* as Sara Bernhardt, what of it? An *actrice* is only imitating other people's emotions; that is not living; that is only being a *cabotine*, nothing else. Have a more worthy ambition, free your own country, free Ireland.[190]

Gonne stated that Millevoye continued: 'Let us make an alliance. I will help you to free Ireland. You will help me to regain Alsace-Lorraine.'[191]

For the next few years Gonne found herself living two lives, travelling between Ireland and France. On 11 January 1890, at a time when she was residing at an apartment in Paris, Maud gave birth to their son Georges Sylvére. The baby died in infancy, but Gonne developed a belief that the child could be reincarnated as a result of sexual intercourse occurring next to his tomb. Perhaps traumatised by the grief of losing a child, Gonne sought refuge in the supernatural, and at Samois-sur-Seine Cemetery the act of intercourse between herself and Millevoye occurred. It led to the conception of their daughter Iseult who was born on 6 August 1894. Gonne's relationship with Millevoye and her motherhood remained totally separate from her political activism and public profile in Ireland.

Today, Gonne is undoubtedly best remembered as the muse and the great unrequited love of the poet William Butler Yeats. Yeats had made her acquaintance before the birth of Georges or Iseult and he was unaware of her secret French affair at that point. He had first encountered Gonne in January 1889, when she arrived as a twenty-two-year-old at his family home, visiting his father John Butler Yeats. W. B. Yeats would recall that with her visit, 'the troubling of my life began'. In his memoirs, he captures the eccentricity and beauty of Gonne, and how he was awestruck by her presence:

> Her complexion was luminous, like that of apple-blossom, through which the light falls, and I remember her standing that first day by a great heap of such blossoms in the window. In the next few years I saw her always when she passed to and fro between Dublin and Paris, surrounded, no matter how rapid her journey and how brief her stay at either end of it, by cages full of birds, canaries, finches of all kinds, dogs, a parrot, and once a full-grown hawk from Donegal.[192]

There was an undeniable connection between Gonne and Yeats, a deep friendship and chemistry which grabbed the attention of many who encountered them. In her autobiography, *Flowering Dusk*, the poet Ella Young mentioned seeing Gonne and Yeats together in Dublin, and noticing the two in the National Library:

> Everyone is conscious of those two as the denizens of a woodland lake might be conscious of a flamingo, or of a Japanese heron, if it suddenly descended among them. Later, in the narrow curve of Grafton Street, I notice people are stopping and turning their heads. It is Maud Gonne and the poet. She has a radiance as of sunlight.[193]

The two maintained a correspondence, in particular when

Gonne was in France, which provides us with an insight into their relationship and their thoughts and observations on others in cultural and nationalist circles. Yeats and Gonne shared political platforms, moved in the same cultural circles, and both developed interests in the supernatural and the occult. In 1891 Gonne briefly joined the Hermetic Order of the Golden Dawn, an organisation with which Yeats was involved. Yeats's biographer Roy Foster has noted that 'in early 1889, as William Butler Yeats was drawn into the world of Maud Gonne, he was simultaneously proceeding with his ventures into occult experimentation. The two obsessions became closely associated in his mind, and would remain so.'[194]

The Hermetic Order of the Golden Dawn drew on a wide variety of influences, and while it certainly drew strongly from Rosicrucianism, 'the society also drew on Egyptian, Jewish and Masonic elements, as well as on the Tarot cards.'[195] It was through friends of Yeats who were interested in the occult, that Gonne developed her ideas about the potential reincarnation of her dead son. She had attended séances with Yeats, asking his fellow occultists if a child could be reincarnated. As far as Yeats was aware, the young boy who had perished was not her own child, born of an affair, but rather a child adopted by Gonne. Yeats recalled that Gonne had arrived in Dublin from Paris in October 1891, in a deep sense of personal grief at the loss of her son, at a time when

Ireland was mourning the loss of Parnell:

> I met her on the pier and went with her to her hotel, where we breakfasted. She was dressed in extravagantly deep morning, for Parnell, people thought, thinking her very theatrical. We spoke of the child's death. She had built a memorial chapel, using some of her capital. 'What did money matter to her now?' From another I learned later on that she had the body embalmed. That day and on later days she went over again the details of the death – speech was a relief to her. She was plainly very ill.[196]

Yeats's infatuation with Gonne was evidently clear, and in 1891 he proposed to her for the first time, though she refused to marry him. Yeats would propose to Maud on several occasions, including in the aftermath of John MacBride's execution in 1916, and the poet would even propose to her daughter Iseult in later years.

Yeats did finally learn the truth about Gonne's French relationship in December 1898. Having dreamt vividly of kissing Gonne, he told her about it over breakfast in the Dublin hotel where she was staying, leading Gonne to confess that she had experienced something akin to that very same dream. For the first time 'with the bodily mouth', the two kissed. It was in the aftermath of this experience that Gonne spoke to Yeats about Millevoye, and about the births of their two children. She admitted to Yeats that she felt 'a horror and terror of physical love', and what occurred next was a sort of 'mystical marriage' between the two. It has been described as 'an asexual commitment to each other, heavily reliant on the idea that they had been paired in a previous life as brother and sister.'[197] Yeats wrote to his close friend and confidante Lady Gregory:

> The fact is that M G has told me with every circumstance of deep emotion that she has loved me for years, that my love is the only beautiful thing in her life, but that for certain reasons which I cannot tell you, reasons of a generous kind and a tragic origin, she can never marry.[198]

When Maud returned to Paris after these incredible confessions, Yeats followed after her, and the series of confessions and insights continued. In February 1899, Yeats confided in Lady Gregory from Paris that:

> I have had a rather depressing time here. During the last months, and most all while I have been here she has told the story of her life, telling gradually, in more detail, all except a few things which I can see are too painful for her to talk of and about which I do not ask her.[199]

Yeats returned to the Irish capital soon afterwards and remained infatuated with Gonne, while greatly pained by her suffering.

Gonne's relationship with Millevoye was in tatters by the

summer of 1900, as by then Millevoye had a new mistress in Paris. Iseult, the surviving child of the affair, was predominantly educated and cared for at a Carmelite convent in Laval, France. In public, particularly in Ireland, she was referred to as Maud's niece or cousin rather than daughter. While her private life was in chaos, a public image of Gonne as a fearless Irish leader of Joan of Arc quality was spreading. In the pages of an 1896 edition of *The Shan Van Vocht*, a poem dedicated to Gonne noted that:

> Uncrowned, save by a nation's love, our island's maiden queen,
> By spell of her young voice alone, unfurls the standard green,
> Where in the days of gallant Hoche, the sword of Tone fell keen.[200]

In a sense, Gonne was at something of a crossroads in her own life by the time she met the returning Boer War hero in France, juggling a complex private life with an active political agenda and public image. Yet MacBride was not destined to spend long in the French capital. As he was unable to return to Ireland as a result of his participation in the war, the belief was that he should tour the United States, speaking on the heroics of the Irish Brigade and fundraising for the *United Irishman*. Arthur Griffith's newspaper had served as an important ally and propaganda tool during the war. Gonne recounts that 'Griffith said he thought it was quite useless for him to take the risk of going to Ireland as things were and MacBride decided to go to America.' To her:

> I felt that little band of Irishmen in the Brigade had done more for Ireland's honour than all of us a home, for it is action that counts. MacBride said the flag sent out by Inghinidhe na hÉireann had been greatly appreciated.[201]

MacBride's presence in Paris and his return from the battlefield attracted considerable attention from the press in Ireland. An interview with the Major, filed by Barry O'Delany from the French capital, appeared in several Irish newspapers. O'Delany basked in MacBride's presence, writing:

> The love of country – the noblest love God ever planted in the heart of man! – must glow indeed but faintly in the breast of the Irishman, or Irishwoman, who could touch unmoved the hand of a brave compatriot who had risked his life for Erin's sake.[202]

During the interview MacBride produced a piece of battled metal, informing O'Delany that it 'is all that is left of the sight of one of the English cannons taken at Colenso; you see it is twisted out of shape.' He went on to state that 'grab-all greed' is what motivated Britain towards war, as 'had there been no gold mines in the Transvaal there would have been no war. The other motives put forward by England are a credit to her hypocrisy.'[203]

Prior to his departure for the United States MacBride was present at a banquet for the Irish Transvaal Committee in Paris, which was attended by President Kruger who had fled South Africa on the Dutch warship *Gelderland*. It was widely reported in the Irish media that Kruger met Irish nationalists such as John O'Leary, Maud Gonne and MacBride at the reception:

> Miss Maud Gonne, as representing the Daughters of Erin, was the first to present an address: 'Monsieur le President' said Erin's lovely delegate, as she curtseyed before the aged hero, 'it is with feelings of the deepest sympathy with your case, which is also our own, and with profound admiration for the heroism with which you have maintained the glorious fight against our common enemy, that I present you this address in the name of the women of Ireland.'[204]

Comically, the Boer emissary Dr Willem Leyds, to whom Maud Gonne had proposed placing bombs disguised as lumps of coal in the holds of British troopships, received a warning from an Irish informant of Maud Gonne's planned presentation prior to the ceremony:

> Adverrissement!! You are warned that the ridiculous Maud Gonne with one of her amoureux, the third-rate poet Yeats, is getting up a present Deputation to meet President Kruger. As she is universally laughed at, she must

be kept to one side.[205]

On being introduced to MacBride, it was recorded that the aging Kruger 'drew himself up to his full height', and 'took the hand of the young soldier into his own.' Major MacBride was reported to have 'seemed touched to the heart's core', and he defiantly told the gathering: 'Monsieur le President, to fight for the liberty of any land could only be a happiness and an honour for an Irishman. But to fight for the liberty of a land whose enemy is also our enemy is the birth right of an Irish Brigade!'[206]

Maud Gonne remembered Kruger as 'a tragic, broken-hearted old man, with rugged dignity. He looked very weary.'[207] By then, however, one suspects Kruger, and indeed MacBride, were well aware of what the outcome of the war would be.

It is worth noting that a curious entry concerning President Kruger appears in the Dublin Castle police intelligence reports of the early twentieth century. While a degree of what appeared in such intelligence files was often hearsay or half-truth, the entry is intriguing as it specifically names two IRB men in Castlerea, a town where MacBride had worked and been actively involved in the Fenians, as well as naming his brother Anthony and Dr Mark Ryan. 'P. Shaughnessy, Con 50609' reported from Castlebar in February 1901 that:

I beg to report that I have been informed on good authority that a considerable sum of money was given by the ex-President of the Transvaal to Michael Davitt when presenting him with an address in France a few months ago, and that a portion of it is now being utilised by IRB men in this country. My informant has told me that he has no doubt, but John Sile and Thomas Egan of Castlerea have been receiving money from some source, for some time past, and he is of the opinion that they are getting it from Dr. Mark Ryan and Dr. A MacBride of London.[208]

Before MacBride's departure for the United States, a crucially important letter of introduction to John Devoy was provided for him by John O'Leary. It was a means by which one respected nationalist would convince another of the importance and sincerity of the young Mayoman. Dated 30 November 1900, O'Leary wrote:

> I write now merely to introduce to you my young friend, the Major, who in my opinion at least, has done us and our country the greatest credit in the Boer War … I knew him long before he went to South Africa, and then, as now, I found him a type of the best sort of young Irishman. I don't know that I need say anything more.[209]

Devoy was born in pre-famine Kildare in September 1842, the third of eight children. Having joined the IRB in 1861, he went on to serve in the French Foreign Legion, gaining military experience. Sentenced to fifteen years' imprisonment with hard labour in 1867 as a result of his political activism, he was later released in 1871. This was as a result of a partial amnesty granted to Fenian prisoners, though they were exiled from British territory until the expiration of their initial sentences. Devoy sailed for the United States on board the steamer *Cuba*, in the company of four other IRB activists, with the five men becoming known as the 'Cuba Five'. In the United States, he joined Clan na Gael, and later he was instrumental is raising vital funds for the Land League movement in Ireland. As Patrick Maume commented:

> Devoy helped to organise the American Land League, a vital source of funds for the Irish organisation. By 1881–2 tensions appeared in the alliance: there was friction between Parnell and Devoy over the question of whether the American organisation should be controlled from America or from Ireland.[210]

Clashing with Parnell and other significant figures over the course of his political career, Devoy was headstrong and often confrontational. In 1903 he established the *Gaelic American* newspaper, which would prove influential. It was perhaps his position as Secretary of Clan na Gael, however, which influenced O'Leary in writing to him prior to MacBride's departure.

In Devoy's book, *Recollections of an Irish Rebel,* which served equally as a historical overview of Irish separatism and a personal memoir, he outlined his belief that in the context of the 1798 rebellion:

> History proves that the only remedy for all of Ireland's ills is Total Separation from England and the setting up of an Independent Government having no political connection whatever with the British Empire. Of course, it is manifest that as England grew stronger and Ireland weaker as a result of the alien, unjust and tyrannical system which England imposed on her, political separation could not have been achieved without foreign aid.[211]

In a sense, that belief in the need for foreign aid was something which clearly motivated Devoy and his associates in the United States, as they were fundraising and drumming-up support for the movement. John MacBride, like many Irish nationalists before him, was destined to move in the same radical circles of Irish America for a period, to try to gain funding for the cause of Ireland in the land of Devoy and Clan na Gael.

Chapter 5

America and Marriage

News of MacBride's visit to the United States was met by excitement in the Irish American press, even before he arrived on American soil. The *Kentucky Irish American* reported on 8 December 1900 that 'John MacBride, who organised and commanded the Irish Brigade in the Transvaal, sailed from Paris Saturday last for New York, where he will begin a lecture tour through the United States.'[212]

Arriving in New York, MacBride was met with enthusiasm from gatherings of Irish nationalists eager to hear about the glories of the battlefield.

MacBride was generally well received in the United States, and in his own words he had gone there to 'lecture in aid of the anti-recruiting movement in Ireland and on behalf of the *United Irishman* newspaper of Dublin. All the money obtained in the United States was devoted to the objects named above and £50 kept by me to enable me to live until I got a position.'[213]

For MacBride, convincing Irish American republicans of the need to support Griffith's paper was crucially important. In his correspondence with Devoy, MacBride outlined the 'absolute necessity for supporting the *United Irishman.* The *United Irishman* at present supplies the place of organisers in Ireland and is at least equal to a dozen.'[214]

MacBride also used the speaking tour to boost morale among the Boer solidarity movement, when defeat seemed imminent on the battlefield. When he was interviewed at the Vanderbilt Hotel, he made it clear to the press that while Winston Churchill and other reporters were adamant that the Boers were a spent force, MacBride's view was that: 'Churchill may say what he likes about the war in South Africa being over, but I tell you the war is not over. The Boers will fight just as long as there is a man, woman or child alive.'[215]

Evidently, Maud Gonne had made a considerable impression on MacBride in Paris, as he wrote to her not long after his arrival in the US, requesting that she join him on his speaking tour. Perhaps he had fallen for Maud, or perhaps the Major was still honing his skills as a speaker, and believed the presence of the charismatic activist Maud Gonne would be beneficial to the lectures. One journalist covering the tour had complained that 'we hope that with a little practice the Major will be able to tell the story off-hand, for having to read it takes away very much from its interest.'[216] MacBride was certainly taken by Gonne's abilities. Soon after her arrival he wrote to his beloved mother Honoria that: 'Miss Gonne astonishes me the way in which she can stand the knocking about. For a woman it is wonderful.'[217]

Gonne's recollections of America included reference to John Devoy, who MacBride was eager to impress. She recalled arriving in New York upon a French Transatlantic liner and delivering a speech the following February evening to an eager audience. The next day she was visited by Devoy:

> He tripped over a footstool and landed on his knees at my head. MacBride and I helped him to rise quickly and got him comfortably seated in an armchair, but this incident was most unpropitious. MacBride told me afterwards that Mr Devoy was extremely temperamental and self-conscious and could not stand anything which upset his dignity.[218]

MacBride spoke in a wide variety of American cities and towns, recounting his experiences to large audiences in traditional Irish hubs such as Chicago, but also to sizeable crowds in places such as Wisconsin and St Louis. He moved among the Clan na Gael community, while Gonne 'was kept busy with reporters and reception committees'. She could clearly see, however, that despite the large and eager audiences which attended their lectures across a variety of cities, MacBride was not satisfied with the state of the movement:

> The men in high places, distinguished lawyers and politi-

> cians, were not revolutionists and they had much control. It was inevitable that they should look on the organisation from an American point of view – the great voting power of the Irish. Many of these successful men were sons of parents who had been driven from Ireland on emigration ships ... but their American education, their successful business careers, made most of them adverse to revolutionary schemes.[219]

Gonne formed the opinion that 'no doubt they would back up the fight in Ireland when it started, but they were happier supporting constitutional leaders like Parnell and were hard to convince that there was nothing to hope from men like Redmond or John Dillon.'[220]

Constitutional nationalists including John Redmond had engaged on speaking tours of the United States in the years prior to the MacBride/Gonne tour. Before he departed from New York in 1892 Redmond had told the American press that 'my reception by the people of New York strengthens my determination to fight for Home Rule on the lines of our dead leader', a reference to Charles Stewart Parnell, who was as revered by sections of Irish America as he was on his home turf[221]. Gonne may have been taken aback by the conservatism of some of the Irish American audience, but constitutional nationalism was deeply ingrained in sections of the community there, from the time of Daniel O'Connell's Repeal and Emancipation movements.

In the United States, MacBride was in written communication with Thomas J. Clarke, the veteran Fenian who would become one of the signatories of the 1916 proclamation. As John and Anthony MacBride had played a prominent role in the Amnesty Association when it campaigned for prisoners such as Clarke during the days of heavy Fenian activity in Britain, the mutual respect and admiration between the two men was not surprising. Clarke had been one of the final Fenian prisoners released after he had been sentenced to penal servitude for life in May 1883 for his involvement in the IRB's Dynamite campaign. Following his release in 1898 Clarke had settled in New York, obtaining employment there in a factory where the foreman happened to be a Clan na Gael member.[222] MacBride had begun his American speaking tour in New York and was destined to return there at a later date. In one letter that April Clarke joked:

> The Mayo ladies are putting their heads together here in order to be ready to make a presentation to Major McBride when he returns. That will be news for you. Don't ask me what it is they are going to present. I don't know. Perhaps it's a wife—with a fervent wish that it may, I'll wind up this note. Trusting you are OK and Miss Gonne likewise.[223]

Within MacBride's private papers is a cut-out from an American newspaper that he had kept as a memento. It tells of a presentation made to him upon his return to New York by 'the women of County Mayo residing in New York':

> No words in print can accurately describe the scene of enthusiasm that occurred In the hall when the Major was presented with a magnificent gold watch and chain valued at $300, which bore a suitable inscription and accompanied the address as a gift from the women of County Mayo residing in New York.[224]

While Clarke joked of the women presenting a wife to Major MacBride, it was Thomas Clarke himself who would be married in the city. In July 1901, Kathleen Daly arrived in New York. She was a Limerick woman from a prominent Fenian family who would play her own part in Irish revolutionary history in the years to come. Her Uncle, John Daly, had been imprisoned with Clarke, also as a result of his Fenian activities, and it was through that connection that Kathleen and Thomas had first met in Limerick. At their New York wedding, MacBride served as best man.

Keeping with the theme of weddings, Gonne would later claim that it was during this speaking tour that MacBride first proposed to her, though she informed him that against the backdrop of the pressing political campaigns in which they were both involved marriage was not in her thoughts.

It was while they were in the United States that Gonne received news from Ireland that their friend Willie Rooney was dead. MacBride and Rooney had moved in the same circles in Ireland, with Rooney the driving force of the Celtic Literary Society. A cable from Arthur Griffith on the Boston leg of the speaking tour in May 1901 informed Gonne of the loss of a man she believed had displayed an influence in his day 'comparable with that of Thomas Davis in his.'[225]

Gonne would receive a further communication from Griffith, while speaking alongside MacBride in St Louis. He was pleading with her 'not to stay too long in America as I was badly needed in Dublin where another Royal visit was threatened.'[226] Gonne concluded her part in the United States tour, leaving the Major to complete the rest of the appearances alone. With his oratorical skills improved and his confidence growing, MacBride continued to speak to large crowds. In San Francisco, he informed a sizeable gathering that 'If freedom is worth having, it is worth fighting for; and if it is not worth fighting for, it is not worth having!'[227]

The Major returned to Paris in July, though lecturing on the Boer War and on his involvement in it would remain a feature of his life in the years that followed.

It was not Ireland Gonne was first destined for after leaving MacBride's tour, even though Griffith insisted she was urgently required, but rather France. Gonne visited Iseult at the convent in Laval where she had placed her in care. The relationship between Maud and Iseult at this point was somewhat distant. Margaret Ward has described Maud's attitude as 'reminiscent of an indulgent godmother who could happily shower gifts on a child, confident that she would not be around to deal with the consequences.'[228] The present Maud brought with her from America was somewhat unconventional to say the least, and truly horrified the nuns at the convent. Certainly, it was not everyday someone arrived to present the gift of a live baby alligator to a seven-year-old child! After her eccentric trip to Laval, Maud travelled onwards to London. She visited her sister Kathleen and met with members of her family who were gathering for the wedding of May Gonne, Maud's cousin. During this short stay in London she also met with Yeats, who was still infatuated with her. Yeats once again proposed to his muse. In her memoirs, she recounted Yeats asking of her to 'marry me and give up this tragic struggle and live a peaceful life.' Maud remembered the conversation they had:

> 'Willie, are you not tired of asking that question? How often have I told you to thank the Gods that I will not marry you. You would not be happy with me.'
>
> 'I am not happy without you.'
>
> 'Oh yes, you are, because you make beautiful poetry of what you call your unhappiness and you are happy in that. Marriage would be such a dull affair. Poets should never marry.'[229]

Maud did finally make it to Ireland after the London wedding, and she threw herself into political activism once again, though she went back to France shortly afterwards.

MacBride also returned to Paris, but for him it was not a city that seemed to offer much opportunity. What kind of employment, if any, would be available for this man of action was totally unclear. MacBride's humble abode in Paris was a small attic room at 30 Rue Gay de Lussac, located in the Latin Quarter of the city. He was financially impoverished and at something of a loss with regards his future. Gonne commented that 'without the language, MacBride, I am afraid, had a hard time in Paris; waiting for a chance is always hard. I felt he would have done better to have stayed in America, where he had many openings.'[230] In returning to Europe, MacBride seemed to be making a conscious decision to be amongst friends in Paris, and perhaps he was also seeking to be closer to Gonne.

In November 1901, he was formally honoured by the presentation of a ceremonial sword and revolver by a visiting Irish delegation, in recognition of his actions in South Africa. Dublin Castle intelligence kept a transcript copy of the address which accompanied the presentation and which was also reproduced in several newspapers at the time. The powerful oration closed by including MacBride in the pantheon of Irish nationalists, and placing great importance on him as a future leader:

> We certify to you that the people of Ireland are true to the first principles of Nationality as stated by Tone, Emmet,

> Mitchel, Davis and others have stated besides; and think you are the man chosen to prepare the scattered Irishman for the last battle to bring back to Erin her rights and Independence. GOD SAVE IRELAND![231]

The speech which MacBride delivered at the ceremony was loaded with passion and fierce rhetoric. It was a call to arms that was met with rapid enthusiasm in the Salons Corazza at the Palais Royal. In the presence of men like John O'Leary and other veterans of the struggle, MacBride outlined his case that Ireland was moving towards its own confrontation with the British Empire:

> The Boers, in their fight against English oppression, have been as one against ten, and sometimes, as even one against twenty or more. The combined population of the Orange Free State and the Transvaal does not equal that of the city of Dublin. Yet the Boer War has already cost England three times as much as the Crimean war did. Let us, then, cease to live in dreams only of Ireland's freedom; if we do not wish to be regarded as slaves and dastards in our own land. England was never weaker than she is at present.[232]

MacBride and Gonne continued to feature in each other's lives, though she was frequently moving between France and Ireland. She rented a small home at 42 Coulson Avenue in Rathgar, and immersed herself in Dublin and Parisian life. In April 1902, she played the lead role in Yeats's *Kathleen Ní*

Houlihan. It was produced at Saint Teresa's Hall in Clarendon Street by the Irish National Dramatic Society and Gonne's Inghinidhe ne hÉireann organisation. Yeats remembered that she played the lead role 'magnificently and with weird power.'[233] Kathleen herself exists as a mythical symbol and emblem of Irish independence, and the play was set during 1798, the year of the United Irish rebellion which MacBride, Yeats and Gonne had all commemorated only a few short years previously. Yeats dedicated the play to the memory of William Rooney. The critic Stephen Gwynn would later note that 'the effect of Kathleen Ní Houlihan on me was that I went home asking myself if such players should be produced unless one was prepared for people to go out to shoot and be shot.'[234]

The actress and republican activist Máire Nic Shiubhlaigh was among those present in the hall on the night the play was first performed, and, like many other members of the cast and audience, her memory of the night was Maud Gonne:

> Watching her, one could readily understand the reputation she enjoyed as the most beautiful woman in Ireland, the inspiration of the whole revolutionary movement. She was the most exquisitely fashioned creature I have ever seen. Her beauty was startling. Yeats wrote *Kathleen Ní Houlihan* especially for her, and there were few in the audience who did not see why.[235]

If Gonne stole the show in Dublin, MacBride was unable to witness her triumph as he still could not return to the land of his birth; nor could be set foot on any part of British soil, as he believed he would be liable for arrest because of his actions in South Africa. In Ireland, his star was still shining bright, with badges and posters of Major MacBride for sale and proudly worn and displayed by nationalists. Poems and songs in his honour were printed not only in nationalist publications like the *United Irishman* but also in regional newspapers.

Though MacBride couldn't have known it there was in fact no plan to arrest him on British soil. Internal correspondence between the London authorities and Dublin Metropolitan Police noted that 'no warrant has been issued for his arrest and his case, for being in arms against our troops in South Africa, has not been considered as far as police are aware with a view to prosecution.'[236] The crucial difference between MacBride and Arthur Lynch, who was successfully tried for treason, was that Lynch had travelled to South Africa following the outbreak of hostilities there; while the authorities recorded that MacBride was already in the country. MacBride's fear of arrest was undoubtedly a major factor in his decision to remain in France, where steady work was increasingly difficult to find.

Employment did come at last, in early 1902. MacBride found a position working as secretary to the correspondent of the *New York Sun* newspaper, at £2 a week. At first, the news horrified Gonne who informed him that his employer was pro-British in his political outlook. MacBride was adamant in his response that: 'I have been converting him and his family to Irish republicanism.' In the end Gonne was just grateful that he had found work 'to occupy his mind and enable him to live.'[237] Among the people MacBride informed of his new employment was John Devoy, with whom he had maintained a correspondence since his visit to the United States: 'You will be astonished to hear that I have been doing newspaper work for the last four or five weeks. It is not a magnificent paying job but it keeps me going.'

Devoy was considering stepping aside as leader of Clan na Gael at this point, an organisation he had aligned with the Irish Republican Brotherhood in the 1870s. MacBride was a strong supporter of Devoy's militarist viewpoint, telling him 'with that policy there is hope for Ireland's future. Without it there is no hope.'

If Devoy was serious about retiring, MacBride outlined his belief that 'the Convention could hardly make a wiser or better choice than plucky Tom Clarke'. Ultimately, MacBride wished of Devoy 'may your policy be one of war on England and everything English.'[238]

MacBride and other militant separatists needn't have worried about the retirement of the firebrand leader. Devoy retained his position of influence in Irish American radical circles and would later prove vitally important in arranging communications between republicans and German representatives in New York, following the outbreak of the First World War.

Gonne and MacBride continued to see each other regularly in Paris, becoming better acquainted with one another and with each other's ways. An anecdote that Maud Gonne related about MacBride gives us an insight into his 'queer conventions' as she termed them, but also tells us something about her own attitudes to social boundaries:

> One day, after a lecture by d'Arboid de Joubainville in the Quartier Latin we had both attended, to avoid going to a café, as he suggested, I insisted instead that he should give me tea in his room, where we would be quieter for a talk, really because I knew the money he would have spent at the café would have probably meant no dinner for him the next day. I think he was shocked at the suggestion, till I told him he must get rid of the English idea that a bedroom was a less proper place than a sitting room, for he was full of queer conventions.[239]

MacBride became aware of Maud Gonne's affair with Millevoye after hearing rumours about it when he returned from the United States. Gonne told MacBride the truth about her relationship with Millevoye, although she did not mention their children. MacBride later noted that she told him 'she intended, of course, to turn over an absolutely new leaf, and she said that she intended to become a Catholic.'[240]

By the summer of 1902, it would appear that Gonne had changed her mind in relation to the proposition of marriage she claimed MacBride had made in America, and she seemed destined to wed him. Having ended her affair with Millevoye she wrote to her sister Kathleen informing her of her intentions, and making it clear that her own personal circumstances were also an influence in her decision:

> Now I see the chance, without injuring my work, of having a little happiness and peace in my personal life, and I am taking it. We are made that way, that we need companionship and with Iseult growing up, I cannot get this companionship outside of marriage. Marriage I always consider abominable but for the sake of Iseult, I make that sacrifice to convention.[241]

Kathleen opposed the planned marriage, proposing instead that Maud wed Yeats. Maud rejected this totally, claiming that she knew MacBride 'very well', undoubtedly a reference to the time they had spent together in the United States and their subsequent social life in Paris:

> As for Willie Yeats I love him dearly as a friend, but I could not for one moment imagine marrying him. I love John MacBride and am going to marry him. MacBride is a man I know very well. I have seen a great deal of him for the last

> two years and I know he is thoroughly sincere and honest and I can trust him entirely and I think I will always be happy.[242]

MacBride would later state that the idea of marriage was entirely Maud Gonne's. This is of course at odds with the claims put forward in her autobiography that he proposed to her in the United States. He commented:

> I was not anxious for the marriage as I knew we were not suited for one another .... Then at last moved by her tears and thinking I was doing good for my country and good for herself I consented to marry her. It was a foolish thing to do. I gave her a name that was free from stain or reproach and she was unable to appreciate it once she had succeeded in inducing me to marry her.[243]

News of the engagement was widely reported. In February 1903, MacBride was briefly interviewed by *The Morning Leader* in Paris, who congratulated him on the planned marriage and asked him if the couple 'proposed to return and live in Dublin.' MacBride laughed, and said that the British authorities would either arrest or shoot him if he did that and neither Miss Gonne nor himself were 'anxious for either contingency just now.' The newspaper noted that MacBride stated 'the almighty never meant Ireland to be governed by Britain, and if readers of *The Morning Leader* care for a message from me you may tell them that I would dearly love to come and deal with the English in their own country as I did when I was fighting with the Boers in South Africa, and maybe I will one day.'[244]

Gonne's daughter also did not welcome news of the proposed marriage. Maud remembered that on visiting Iseult at Laval, the young child was devastated by the news, and that 'she had cried when I told her I was getting married to MacBride and she hated MacBride. I had felt like crying too. I told her I would send her lovely things from Spain, where we were going for our honeymoon, but she was not consoled.' Gonne remembered that the youngster had to be dragged away from her sobbing.[245]

News of Gonne's decision to convert to Catholicism in preparation for the marriage was printed in the *United Irishman*, where it was noted that: 'Miss Gonne, who some time ago became a Catholic, will be formally received into the Catholic Church on Tuesday, at the Chapel des Dames de St. Thérese, Laval, and her marriage will take place before the end of the month.'[246] Gonne was baptised into the Catholic faith on 17 February 1903, and for her confirmation name she took Honoria, the name of MacBride's mother.

Gonne claimed that shortly after the heart-breaking moment with her daughter, she was waiting in her apartment for John to collect her one evening, as they were going to dine at a nearby restaurant. Tired, she lay down and closed her eyes, and heard her deceased father Tommy speak:

'Lambkin, don't do it. You must not get married.'[247]

When Gonne informed MacBride of this, he showed her a letter from his mother Honoria in Westport:

> I have seen Maud Gonne. She is very beautiful; she is a great woman and has done much for Ireland but she will not make you happy. You will neither be happy, she is not the wife for you. I am very anxious. Think well what you are doing.[248]

Similarly, Major MacBride's brother Joseph was dead set against the marriage:

You know of course what you are doing, but I think it most unwise. Maud Gonne is older than you. She is accustomed to money and you have none; she is used to going her own way and listens to no one. These are not good qualities for a wife. A man should not marry unless he can keep his wife.[249]

Arthur Griffith, a friend to both parties, wrote to Gonne begging her not to marry MacBride. He pleaded with her 'for her own sake and for the sake of Ireland to whom you both belong' not to marry the Major. Griffith believed that 'I know you both, you so unconventional, a law to yourself; John so full of conventions.'[250]

It seemed that proponents of the marriage were near impossible to find. While her daughter Iseult, Joseph and Honoria MacBride, Arthur Griffith and Maud's sister Kathleen were all opposed to the planned marriage, it was from William Butler Yeats that the most emotional of pleas would come. The news of Maud converting to Catholicism brought about a great emotional outpouring from Yeats in a letter from late January 1903. It began with the words: 'I appeal to you in the name of 14 years of friendship to read this letter. It is perhaps the last thing I shall write you.' Yeats appealed to Gonne spiritually, telling her: 'If you carry out your purpose you will fall into a lower order and do great injury to the religion of free souls that is growing up in Ireland, it may be to enlighten the whole world.' A common theme in the various letters of concern from their family and friends were the class differences between Gonne and MacBride, but in Yeats's letter these concerns were most profoundly evident: 'You possess your influence in Ireland very largely because you come to the people from above. You represent a superior class, a class whose people are more independent, have a more beautiful life, a more refined life. Every man almost of the people who has spoken to me of you has shown that you influence him very largely because of this.' Yeats believed that 'it is not only the truth and your friends but your own soul that you are about to betray.'[251]

Gonne replied to Yeats from Laval, beginning by telling him his letters 'have made me sad, because I fear that you are sad and yet our friendship need not suffer by my marriage.' Her letter focused on the spiritual and religious issues which so troubled Yeats:

> About my change of religion I believe like you that there is one great universal truth. God that pervades everything. I believe that each religion is a different prism through which one looks at truth. None can see the whole of truth. When we do, we shall have merged in the deity, and we shall be as God but that is not yet. In the meantime our nation looks at God or truth through one prism, The Catholic Religion.
>
> I am officially a Protestant and supposed to look at it from another and much narrow one which is moreover the English one. I prefer a truth through the same prism as my country people – I am going to become a Catholic. It seems to me of small importance if one calls the great spirit forces the *Sidhe*, the Gods and the Arch Angels, the great symbols of all religions are the same. But I do feel it important *not* to belong to the Church of England.'[252]

None of this would have been reassuring to Yeats in the slightest. If he was baffled by Gonne's decision to marry MacBride, it is clear to us now that Gonne was drawn to MacBride as the embodiment of the Irish nationalist tradition she idolised and dedicated herself to. There had been clues in her letters to Yeats of what was to come. She had written to him in the summer of 1902 of a visit she had made to the MacBride family in Mayo, during one of her stays in Ireland:

> I have had a very pleasant time. Joseph MacBride took me out conger eel fishing, we didn't get back till one 'clock – It was too lovely among the islands in Clew Bay .... Joseph MacBride is very nice; he reads a great deal and knows all your books. He lives in a charming cottage on the edge of the bay, where we all went to tea yesterday. By the way he told me to tell you than any time it suited you to come and spend a quiet time in the country, you would greatly please him if you would write and tell him you were coming to stay with him in that cottage.[253]

While she was undoubtedly drawn to MacBride and all he, and indeed his family, embodied, Gonne believed that by marrying MacBride, she could further the cause of Irish independence to which they were both committed. She informed her friend Madame Avril that by marrying MacBride she expected: 'I shall be able to more effectively serve the cause of independence.'[254]

The marriage of Maud Gonne and John MacBride took place on 21 February 1903, in the most unusual of locations. A civil ceremony was to occur at the British Embassy in Paris, before the marriage rite could take place at the Church of Saint-Honoré d'Elyau. That John MacBride, who had taken the fight to the British Empire in South Africa, should be forced to partake in a civil ceremony in the British Embassy prior to marrying Maud Gonne was a great irony. MacBride was also conscious of the risks it brought: 'We had to go to the British Consulate to have the civil ceremony performed and I kept my hand on my revolver while the deed was being done as I was under the British flag while there and I was not going to allow them any tricks.'[255]

A detailed report of the wedding appeared, naturally, in the *United Irishman*. It was reprinted in several regional newspapers, indicating the broad interest in the marriage throughout Ireland. The priest chosen to perform the duties was none other than Father Van Hecke, former chaplain to the Irish Brigade in the Boer War – and the marriage ceremony was loaded with other symbolism. The flags of the Irish Brigade from South Africa, including the flag Maud Gonne's organisation had sent to the Brigade, were present in the church. Even the breakfast on the following day was politicised, with the *United Irishman* noting: 'The wedding breakfast took place in the Hotel de Florence. The centre of the table was decorated with a lovely basket of shamrocks and violets, entwined with green, white and orange ribbons, sent over by Inghinidhe na hÉireann.'[256] Among the gifts presented to the newly-weds were a 'beautifully decorated Irish harp' from Belfast, 'Mother Nolan's Irish Prayerbook' and a rather curious 'lizard-skin cigar case'. Father Van Hecke rose to the occasion, telling those gathered about shared moments with MacBride in South Africa:

> We have slept side by side sometimes under the open sky, covered by the same rug, as other times drenched to the

> skin, and I can bear witness that never did I hear a murmur or a word of complaint for all he was enduring the cause of freedom. It is with the greatest pleasure that I came from Belgium to unite him to that peerless woman of the Irish race …[257]

Privately, Yeats would confide his heartbreak to Lady Gregory, with whom he maintained an ongoing correspondence. Publicly, his heartbreak would lead to some of his most celebrated poetry. 'Never Give All the Heart', written in 1903 and published in 1905, perhaps best captures the poet's heartbreak. As Yeats critic David A. Ross has noted, 'cynically and worldly, the poem represents Yeats at his farthest remove from the romanticism that was almost innate to his personality.'[258]

> Never give all the heart, for love
> Will hardly seem worth thinking of
> To passionate women if it seem
> Certain, and they never dream
> That it fades out from kiss to kiss;
> For everything that's lovely is
> But a brief, dreamy, kind delight.
> O never give the heart outright,
> For they, for all smooth lips can say,
> Have given their hearts up to the play.
> And who could play it well enough

If deaf and dumb and blind with love?
He that made this knows all the cost,
For he gave all his heart and lost.

Chapter 6

A Marriage in Tatters

The marriage of Maud Gonne and John MacBride was heralded by Irish nationalists as the coming together of two great patriotic figures. After their wedding, the newly-wed couple settled into their residence Les Mouettes in Colleville-sur-Mer, Normandy. Maud had purchased the house from the sizeable inheritance left to her by her great-aunt Augusta. Les Mouettes was to be home to what was in reality a family, including Maud and her daughter Iseult, but also Eileen Wilson, Maud's half-sister, who was to be Iseult's governess. In addition to this, Maud hired housekeeping staff.

Gonne found Colleville beautiful and relaxing, later writing to her sister Kathleen:

> The more I see of this place the more I love it. It is so wild and so country. The garden goes down to the sea and the fields full of wild flowers come down to the garden, and there is no one but ourselves. We go about most of the day

> in bathing dresses and shrimping and fishing take up a lot of the time.[259]

Great mystery has always surrounded the honeymoon of Major MacBride and Maud Gonne, which involved a trip to Spain. What is known for certain is that the honeymoon was a most unhappy one, though the circumstances have been contested. Maud Gonne would later confide to a friend that when she and MacBride were informed of a planned visit by the King and Queen of England to Spain, the two newly-weds organised a trip which would allow for the assassination of British royals at Gibraltar. Their honeymoon would provide the cover for allowing them to be in Spain at the time of the royal visit. Margaret Ward has noted that 'it sounds like an adventurous fiction, but some may feel that this offers a plausible explanation for what finally precipitated Maud into marriage.'[260] In *The Gonne-Yeats Letters, 1893–1938,* it is argued that this was not 'adventurous fiction', but rather a plan which was first muted in the United States in 1901. MacBride was eager for militant action, and had written to John Devoy informing him 'should my services be required for work you can promise for me', and it has been argued in the edited collection of letters that this was one such example of action MacBride was willing to take:

> MacBride went to meet with his friends to carry out the mission, but that night he came back to the hotel drunk

> and would not say what had happened. This was the final blow in a honeymoon that from the start had not been auspicious.[261]

MacBride would later write to his brother Anthony that, 'needless to say I did not put foot on Gibraltar and consequently do not know how the C.B.s are doing there. We were at Algeciras (opposite Gib) the day the king arrived and as he forgot to send me an invitation I did not go.'[262] It is all somewhat unclear, but an intriguing story none the less.

MacBride would claim the unhappiness of the honeymoon was brought about principally by the fact that his new wife wished to maintain a correspondence with former lovers. He would recall that 'during our honeymoon (what a misnomer!) she was sending messages to her principle ex-lover', a reference to Millevoye. It appears that right from the beginning there was deep unhappiness and tension in the relationship because of this issue. MacBride later remembered, 'From the very day we were married she wanted to keep up a correspondence with her ex-lovers and bring them to the house for me to entertain. Of course, I would not allow such a thing, I knew she had an evil life before our marriage.'[263] MacBride totally opposed any contact between Maud and Millevoye. A decision was eventually reached that Millevoye would see Iseult twice a week, when in Paris, at the home of Maud Gonne's friend Madame Avril. While MacBride was greatly pained by the idea of Millevoye and Maud being in contact with one another, their relationship continued.

John MacBride was no doubt somewhat ashamed of the extent to which he had become economically dependent on his wife. She had given him a wedding gift of £3,000, which he regarded as something of an insult. Yet this money was crucially important to him, as he had given up his job prior to the marriage. He found himself relying on his wife, living in a house which she owned, and sharing it with women only she was related to.

Within a very short period of time, it was evidently clear to both parties – and to their broader networks – that the relationship was unsustainable. Against the backdrop of a marriage that was deeply unhappy from early on and indeed perhaps because of it, Gonne continued to travel forward and back to Ireland to engage in political activities, for example opposing the Royal visit of Edward VII to Ireland. She would also visit her sister Kathleen and Willie Yeats in London. She informed Yeats of her deep unhappiness within the relationship, telling him she had 'married in a sudden impulse of anger.'[264] As Anthony Jordan has stated, the marriage must surely have been 'a public humiliation for Willie Yeats. The world knew of their long-standing relationship, and Maud was the muse of all his output of love poetry.'[265] After their London encounter Yeats retained a hope that the spark could be relit, captured in his poem 'Reconciliation':

> 'But dear, cling close to me; since you were gone.

My barren thoughts have chilled me to the bone.'

MacBride had little regard for Yeats, who he viewed with a degree of suspicion. He referred to Yeats as 'weeping Willie' in private correspondence, noting that he was 'glad weeping Willie has retired into solitude he so richly deserves, and from which he should never have emerged. He has set a good example to the other spouting patriots.'[266] MacBride allegedly removed Yeats's books from the couple's household, and Gonne stated that MacBride had even threatened to shoot the poet on one occasion – 'the only cheerful piece of news I have had in days', wrote Yeats to Lady Gregory; 'it gives one a sense of heightened life.'[267]

In Dublin political life, Maud's actions included forming a 'People's Protection Committee'. Its aim was to challenge Dublin's Lord Mayor, Tim Harrington, over claims that Dublin Corporation intended to issue a welcome address to the visiting monarch, Edward VII, in 1903. There were boisterous scenes at a meeting in May at the Rotunda, when Gonne and others confronted Harrington, John Redmond and other members of the Irish Parliamentary Party on the issue. It proved quite the occasion, as 'chairs were thrown, the hall erupted, and Gonne was carried away from her seat for her own protection.'[268]

When recalling this event many years later for the Bureau of Military History, Gonne believed that 'The Battle of the

Rotunda', as some in the press called it, was a significant moment. To her 'it marked the first open clash' between what she termed the 'decaying parliamentary movement' and militant separatists. Gonne took pride in the fact that:

> Its result was even more important as being the first time since the Union in 1800 when officially Ireland refused to recognise the English Crown and Edward VII on his first visit to Ireland after the coronation received no official welcome in Ireland's capital – an event whose significance got much publicity in the foreign press.[269]

MacBride cabled congratulations to his wife on hearing of the successful disruption of the Rotunda meeting, indicating that there was contact between the two of them while Maud was in Ireland. John MacBride was reported in the press as stating 'if there are any who feel aggrieved at my wife's action, I shall be most happy to afford them satisfaction in this accommodating country of France.'[270]

By May 1903, Maud had discovered that she was pregnant. She returned to France, but the relationship between her and MacBride continued to deteriorate over the following months. Their son, Jean Seágan (later Seán) Gonne MacBride was born on 26 January 1904.

As with the earlier symbolism of their wedding, the provisional baptism of young Seán took place in the presence of flags and symbols such as MacBride's ceremonial sword, which had been presented to him by an Irish delegation in Paris. The Irish media reported excitedly on the birth, as did sections of the international press: 'Major MacBride, who married Miss Maud Gonne, has expressed the hope, wrote the *New York Sun*, that their little boy Seán will be the first president of the Irish Republic.'[271]

The boy was to be formally christened in Ireland, and while this of course excluded MacBride from proceedings, he supported the decision. His mother and brothers living in Ireland were present at the christening, with Honoria serving as Seán's godmother. The ceremony took place at the Church of the Three Patrons in Rathgar on 1 May 1904, attracting the attention of intelligence police officers. Gonne later recalled that:

> The ceremony nearly ended in disaster when the priest objected to John O'Leary, a Fenian, standing as godfather, but somehow, Joseph Mac Bride got over the difficulty with the priest and after long delay Seán was satisfactorily christened, though John O'Leary proudly stated he was a Fenian and I was adamant that John O'Leary and no other should be his godfather. It would have greatly distressed old Mrs. MacBride if the ceremony had not taken place.[272]

With his wife and child in Ireland, MacBride once more returned to the United States. He set out for New York on the French liner *Bretagne* shortly after his wife's departure for the Dublin christening. MacBride remained a hugely popular figure to sections of the Irish American community, and, just as at home, his name was adopted by GAA clubs and societies across America. A San Francisco newspaper for example reported in May 1904 that the MacBride Club was taking on numerous others, including the Wolfe Tones and the Parnell Club, in a GAA competition there.[273]

The return of the 'gallant Major' was heralded in the press, with John Devoy's *Gaelic American* intriguingly noting that:

> Major MacBride pronounces as a lie made out of whole-cloth the alleged interview cabled to this country recently stating that the object of his visit was to organise a Brigade for the Russian army in the Far East.[274]

It is likely that such an undertaking was the last thing on MacBride's mind at this point. He did spend some of his time in 1904 writing up his memoirs of the Boer War, which were printed in a wide variety of regional papers, though he would later expand on these recollections for the *Freeman's Journal* in 1906.

From America, MacBride later claimed that he wrote to Gonne, telling her he was anxious they should live there, rather than in Paris:

> While he was in America he wrote a letter to his wife saying that he thought he would settle in America and that it would be the best place for them to live. He said that Paris

> life was not a happy one and that his feeling was that the best thing for her and for him and for the future happiness of both was to sever all connection with her other life ....[275]

MacBride was unable to convince his wife to move to America and thus lose all contact with her former life. If Gonne's previous relationships were a major source of contention in the household, the issue was about to explode by the summer of 1904. MacBride would later claim that it was at this point that he became aware of the extent of Gonne's former relationships. He also maintained that Maud kept pictures of ex-lovers about her house and that by her own admission 'she had been the mistress of three different men'. One issue which grated with MacBride was (he alleged) her desire to bring former lovers into their home:

> She got me to write to another of her lovers giving him an invitation to stay with us for a week, which I did and which he accepted. Needless to say in this instance I was not aware of the relationship that had existed between them. She is a vile woman, 'Woman' – it is a disgrace to womanhood to call her by that holy name.[276]

John was deeply upset by the revelations about her past, writing: 'I knew she had led an evil life before our marriage but did not know it was as bad as I found out afterwards.'[277] MacBride also alleged that he received anonymously 'a portion of a letter written by his wife to her cousin, Mrs. Clay', in which Maud said that she was so pleased 'that the child was a boy and that she thought it resembled George', it was claimed by MacBride's legal team that 'she did not tell this to John as he did not believe in the transmutation of souls.'[278]

On 25 November 1904, John MacBride left for Ireland, leaving Paris at a time when his wife was also out of the country. This, he believed, would throw detectives off the scent. Behind him, he left a note stating in summary:

> That their married life was not a happy one owing to her being unable to rise above a certain level; that is was very painful to him to see that she was only a weak imitation of a weak man. He also advised her, in case he was hanged or died in prison, to get married again, as she was a woman who could not live without some man or other behind her.[279]

With MacBride's departure for Ireland, Gonne began the process of initiating the dissolution of the marriage. She travelled to London, and there laid out the claims against her husband before his brother Dr Anthony MacBride. Anthony was told that 'his brother had been guilty of indecent behaviour towards Iseult, the illegitimate child of his wife.' Dumbfounded by the allegations, Anthony 'asked what the indecent behaviour was specifically and she told him there was no assault but indecent exposure. He expressed great surprise and utter disbelief of the conduct ascribed to his brother.'[280]

Maud informed Anthony that in addition to this, 'his brother had acquired drunken habits and was generally acting badly.'[281] While MacBride took issue with what he saw as the low morals of his wife, Maud would also raise a number of issues during their divorce and the fallout that surrounded it. In private correspondence at the time of the separation, she alleged:

> I have hidden from everyone what I had suffered from John MacBride's drunkenness during my married life. It has been terrible; it is drunkenness that has lowered his moral character so that he has done the acts he has ....[282]

Rumours of MacBride's drinking habits were whispered beyond the halls of the MacBride household too during the course of the marriage. In November 1903, Willie Yeats would write to Lady Gregory, 'have just heard a painful rumour – Major MacBride is said to be drinking. It is the last touch of tragedy if it is true.'[283] Maud Gonne would later place the blame for MacBride's excessive drinking on his friend Victor Collins, claiming that 'despite my warning John became the inseparable companion of Collins, who introduced him to a rather undesirable drinking set who usually foregathered in the American Bar.'[284]

Certainly, MacBride seems to have found some solace in excessive drinking bouts in France. Collins, a friend to both partners in the relationship, discussed the failing marriage with Maud Gonne and wrote to MacBride that among her complaints was her husband 'coming home too drunk to get out of the cab'. MacBride refuted the allegations, replying that he was:

> … under the influence of drink once while she was in the house and that was on Christmas night 1903 and about two or three times at the most when she was away and then it was to drive thoughts of her out of my mind …. Her life was not a life for an honourable man to think over. It is a wonder she did not succeed in making me a drunkard.[285]

MacBride first heard of the allegations of impropriety levelled against him from Anthony's wife, who travelled to Dublin to inform him. He strongly denied all of Gonne's charges, and went to London to confront her. He wrote a letter to his wife from the Euston Hotel on 21 December, telling her that he totally rejected 'the scandalous charges you and your English friends have been making against my character.'[286] MacBride attempted to meet his wife in London on Christmas Eve 1904, but she refused to see him.

The conditions put forward by Maud Gonne in a letter two days later, were that MacBride would emigrate to the United States and she would retain sole custody of their son Seán. Visitation rights would only be granted if MacBride could prove he was capable of leading 'a sober decent life' in future.

Gonne wished for the terms of separation to be agreed quickly and out of the public eye. She was perhaps fearful that if the separation should become a significant public scandal and media circus, the nature of her previous relationships would be exposed, at potentially great risk to her reputation and her standing in nationalist circles. On the issue of custody of Seán, MacBride put forward a most unusual suggestion: that a panel of Irish nationalists, including John O'Leary, serve as arbitrators in the issue of deciding the child's future. As Dr Caoimhe Nic Dháibhéid has noted, 'these appealingly ludicrous suggestions were dismissed out of hand by Gonne's legal team, which was already looking towards the more favourable surroundings of the divorce courts.'[287]

MacBride consulted Richard Barry O'Brien, who was a highly regarded solicitor in nationalist circles. Reproductions of the correspondence between O'Brien and Gonne exist today in MacBride's private papers, and give us an idea of her mindset during the separation. Gonne made it clear to his solicitor that she wished for the child to be raised in Ireland. She wrote that 'If John keeps from drink and does not otherwise annoy me, I am not selfish and would gladly increase the opportunities for him to see the child, but it must be left to my discretion.'[288] In replying to Gonne, O'Brien clearly believed there were hugely important issues at play and he warned her to 'take care that you do not allow yourself to be dominated by English political and family interests in a manner where the interests of your country are concerned.'[289] MacBride shared this belief, writing to O'Brien:

> I am well aware that whatever we do a public scandal ought to be avoided in the interests of Ireland as we both have played a part in Irish politics. I have risked my life for Ireland and I am ready and willing to risk everything for her but honour.[290]

The most hotly debated aspect of the MacBride/Gonne separation has always been the allegations of MacBride's abusive and highly sexualised behaviour towards female members of the household, and in particular the alleged abuse of Gonne's eleven-year-old daughter Iseult. Not long after Gonne's confession to MacBride of the extent of her relationship with Iseult's father, her friend Madame Avril alleged to Maud that Iseult had been molested by MacBride.[291]

When W. B. Yeats learned of these allegations in early 1905, he wrote to Lady Gregory of his revulsion on hearing of 'the blackest thing you can imagine'. Yeats would prove instrumental in collecting evidence to be used against MacBride with regards his drunken behaviour. Roy Foster noted that Yeats tried to marshal evidence against MacBride via the solicitor John Quinn in New York, as well as 'from old United Irish League enemies in Mayo.' Yeats wrote to Quinn commenting that: 'this man has been a drunken cad from the first.'[292] Quinn found it difficult to gather any information on MacBride's behaviour in the US. He wrote to Yeats that:

> 'MacBride had had his friends here notified and they apparently take his side of the case generally and those who do not say the scandal is hurtful to the cause generally and that the sooner it is hushed up the better.'[293]

Statements that did come forward from the United States came from Mary T. Quinn of the Irish National Theatre Company, and also of a member of Gonne's Inghinidhe organisation. She described encountering MacBride during the summer of 1904 at the St. Louis World Fair. She stated that she saw MacBride 'many times during the month of July 1904 and on nearly every occasion when deponent saw the said MacBride he was more or less intoxicated.' It was claimed that 'on some occasions MacBride was so intoxicated that he was maudlin and incoherent in his speech.'[294] In correspondence with Gonne, Quinn claimed that MacBride was often to be found with Joe Wade, a fellow veteran of the Irish Brigade, who 'went after him and took care of him all the time when he was wandering about drunk and half insane.'[295]

Accusations that MacBride had been a heavy drinker in South Africa were levelled against him too, coming from one Fritz Joubert Duquesne. This led to a letter of response being produced, signed by General Louis Botha and General de

Wet amongst others, distancing themselves from Duquesne's claims and claiming not to know of any such individual.[296]

Gonne found little sympathy from leading Irish nationalists. She wrote to John O'Leary on 9 January 1905 that:

> My husband has done things which make it impossible for us to live together. To avoid going into the law court, where I should have to publicly dishonour a man who fought against England, I have offered terms of separation which my family, who know the whole circumstances, consider too generous.[297]

O'Leary replied on 14 January 1905, telling Gonne:

> Knowing your husband as I do, I cannot believe he has done anything that would make it impossible for you to live together. But whatever he has done, or whatever you think he has done, is a matter, which, as far as I can see, need not enter into the question of separation at all.[298]

Gonne was clearly unhappy with O'Leary's response, informing him that 'I am sorry that you do not approve though I think if you knew the whole circumstances you would understand that I must safeguard my little son from the example of his father.'[299] Gonne alleged that she believed MacBride to be 'actually mad' at times.

Aware of this series of letters between Gonne and O'Leary, and with copies of the correspondence, MacBride noted that he was inclined to agree with Gonne on the question of his madness, as 'I must be at times 'actually mad', for undoubtedly it was the act of a madman to marry a woman who has led such an evil impure life.'[300]

Details of the allegations against MacBride became public in a variety of ways. Augustine Ingoldsby, Secretary of Cumann na nGaedheal, remembered a letter arriving at a convention in Dublin, when John MacBride was in attendance:

> I knew John McBride well. I remember I was sitting beside him at a Cumann na Gaedheal convention. As Secretary of the Cumann na Gaedheal I had received a letter from his wife in which she made accusations against her husband about his conduct and that of his friends in Paris. I asked whether I should read the letter and the chairman, P. T. Daly, said yes. John McBride asked leave to retire while it was being read. After I had read a few lines some of the members, including John O'Byrne and Joe Ryan, said I should read no more, of which I was very glad, as it was very unpleasant. The members all took John MacBride's part with the result that he was appointed on the committee and she was voted out.[301]

Among those utilised by Gonne and Yeats to acquire information on MacBride was Annie Horniman, a key figure in the Abbey Theatre. MacBride had argued that his mother could serve as primary carer for Seán, and for that reason Gonne believed it worthwhile to gather information on the business premises Honoria maintained, which functioned as a public house as well as a licensed shop. Horniman visited Mayo, but found that the MacBride family were highly regarded and respected locally. She reported that 'the MacBride business 'is most assuredly not what could be considered a low public house where peasants and workmen would go to.'[302]

In February 1905, Gonne formally appealed to the law courts in France. In the 'Petition of Maud Gonne MacBride to the President of the Civil Tribunal, Paris' it was alleged that MacBride's drunkenness was uncontrollable, that he had made improper advances towards female members of the household and that that he had a 'jealous, suspicious and violent temper.'[303]

The allegations against MacBride were reprinted in the *Irish Independent* newspaper, which he subsequently sued for libel. As a result of his South African citizenship from the Boer War, MacBride needed to first prove Irish citizenship, which he was successful in doing. Establishing Irish domicile for MacBride was crucial as it would decisively shape the Paris case, as it meant the French court was then limited to granting a legal separation.

The Parisian divorce case proved incredibly bitter. In the

notes of MacBride's legal team it was stated 'there was also a distinguished Irish literary man who was in love with Mrs. MacBride before her marriage. How far there were any immoral relations between them cannot be said with certainty.'[304] Gonne's Irishness was also up for question:

> How Maud Gonne came originally to take part in Irish matters is more or less a mystery, in fact her nationality itself seems in some respects to be in doubt. Her father, however, was a Colonel in the English army and she says she was born in the camp near Aldershot. The question has been raised as to whether her family were Irish at all, she herself has asserted that they were and the opinion seems to have gained ground that the Gonne's had for some time been settled in Ireland …. Why Maud Gonne ever came into Irish politics seems strange to many people; those who met her at the time say that she knew nothing of Irish matters, nothing of Irish history, nothing of Irish politics, and there was no patriotism in her blood as there was patriotism in the blood of her husband.[305]

The final verdict in the Paris case was not reached until August 1906 and a legal separation was duly granted. Gonne was given sole custody of their son Seán and MacBride was allowed the right to weekly visits at Gonne's residence. The court accepted the charges of drunkenness against MacBride but did not uphold the immorality charges. It is important to note that the alleged sexual impropriety towards Iseult was raised in the courts, but it was alluded to only by MacBride's side who wished to confront the allegation. Dr Anthony MacBride insisted on raising the issue during the case, highlighting that Gonne had not mentioned it in court. Gonne complained in correspondence with W. B. Yeats following the trial that the accusation being made against her now was that 'I had accused him before members of his own family but knowing this accusation to be false I had not brought it forward in the divorce suit.' She stated:

> This may mean that I will have to prove this horrible thing, I shrink from doing it because it means that poor little Iseult will have to appear in court and be questioned and cross questioned on this hideous thing which I want her to forget. She is a nervous child and was ill for days after the terror of it and used to wake at nights screaming that MacBride with his "eyes of an assassin" was running after her, even now she hardly likes going up stairs after dark alone because as she told me last week when I was laughing at her for being afraid, she is always afraid MacBride may be hiding and run after her. Still it is possible it will have to be proved.[306]

MacBride notes that there was an incident during which Iseult had entered his bedroom one morning 'when I had the chamber pot in my hand'[307], and it is possible that from this incident emerged the broader issue. Many years later, Iseult's husband, the celebrated writer and poet Francis Stuart, would write in his semi-autobiographical *Black List Section H* that his wife could relate 'an anecdote about how her step-father, John MacBride, had made advances to her as a child with [a] detached air.'[308] As a result of Gonne's insistence on not bringing her daughter into court, the allegations of sexual impropriety went untested.

On the issue of Eileen Wilson, Gonne's half-sister, it was alleged in court by a servant of the household that MacBride had engaged in inappropriate contact with Eileen. Evidence of MacBride kissing Eileen was brought forward by several witnesses, including Gonne's midwife. There were poor relations in the household between MacBride and the midwife, and in MacBride's legal team notes it is stated:

> Mrs. MacBride had a midwife who was an objectionable woman to Major MacBride in consequence of the conversations which she carried on during her stay in the house with Mrs. MacBride, the conversations were always relating to sexual connection. Major MacBride heard these Conversations going on one day through the partition which separated the room where his wife and the midwife were from the room where he slept. The Major had a quarrel with his wife on this subject, objecting strongly to the presence of this midwife. He treated the midwife with marked disdain, not speaking to her and taking no pains to conceal

his displeasure at her presence in the house.[309]

Where was Eileen Wilson while all of this controversy was occurring? By the time of the trial, Eileen was in fact married to Joseph MacBride, John's brother. They had been married in July 1904 at Ely Place in London, and it was reported at the time in the press that 'Miss Wilson comes of a prominent Parisian family, and is a connection of Mrs. Maud Gonne MacBride.'[310] Eileen ultimately settled in Westport with Joseph, in a happy relationship that produced several children. As Gonne wrote to Yeats, Joseph MacBride announced in court that 'all those who slandered his wife were vile women in the pay of the vilest creature upon earth'. Eileen herself denied that anything improper had occurred.

It was also alleged in court that John MacBride had made indecent proposals towards Barry O'Delany, Iseult's governess. MacBride noted 'it is absolutely false that I offered to show myself naked to this witness. Her looks would not tempt any man and her age is such as to render the suggestion preposterous.'[311]

Historians have long differed on the issue of MacBride's behaviour towards the female members of the household, with some noting the alleged sexual assaults as undisputed fact. It is important to note that MacBride defended himself successfully against the accusations that were put before him, but claims and allegations like those made later in Francis Stuart's work should be considered or at least acknowledged too. Anthony J. Jordan, having examined the case in detail, believes that the letters of Gonne and Yeats have been adopted too easily by biographers and historians as the total truth on the issue, and that the alleged incident with Iseult Gonne and alleged infidelity with Eileen Wilson have been written of repeatedly as fact: 'This, despite the fact that he faced the latter charges, at Maud's insistence, and the former at his own insistence, in a Parisian court, and neither was upheld.'[312] Others, such as Dr Caoimhe Nic Dháibhéid, author of an excellent biography of Seán MacBride and the author of an academic article examining the divorce, have argued that 'far from a proof of fabrication, this reluctance is more accurately interpreted as the material impulse to preserve Iseult's reputation.'[313] Jordan is certainly correct to take issue with statements such as 'MacBride in a drunken fit had sexually assaulted members of his own household and had even molested the eleven-year old Iseult', owing to the fact these issues were not ruled on by the courts of law.[314] The celebrated poet Paul Durcan, the grandson of Joseph MacBride and Eileen Wilson, fiercely opposed the allegations of abuse towards Eileen, noting that his grandmother always spoke of John MacBride with warmth. Durcan believes that MacBride was 'unquestionably defamed', and lays much of the blame on the 'the people in the Yeats-Maud Gonne Industry'. He asserts that such people 'would not have published this story about my grandmother, Eileen, until she was dead.'[315] Durcan recalled that a portrait of John MacBride hung over the mantelpiece in the family home, and that MacBride was godfather to their daughter Síle. John MacBride has featured on several occasions as a subject of Durcan's poetry, most recently in his 2015 collection *The Days of Surprise*. In his memoir, *Paul Durcan's Diary*, he stated that 'The heroes of my childhood and youth were John MacBride, Patrick Pearse and General Sean MacEoin.'[316]

The effects of the brutal separation would reverberate in Irish nationalist circles for some time, driving a wedge between individuals and even impacting on the relationships between organisations. In October 1906 Gonne attended the Abbey Theatre premiere of *Deirdre, The Gaol Gate* and the *Mineral Workers* in the company of W.B. Yeats, and she was reportedly hissed by supporters of MacBride. Gonne was a woman who had not alone left the hero of the Irish Brigade, but who had broken her Catholic wedding vows, and the hostile reception must have been quite the shock to a woman who had been the darling of Irish nationalism at one point, 'Ireland's Joan of Arc'. Maud Gonne MacBride was beginning to realise that the doors of the broad nationalist movement in Ireland were closing to her.

If proof of this was needed, it came at the annual convention of Cumann na nGaedheal in 1906, where an attempt was made by some IRB men to exclude Maud Gonne from a position. Cumann na nGaedheal had been established in 1900 by Arthur Griffith, and was intended as a broad umbrella group which would bring together literary and political nationalist associations and groups. Griffith had argued strongly in the pages of the *United Irishman* that the various nationalist forces in the country needed to be united and Cumann na nGaedheal can be seen as the forerunner of the Sinn Féin party he founded in 1905. Denis McCullough, at the time a leading member of Cumann na nGaedheal in Belfast, recalled that:

> I was a member of the Belfast Executive of Cumann in nGaedheal and, I believe, acted as its secretary for some time. With Bulmer Hobson I attended the annual conventions of the organisation in Dublin. At one of these I remember very serious differences arising. Following the divorce proceedings in Paris between Major John MacBride and Maud Gonne, an attempt was made, I believe by the I.R.B. group, to have John MacBride elected as Vice President of the organisation and to exclude Maud Gonne from this office.
>
> The women's organisation …who had delegates at the convention, opposed this move fiercely. Attempts were made to 'nobble' Hobson and myself on our arrival at the Mansion House, where the convention was being held, by P. T. Daly – the I.R.B. leader in Dublin – by giving us "orders" to vote for MacBride and against Maud Gonne.[317]

In the end, both MacBride and Gonne were made Vice

Presidents of the organisation, in an attempt to calm tensions between the two factions at the conference. During the tense debate on the subject, McCullough briefly left the hall:

> During the debate on this matter I went to the foyer for a cigarette. MacBride followed me out and assured me that he was not party to the move on his behalf and urged me to vote as I thought right. I treasured his friendship always afterwards.[318]

In a sense, MacBride and Gonne had become 'the first couple of Irish nationalism' during their brief love affair. As a result of the huge publicity generated by their marriage and the birth of their son, the fallout from their contentious separation was always destined to have an effect on Irish nationalist circles, splitting organisations and dividing loyalties.

Chapter 7

Returning to Ireland

In July 1904, it was noted in John MacBride's Dublin Castle intelligence file that:

> I beg to report that I have received information from a reliable source that Major John McBride is about to leave Paris, and is proceeding to the Seat of the Japan and Russian war – ostensibly as a war correspondent.[319]

In reality, this was when MacBride's relationship was crumbling around itself in Paris, and little did intelligence gatherers know that they would soon be following him on the streets of Dublin once again. MacBride arrived in Dublin before the commencement of the separation case in Paris, and from that point onwards clearly moved freely between Dublin, Westport and all other places.

From the time that the authorities were aware of his re-emergence on Irish soil, shortly after his arrival in November 1904, he was actively monitored by intelligence officers.

They noted that he was 'visited by some of the most active Secret Society men in the city'[320] during his early weeks in Dublin. In particular, MacBride's association with Arthur Griffith, Fred Allan, P.T. Daly and John O'Leary was commented on by police. It was clear that MacBride was going to attempt to involve himself in radical political circles at home despite his ongoing legal woes in France.

The fact that MacBride was able to return to Ireland was raised in Westminster, albeit long after his return to Irish soil, but there was no attempt made to arrest him in relation to his activities in the Irish Brigade. John Lonsdale, an Armagh man by birth and a vocal unionist MP, asked in the House of Commons in June 1906 if it was known John MacBride had been sighted in Dublin on 1 June of that year, and if John MacBride had been given permission to return to Ireland. Lonsdale's question was enough to spark a reply from the Major himself, who delighted in writing to the press that:

> I am at a loss to understand why Mr Lonsdale – who I am informed is one of the Orange deadheads – wants to know if I was in Dublin on the 1st June. Why the 1st June, any more than the 1st January or the 12th July? I returned to my country on November 25th 1904 and have been in permanent residence here since. I am on no 'visit'. [321]

A 'reliable' informant in Mayo suggested to State intelligence that MacBride was no longer a threat. What is telling about the entry in MacBride's intelligence file is that it indicates the State regarded not only John MacBride, but his family, as being of considerable importance:

> This informant has special facilities for knowing the intentions of the MacBride family in Mayo. This informant in the past has proved to be reliable. It remains to be seen however whether his information with regards Major MacBride's plans are equally trustworthy.[322]

Regardless of whether or not the authorities believed such reports to be true, intelligence officers still kept a close eye on the Major's activities in Dublin. They recorded in January 1905 that 'McGarveys shop was MacBride's chief resort while here and in it he was socially met by Secret Society men.'[323] McGarvey's of North Frederick Street was much more than a shop. Having been established in the late nineteenth century by Cathal McGarvey, the premises at 30 North Frederick Street was popularly known as 'An Stad'. It played host to all sorts of nationalist and cultural gatherings, ranging from Gaelic Leaguers to GAA athletes, and from Abbey Theatre performers to militant separatist nationalists. Henry C. Phibbs, once a member of the Celtic Literary Society, remembered that 'An Stad' drew all sorts, from James Joyce to Patrick Pearse, and including a certain Michael Cusack:

> One of the people who would occasionally wander in was

'old man Cusack', a bearded old stalwart who called himself 'Citizen Cusack'. He always carried a green muffler around his neck and wielded a heavy blackthorn stick. It was said that he was the founder of the Gaelic Athletic Association.[324]

The authorities seem to have believed that the plan in nationalist circles was for MacBride to stand for election to Dublin Corporation. It was discovered, however, that he would be invalid to contest an election. An intelligence report early in 1905 noted:

> It was at first intended that he should be nominated for municipal honours as a National Council candidate but it was discovered that his nomination would be invalid in so much as his name does not appear on the Burgess role. He applied for a position in at least two city firms to the managers of which he had been previously known but in each case he was met with a prompt refusal.[325]

As MacBride continued to try to find employment in Dublin, that same year would witness the foundation of Arthur Griffith's Sinn Féin party. The new movement emerged from the coming together of Cumann na nGaedheal with the northern Dungannon Clubs, which had been established by Northern-IRB men Bulmer Hobson and Denis McCullough. Beyond his words of warning to Maud in advance of the wedding, which were proven totally accurate, Griffith had succeeded in staying out of the intensely bitter separation of Gonne and MacBride, remaining a respected figure to both. Branches of the new Sinn Féin party were quickly established across the country, and, as Joost Augusteijn has noted, the MacBride brothers in the West of Ireland were instrumental in establishing one of the first provincial branches of the new movement there.[326] The name 'Sinn Féin' or 'We Ourselves', was coined by Máire Butler. She was an activist within the Irish language revivalist movement, who also happened to be a cousin of leading unionist Edward Carson. Griffith had developed the ideology and philosophy of this new party in the *United Irishman* and in his book *The Resurrection of Hungary: A Parallel for Ireland*, published in 1904. There, Griffith had argued for a dual Anglo-Irish monarchy, and for the re-introduction of a parliament, styled on that of Henry Grattan. The Sinn Féin movement proposed economic nationalism and protectionism, as well as arguing for an abstentionist approach to the Westminster parliament. Certainly, this wasn't the militant separatism associated with men like MacBride, but the organisation attracted a broad network of nationalist membership, including radical separatists, who may have recognised its potential to draw popular appeal.

Among those active in Sinn Féin from the beginning were important IRB figures. They had come from the Dungannon Clubs, whose manifesto and constitution preached a political line of dissent by comparison to Griffith's ideology:

> Ireland stands today in the midst of the strong and powerful people's weak and miserable, among the wealthy nations we are poor and beggarly, among the proud we cry with a weak voice faint-heartedly for that strong and independent national life than can only be won by strenuous effort and great sacrifice.[327]

For many in the ranks of the IRB, supporting Sinn Féin was more about pragmatism than general enthusiasm. George Lyons would recall in his statement to the Bureau of Military History that 'the IRB approved of the Sinn Féin policy as a bridge between London and the Irish Hillside and frequently had to finance the Sinn Féin candidates for local bodies. It was considered at this time that open advocacy of republicanism would cause suppression by the Eng1ish authorities.'[328]

Major MacBride's public support for Sinn Féin in its early years saw him speak on a number of platforms, while at a meeting of Sinn Féin in Castlebar in December 1907 a letter from the Major was read out. He encouraged those present to 'boycott everything English, to support Irish industries and the Language revival, and to do all in their power to encourage the anti-enlisting campaign.'[329]

While MacBride found time to publicly support Sinn Féin, he was also focused on revisiting his memories of the war in South Africa, and at this point he wrote the popularly received collection of articles for the *Freeman's Journal.* Thirteen articles by MacBride were printed in total, beginning on 13 October 1906, and they were reprinted in many regional newspapers. Given the recent embarrassments of the divorce case, and the libel action against the *Irish Independent,* this must surely have provided welcome relief and distraction.

In the years following his return to Ireland, he lodged primarily with Fred Allan, a veteran IRB member. In the 1911 Census for example, MacBride is listed as a boarder at Allan's household in Spencer Villas, Glenageary. Allan was born in 1861 into a Methodist family with unionist political ideas, though as a young man he had been shaped by the political writings of Karl Marx and John Mitchel. He joined the IRB in 1880 and by 1883 he was secretary of the movement in Leinster. Allan was a very capable organiser and political thinker, and as Owen McGee has noted:

> The most striking fact about Fred Allan's career was his exceptional organisational and entrepreneurial ability. This enabled him to give very valuable assistance to, and to earn the highest respect from, each successive body with which he was involved.[330]

Allan was also a significant figure within Dublin Corporation and held a number of positions in the body, for example becoming secretary of Dublin Corporation's Electric Light Company in 1901.

Dublin Corporation had become an increasingly nationalist body from the late nineteenth century onwards. In 1885, the Corporation voted by forty-one votes to seventeen not to take part in welcoming the Prince of Wales to Ireland, and indeed the 1903 royal visit to Dublin had included no loyal address from Dublin Corporation. It was perhaps because of the nationalist sentiment of the Corporation that MacBride was hopeful of gaining employment there. In January 1905, intelligence reports noted that an informer stated that MacBride 'is looking for a situation under the Dublin and that when this has been secured very little will be again heard of him.'[331] Evidently, the authorities believed that if MacBride secured employment he would fade into obscurity.

MacBride seems to have spent much of his time in Ireland living in the capital. He did also frequently travel to visit his family in Westport and Mayo, with his movements closely monitored at all times. Ernie O'Malley, who would go on to play his own important role in the revolutionary period, remembered the presence of Major MacBride in his west of Ireland childhood, and that:

> He had been kind to us as children .... With him we dropped our best company manners and felt at ease. Story-tellers, sailors and soldiers were very important –and he had been a soldier. He told us about the Boer War. He showed us

> an unminted gold coin, which had once been in the Boer mint .... We knew the stories of Boer commanders and the names of offices, long rides searching for food in the burnt ruin of farmhouses and the bitter hate of men who had fought while their women and children huddled in death in British internment camps.[332]

The presence of the Major at meetings in Mayo was recorded in the regional press there, with the *Connaught Telegraph* reporting that John and his brother Joseph were present at a meeting of the Mayo Industrial Development Association in August 1906. Reports of the meeting give an insight into the perilous economic conditions in the county in the early twentieth century. Those gathered were told that 'during the past half a century, 75,000 persons had emigrated from Mayo; and during the same period, over 30,000 houses had disappeared.'[333]

Mayo may have offered a welcome distraction from the capital, where MacBride's libel action against the *Irish Independent*, for publishing the details of the Parisian divorce case, had backfired in spectacular fashion in June 1906, becoming a major source of public humiliation. Amongst other things, MacBride's so-called allegiances to the *Freeman's Journal* newspaper, owing to their printing his memoirs of South Africa, were dragged up in court. He was accused of seeking to undermine the *Irish Independent*, which was an opponent of that paper. Allegations were made that MacBride had not written the pieces in the *Freeman's Journal* himself, and the allegation that MacBride was 'in reality almost an illiterate man, without education' was put forward.[334] MacBride's 'hard drinking' was also referenced. It resulted in MacBride winning only £1 in damages and no legal costs, despite seeking £5,000. The jury found that of the two allegations printed about MacBride in the newspaper, one allegation, drunkenness, was proven but that the allegations of immortality were unproven in the Paris courts. If the libel case had been taken to undo some of the damage of his separation from Gonne, in reality it served only to increase public awareness of the allegations against the Major.

MacBride was also saddened by the death of a mentor and friend. In March 1907 John O'Leary passed away, a man who had been such a significant figure in nationalist circles all his life. In London, *The Times* obituary noted:

> He seems to have drifted into Fenianism, not because he was an Irish Nationalist, but because he was a hater of established institutions. Once he was condoled with on the neglect shown him by the people of Ireland in his old age. 'Ah,' he replied with characteristic irony, 'they'll make up for it by giving me a grand funeral.'[335]

W. B. Yeats would later recall:

> When O'Leary died, I could not bring myself to go to his funeral, though I had been once his close fellow-worker,

> for I shrank from seeing about his grave so many whose nationalism was different from anything he had thought or that I could share.[336]

At O'Leary's funeral, the coffin was carried by MacBride along with P.T. Daly, James O'Connor and John O'Hanlon. Fred Allan, Arthur Griffith and others were in attendance to pay their respects. It was not the 'grand funeral' O'Leary had hoped for. He was buried in Glasnevin Cemetery, without as much as a graveside oration.

The Fusilier's Arch memorial was unveiled in the capital later that year, commemorating the men of the Royal Dublin Fusiliers who had fought in South Africa. One wonders what MacBride thought of the grand spectacle of its inauguration. The nickname 'Traitor's Gate' was almost instantaneous in Dublin, and would stick. The *Freeman's Journal* poured scorn on the monument, 'with its false dedication, to the dead Fusiliers, while the living are left to starve.' The paper commented that: 'From first to last Dublin believed, and believes, the war in which those men were engaged to be unjust and disgraceful. From such a war no glory is to be gained; such a war deserves no memorial.'[337]

Struggling to find any kind of regular employment, and without so much as a permanent address of his own, MacBride was at something of a loss in Dublin. With his son in France, and the details of his private life printed in various sections of the media, this was undoubtedly a difficult period for him. Rumours of his drinking continued, and Maud Gonne wondered from Paris what had become of him, writing to Yeats in March 1907 that 'beyond a paragraph in the *Freeman's Journal* contradicting a report of an Australian paper saying MacBride had committed suicide I have no news of him and do not know what he is doing. If you hear anything in Dublin by chance let me know.'[338]

However, in time, MacBride did finally find work via Dublin Corporation. In 1908, it was reported in the press that John MacBride had become Petroleum Inspector of the Dublin Corporation.[339] Later, he acquired the position of Assistant Water Bailiff and by January 1911 he had become the city Water Bailiff. Sean T. O Kelly, himself a member of the Corporation at the time, remembered that 'this post had been secured for him through the influence of Alderman Tom Kelly, Councillor P. T. Daly and myself.'[340] Daly, a Dubliner by birth, had been a member of James Connolly's short-lived Irish Socialist Republican Party, and by the early twentieth century had become a senior figure in the IRB. He was elected to Dublin Corporation in 1903. Patrick McCartan, senior IRB member, would remember that 'until the advent of Tom Clarke, P. H. Pearse and the others, P. T. Daly was the outstanding man in the IRB of the time, an outstanding nationalist who always worked consistently for the goal of a free Ireland.'[341]

W. B. Yeats's sister Lily would joke some years later in correspondence with the poet that 'it must have been some humourist who got him the post of water bailiff to the corporation'[342], a reference no doubt to MacBride's drinking during his marriage. The job evidently gave MacBride a sense of purpose, as was clear in the recollections of Gearoid Ua h-Uallacháin, who played a leading role in the Fianna youth movement during the revolutionary period. He remembered MacBride's daily journey to the Corporation:

> I used to see Major MacBride every morning walking to his office. He always dressed smartly, and carried his umbrella under his arm like a walking stick or a rifle. When he would be passing the works I would say to Tom Kane, an ex-British soldier, 'There is the man who made you run in Africa', and Kane would boil with temper. Poor Tom Kane was blown up in the First World War.[343]

During this time, MacBride was speaking around the country, giving talks outlining the history of the Irish Brigade, similar in content to his American tour in the aftermath of the war. Police intelligence noted of one meeting in Cork:

> The Hall was only half-full – from 250 to 300 people – quite one third being under the age of eighteen years. There were many ladies and girls. The class of the audience was mixed, but I certainly felt it was a strange gathering ....
>
> A very dangerous orator at times of political unrest, but

> I hold the impression that just now, his speech fell somewhat flat.[344]

On occasion, MacBride's speeches were anything but 'somewhat flat', with a speech in Belfast in 1909 triggering complaints from unionist politicians and the press, and even finding its way into unionist propaganda as proof of the revolutionary scheming underway on the part of republicans. The 'Union Defence League', who were militantly opposed to any attempt to introduce Home Rule into Ireland, reprinted sections of his speech in a pamphlet designed to whip unionists into frenzy:

> I appeal to you most earnestly to do all in your power to prevent your countrymen from entering the degraded British Army. If you prevent 500 men from enlisting you do nearly as good work, if not quite so exciting, as if you shot 500 men on the field of battle, and also you are making the path smoother for the approaching conquest of England by Germany. Let one of your mottoes be: 'No recruits for England.'
>
> Should they [the Germans] land in Ireland, they will be received with willing hearts and strong hands, and should England be their destination, it is to be hoped that they will find time to disembark 100,000 rifles and a few score of ammunition for the same in this country, and twelve months later this island will be as free as the Lord God

> meant it should be, such is the hatred of England felt by many Nationalists.[345]

Unsurprisingly, complaints were made by some in political circles that a member of Dublin Corporation was delivering such explicitly republican speeches. The *Belfast Evening Telegraph* reported on a speech given by MacBride in early March 1911, during which he had stated, in reference to a forthcoming planned royal visit, that 'a foreign ruler was about to visit Ireland in order to receive the grovelling homage of his garrison and the whinging adulation of his place-hunters.' Seizing upon this, the 'City of Dublin Unionist Association' complained to Dublin Corporation. The response from Dublin Corporation was to put forward a motion stating:

> That a reply be sent to the Association to the effect that the Corporation does not invite opinions from its officers, nor does it wish to impose its opinions upon anyone in the service of the Corporation.[346]

MacBride's Belfast speech caused some annoyance in Westminster too. The Chief Secretary was challenged and asked if the government 'intended to take any action in regard to it.' He was also asked if he was 'aware that this Major MacBride is a paid official of the Dublin Corporation, and that his treasonable utterance has given great offence to the Loyalist ratepayers of that city.' Augustine Birrell, as Chief

Secretary, replied that while he believed MacBride's speech had been 'a tirade of ridiculous and dangerous nonsense', no action would be taken against him.[347]

At times, MacBride and his former wife were in Dublin during the same period, but there are no references to them crossing paths. She would arrive sporadically in the capital, involving herself in various political campaigns. In 1910 and 1911 she was campaigning feverishly on the issue of child poverty and hunger in the city. Helena Molony, secretary of Inghinidhe na hÉireann, recalled that despite Gonne's unpopularity in some nationalist circles and her living in Paris, she had remained active politically in that movement. Molony stated: 'She never lost touch with the work, weekly correspondence passed between her and the Society, and she paid lengthy visits two or three times a year. She was responsible for getting us to agitate for school meals.[348]

Gonne worked alongside James Connolly and other activists on the left in the campaign for the Education (Provision of Meals) Act, introduced into England in 1906, to be extended to Ireland. The campaigners finally achieved their goal in 1914 when free school meals became available in Ireland.

Despite Gonne's visits to the city, MacBride did not see his son, as Seán usually remained in France. According to Molony, Gonne feared that: 'her son would be likely to pass out of her care if she brought him to Ireland.' In Paris, the young boy may not have known John MacBride intimately, but he did become familiar with other Irish nationalists. In his memoirs, he recalled:

> I had known Roger Casement fairly well as a child, because when passing through Paris, he used to usually try to visit our house. I was always impressed by this tall, gaunt figure with a beard. He was always very nice to me and patted me on the head.[349]

Other visitors the youngster became familiar with included the novelist James Stephens and W. B. Yeats. Of Stephens, Seán remembered that 'when I was in Paris at school, he used to take me out for a whole day.... The day would end up at Rumpelymeyer's in Rue di Rivoli where they had marvellous cakes made from chestnuts, whipped cream and meringues.'[350]

It appeared a happy childhood, though his father rarely featured. In a television documentary broadcast in the late 1980s, Seán MacBride claimed that there was not much contact. 'I saw him three or four times, in summer periods ... and I used to get occasional postcards from him.'[351] The young boy did visit Ireland on summer holidays in 1910 when Maud brought her two children to Mulranny in Mayo. Maud was still nervous of allowing Seán to spend much time in Ireland. She had once written to her American solicitor John Quinn, that 'MacBride and the English law makes it impossible for me to have him in Ireland until he is old enough to defy both'[352]. From Mayo, she wrote to Yeats that: 'I have been meaning for days to write to you but in this place time passes so. It is so good to be back in Ireland that even the rainy weather does not depress me.'[353]

Maud had maintained cordial relations with the MacBride family. As Joseph MacBride had married her half-sister Eileen, this was particularly important for all concerned. State intelligence had predicted, wrongly, that from the time Joseph married Eileen he 'will take no further part in politics'.[354]

As he continued to move between Dublin and Westport, John MacBride remained an active 'Secret Society' man. He served briefly on the Supreme Council of the IRB in 1911, as representative for Connaught. In November 1910, the IRB were central to the launch of *Irish Freedom*, a radical newspaper which was unapologetically separatist. The first issue of the paper laid out their ideology, plain and simple for readers: 'The Irish attitude to England is war yesterday, war today, war tomorrow. Peace after the final battle.'[355]

John MacBride contributed to this paper. One of his early contributions was controversial as it was an interview in connection with the Siege of Sidney Street. Two members of an anarchist gang, supposedly led by the mysterious Peter Piatkow, now better known as 'Peter the Painter', were shot dead following a prolonged gunfight with the police and the military. The politically motivated gang had attempted to break into a London jeweller's, and a notorious shootout followed as police moved in on the suspects. Winston Churchill, as Home Secretary, had arrived on the scene of the gunfight to observe it all unfold. MacBride believed that 'the whole business should put heart into the younger generation of Irishmen'. When he was asked what could be learned from the event, he commented 'as to that it is the lesson I learned on the battlefields of South Africa – that the English army is of very little account as a fighting force.'[356] MacBride later stated boldly in the pages of *Irish Freedom* that 'my command of the English language is not sufficiently wide to allow me to put into words the intense hatred and detestation I have for England.'[357]

A letter writer to *Irish Freedom* felt compelled to ask why the present generation of republicans had become so inactive, noting:

> I have been trying to find out why Ireland is so quiet and peaceful at present. When I was a young man the Land League kept things lively and there was always some movement which kept things on the move and kept the people thinking about Ireland's rights ... At any rate we kept the peelers going and made them earn their wages – while now they are loading around the country – the lords of a peaceful and apparently contended land.[358]

The newspaper provided a platform for the Major and other public figures, reprinting their speeches as well as publishing letters. In a March 1911 edition, MacBride sounded a note of incredible optimism stating that: 'England's days are nearly done. Fifty years hence there will be nothing left of her empire but an evil memory .... India and Ireland hate her and are longing for the day when they are strong enough to throw off her yoke.'[359]

Yet, for the majority of Irish activists, such a day could hardly have felt further off. Behind-the-scenes, there was a power struggle going on in the Irish Republican Brotherhood. Bulmer Hobson would recall that: 'The membership of the whole IRB at this time, 1911, was, I think, about 600–700 in Dublin and about 300–400 elsewhere, the total being probably about 1,000 and certainly not more than 1,500.'[360]Hobson remembered this as a time of friction between the 'old guard' of the IRB and an emerging younger generation of activists, who were seeking more militant action:

> In 1911 the I.R.B. in Dublin was practically controlled by three members of the Supreme Council – Jack O'Hanlon, Fred Allan, who was of the Supreme Council, and P. T. Daly, and their influence almost stifled all activities. Other members of the Supreme Council were, P. S. O'Hegarty from London, South of England representative, and Denis McCullough from Ulster. John MacBride was representa-

> tive for Connaught, in which capacity he was later succeeded by Seán McDermott. Tom Clarke returned from America to Ireland in 1908, and was co-opted a member of the Supreme Council sometime after. He always demanded a more active policy and supported the younger men.[361]

An eventual split was brought about over the issue of a 1911 Royal visit to Ireland. The visit of King George V had the potential to create massive embarrassment for the IRB, with Fred Allan serving as secretary to the Lord Mayor at that point. The Supreme Council forbade members from partaking in demonstrations against the visit. Instead they emphasised the importance of the Bodenstown commemoration in July for Theobald Wolfe Tone.

Wolfe Tone, often considered the founding father of Irish Republican ideology, is commemorated annually in a cemetery on the outskirts of Sallins, County Kildare. A long-established ritual for the republican movement, there was a real prestige attached to being asked to address the annual gathering. MacBride had spoken at Bodenstown in 1905, and defiantly stated that if the money that had been squandered on parliamentary politics had been spent on arms for the revolutionary movement 'we would be in a position to add another republic to the republicans of the world.'[362] Yet Bodenstown 1911 was to prove a lacklustre affair, with the *Irish Independent* reporting:

> The annual pilgrimage to Wolfe Tone's tomb at Bodenstown took place yesterday, and compared with previous functions of the kind, was not well attended. Only one band was present, though it was nothing unusual to see ten and even a dozen bands in former years.[363]

Patrick McCartan and Tom Clarke both opposed the decision not to organise a protest against the Royal visit with the result that the ideological differences within the IRB Supreme Council were becoming more and more apparent. Fred Allan and Jack O'Hanlon resigned, paving the way for a new and younger leadership to emerge. Despite his age and status as a veteran of the movement, Thomas Clarke backed the younger and more proactive members of the organisation.

In addition to Allan and O'Hanlon, MacBride lost his place on the Supreme Council. MacBride's tenure on the body was incredibly brief as he joined and left it in the same year. It is interesting that Thomas Clarke was instrumental in the replacement of the Major – not least given that MacBride had served as best man at Clarke's wedding. Brian Barton has argued that perhaps MacBride's 'excessive drinking raised doubts as to his reliability and discretion, and his personal life was regarded as a source of embarrassment.'[364] MacBride appears to have been able to maintain his role in Dublin Corporation, however, and his abilities were favourably reported upon, indicating that he had regained some control over his drinking.

MacBride continued to attract public interest as a speaker and as a symbolic figure – a man who had taken the fight directly to the British Empire. In December 1911 he travelled to Glasgow to address a Manchester Martyrs commemoration. In the late nineteenth and early twentieth centuries, the Manchester Martyrs – William Philip Allen, Michael Larkin, and Michael O'Brien – were a central part of republican commemorations. They were members of the IRB and among a group of several dozen activists who laid siege to a police van in 1867. It was transporting two leaders of the IRB, Thomas J. Kelly and Timothy Deasy, to a Manchester prison. Allen, Larkin and O'Brien were hanged for their activities and their deaths served as the inspiration for the popular nationalist song 'God Save Ireland'. At the time of their executions, Frederick Engels, who was then living in Manchester, wrote to Karl Marx:

> The *only thing* that the Fenians still lacked were martyrs. They have been provided with these by [Prime Minister] Derby and [Home Secretary] G. Hardy. Only the execution of the three has made the liberation of Kelly and Deasy the heroic deed as which it will now be sung to every Irish babe in the cradle in Ireland, England and America.[365]

The death of the three Manchester Martyrs became an emotive rallying call for Irish nationalists, not least because their bodies were not returned to Ireland. There were sizeable demonstrations annually right across the island of Ireland, and also in Britain. When MacBride was due to speak at Port Glasgow in 1911, news of his forthcoming visit was enough for the Glasgow newspaper *The Evening Times* to condemn him as a 'disloyalist' for his actions in the Boer War. To many cheers, MacBride told the town he was the very opposite – always loyal to his country and its cause.[366]

MacBride also spoke at the Manchester Martyrs commemoration in Tralee that same year, and would be a frequent sight at commemorations in honour of the trio in the years that followed. He informed the large crowd in Tralee that: 'Home Rule, if passed, could never solve the Anglo-Irish difficulty; it could never be considered a final settlement of the claim of Ireland to independence and nationhood.'[367] Manchester Martyrs commemorations drew the scorn of unionists, who regarded the men as mere criminals. The newspaper *The National Student* would complain of annual enormous meetings to commemorate 'the hanging of three felons'.[368]

The war hero's fierce and unapologetic rhetoric and popular reception at such gatherings attracted the attention not only of the police, but also of Patrick Pearse. In February 1912, MacBride received a letter from Pearse, Principal of Scoil Éanna in Rathfarnham, a bi-lingual school which had been described in *An Claidheamh Soluis* as seeking to be 'a nursery of character, intellect, patriotism and virtue, which may eventually exert a benign influence on the private and public life of our country.'[369] The letter was an invitation to speak before the boys of the school, and Pearse told MacBride that 'what the boys would really like, is an account of your experience in the South African War.'[370]

MacBride had a number of haunts in Dublin and was a frequent visitor at two in particular. Tom Clarke's newsagents and tobacco shop, located on what is now Parnell Street, was visited regularly by the Major.[371] Among other publications, it sold the *Gaelic American* and *Irish Freedom*. The shop was something of a headache for the authorities, as they knew it was a rendezvous point for separatists. Countess Markievicz would recall of Clarke that: 'His advice was always so well thought out and so sound, and the little shop at the corner of Parnell Street so handy, that one could always find a moment to run in and hear what he had to say on any trouble or complication that might arise.'[372]

Séan T. O'Kelly remembered MacBride as a frequent visitor at the Irish Farm Produce Company, which was operated as a shop and café by Jenny Wyse Power, a well-known nationalist activist in the city. Located on Henry Street, O'Kelly remembered that at one point 'I think I had lunch most days of the week' there, and that Arthur Griffith and MacBride were frequently to be found there. Today, a small plaque marks the location of this shop amidst the hustle and bustle of the modern city, as it was in Irish Farm Produce

Company that the 1916 proclamation was signed in the days before the rebellion began.[373]

MacBride's return to Ireland had brought with it public humiliation and scandal, in the form of the *Irish Independent* libel case, but also a renewed sense of personal importance, through his lecturing, political activism and employment with Dublin Corporation. The IRB was certainly at a low ebb, but MacBride had re-established contact with individuals from the days before his exploits in South Africa and was amongst family and friends again. While the movement had become a marginal force as 1911 drew to a close, the emergence of armed volunteers, north and south, was about to revitalise their campaign.

Chapter 8

• • • • •

Home Rule and the Volunteers

For successive generations of constitutional nationalists, and from the time of Daniel O'Connell's mass Repeal movement, the demand for the restoration of an Irish parliament in Dublin had been the popular rallying cry. While O'Connell had ultimately failed in this ambition, and Charles Stewart Parnell did likewise, by 1912 constitutional Irish nationalists believed that they were on the cusp of victory. Prime Minister Henry Asquith, a Liberal, had introduced the Third Home Rule Bill into the Westminster House of Lords in April 1912. While it encountered vocal opposition from sections of the House of Lords, the use of the Parliament Act would ensure that the Bill would become law by 1914, as the House of Lords could not bury such a Bill, merely delay it.

In Ireland, the looming spectacle of Home Rule brought a variety of responses. In much of the south, John Redmond of the Irish Parliamentary Party was hailed as a hero. His party stood for greater Irish legislative independence within the existing framework, and for that reason stood in stark contrast to the ideology of the IRB. Redmond, who had denounced Britain's war in South Africa during the days of MacBride's Irish Brigade adventures, was heralded in the Irish media as *the* 'Irish leader'. He stood on the verge of what for so long had seemed near impossible. In Dublin, thousands gathered to hear Redmond speak, in the belief that Home Rule was imminent. He told the crowd:

> This gathering, its vastness, its good order, its enthusiasm, and its unity is unparalleled in the modern history of Ireland. In point of numbers it recalls the monster meetings of O'Connell, but never, at the best of his days, did he assemble a gathering so representative of all Ireland as this meeting today. Every city, every town, every county, I think I can truly say every parish is represented in the capital of Ireland today.[374]

Home Rule presented a dilemma for some nationalists. For militant separatists, the question of whether limited self-government would be a help or a hindrance to their ultimate aspirations was one which had to be answered. Desmond Fitzgerald, later to fight in the Easter Rising, certainly believed, or at least hoped, that, '... a fairly large number of the people who supported Mr Redmond's party were inclined to be critical and possibly cynical. If Home Rule came quickly, well and good. No doubt it could be used beneficially as a point from which we could evolve nationally. But if it did not come soon, then it would be time to try something else.'[375]

There was little ambiguity in MacBride's position on Home Rule – he had no hope that it would lead to a further state of independence. Writing to John Devoy in 1911, he told the veteran leader that he believed a section of the movement in Ireland was losing focus, and that:

> The prospect of a so-called Home Rule Bill seems to have muddled the brains of a considerable number of them, and they evidently cannot see beyond the tips of their noses. Men that were fairly staunch a few years ago are now something akin to blithering idiots, and hold up their hands in holy terror if one ventures to question the good faith of the Liberal Government and the great British democracy.[376]

Yet if advanced nationalists were confused by the dilemma of Home Rule, there was no such confusion among unionists in the north-east of the country. In Ulster, unionists rallied behind their own political leadership, who encouraged them to stand firm against any attempt to introduce Home Rule there. Unionist opposition to the Home Rule Bill was spearheaded by Edward Carson, in some ways an unlikely icon. Born into a professional Dublin family at 4 Harcourt Street, Carson was a graduate of Trinity College Dublin and a former member of the college hurling team. A charismatic figure, he had been elected an MP for Trinity College Dublin in the 1892 General Election, and he was a formidable opponent. Famously Carson had cross-examined another Trinity graduate, Oscar Wilde, with devastating consequences in 1895. Carson's son, Harry, had fought in the Boer War, taking up arms for the Empire, while Carson himself was instrumental in the prosecution of Arthur Lynch, who had fought alongside the Boers. In September 1911 Carson informed a monster rally at Craigavon, County Armagh that 'we must be prepared, the morning Home Rule passes, ourselves to become responsible for the government of the Protestant Province of Ulster.'[377]

In addition to Carson, other unionist figures included James Craig, later to become the first Prime Minister of Northern Ireland. Craig was a veteran of the Boer War and had fought in South Africa as a captain in the Royal Irish Rifles.

During the Boer War, the *United Irishman* had proclaimed of John MacBride: 'We claim him as an Ulsterman – though his father's clan dwelt, generation after generation, in the Glens of Antrim, and their sturdy spirit is alive today in this young descendant.'[378] It was clear during the Home Rule crisis, however, that MacBride and the Boer cause he had fought for held little appeal to Ulster unionists. Anti-Home Rule postcards from 1912 onwards depicted a nightmare scenario of Home Rule with monuments of President Kruger and other Boer figures erected in Ulster towns. One postcard showed a statue of MacBride himself, rifle in hand, outside Belfast City Hall, with a green flag emblazoned with a gold harp flying from the roof of the building – an image guaranteed to enflame any Ulster unionist!

Public expression of opposition to Home Rule took several forms in Ulster but two in particular were hugely symbolic as expressions of defiance. Firstly, there was the creation of Ulster's Solemn League and Covenant, a declaration of intent to resist Home Rule. Those who signed the Covenant pledged:

> … to stand by one another in defending for ourselves and our children our cherished position of equal citizenship in the United Kingdom and in using all means which may be found necessary to defeat the present conspiracy to set up a Home Rule parliament in Dublin.

On 28 September 1912 – 'Ulster Day' – a Dubliner, in the form of Carson himself, became the first man to sign this pledge at Belfast City Hall. Between it, and a similar declaration which women signed to show their 'desire to associate ourselves with the men of Ulster in their uncompromising opposition to the Home Rule Bill', 471,414 people vowed to resist any attempt at introducing Home Rule.

Secondly, the threat of Ulstermen to take up arms in opposition to Home Rule was something which alarmed

Maud Gonne MacBride, shown with a young Seán MacBride and her daughter Iseult. The marriage of Gonne to John MacBride saddened the young Iseult.

TO-NIGHT! TO-NIGHT!

GRAND • RECEPTION

TO

MAJOR JOHN McBRIDE,

Leader of the Irish Brigade in the Boer War, in South Africa, and

MISS MAUD GONNE

"Ireland's Joan of Arc," by the

United Irish Societies of Providence

AT THE

EMPIRE THEATRE,

SUNDAY EVENING, APRIL 14, 1901

MAYOR JOHN J. FITZGERALD, of Pawtucket, will preside.

THE FOLLOWING TALENT WILL TAKE PART:

MR. DENNIS O'REILLY, - - - - - Reader
MISS MARY McGOVERN, - - - - - Soprano
MR. ROBERT J. CASEY, - - - - - Baritone
MISS MARGARET V. MAHONEY, - - - Reader
MR. EDWARD P. TRACY, - Selections on Irish Bag Pipes
Accompanists, Mr. Frederick G. Gorman and Miss Mary V. Casey.

Grand Street Parade by the Third Regt., I. V., Colonel John T. Flynn, Commanding, from Hotel to Theatre.

TICKETS, 35, 50 AND 75 CENTS.

Doors open at 7.15. Exercises commence at 8 o'clock.
Tickets can be secured from any of the members.

The Exercises will close with the singing of "GOD SAVE IRELAND."

High upon the gallows tree
Swung the noble-hearted three.
By the vengeful tyrant stricken in their bloom;
But they met him face to face,
With the courage of their race,
And they went with souls undaunted to their doom. CHORUS

"God save Ireland!" said the heroes;
"God save Ireland!" said they all.
Whether on the scaffold high,
O'er the ocean's swelling wave,
And the friends in holy Ireland ever dear.

CHORUS.

Climbed they up the rugged stair,
Rung their voices out in prayer.
Then with England's fatal cord arond them cast,
Close beneath the gallows tree,
Kissed like brothers lovingly,
True to home, and faith, and freedom to the last. CHORUS.

A promotional leaflet for one of MacBride's speaking engagements in the United States. Maud Gonne was frequently described as Ireland's Joan of Arc.

Above: John MacBride was a participant in the O'Donovan Rossa Funeral Committee. The 1915 funeral of the veteran Fenian proved a propaganda spectacular, with the Irish Volunteers and the Irish Citizen Army taking part.

Right: William Butler Yeats pleaded with Maud Gonne not to marry MacBride. He would later describe the Boer War fighter as a 'drunken, vainglorious lout' in his celebrated poem 'Easter 1916'.

Above: John O'Grady, the only member of the Jacob's garrison to die during Easter week. He was shot while on a reconnaissance mission near the factory.

Above: The imposing Jacob's biscuit factory. The garrison here encountered real hostility from the working-class Dubliners of the district, many of whom had loved ones fighting in the British armed forces during the First World War.

Left: The poet, playwright and educationalist Thomas MacDonagh. A signatory of the 1916 Proclamation, he was Commandant at the factory. MacBride's military experience proved important, however.

Left: MacBride in Dublin in the later years of his life, having acquired work with the nationalist-inclined Dublin Corporation.

Below: The Fusilier's Arch memorial at St Stephen's Green, derided by nationalists as Traitor's Gate. It commemorates the Royal Dublin Fusiliers and their exploits in South Africa. It was unveiled in 1907 before a huge crowd.

Left: John MacBride at Richmond Barracks in the aftermath of the uprising. It would appear from contemporary eyewitness accounts that he was aware of what awaited him.

Right: Father Augustine Hayden, who attended to MacBride in his last hours.

FIRST ANNIVERSARY.

I gCuimhne Ar.

Seaġan Mac Giolla Bríġde,

MAJOR JOHN MacBRIDE,

Vice-Commandant Irish Republican Army,

Major in the Army of the South African Republic,

Organizer of the Transvaal Irish Brigade,

WHO DIED FOR IRELAND

5TH MAY, 1916.

Go nDeanfaidh Dia Trocaire ar a anam.

"No man can claim authority to whittle down or barter away the immutable rights of nationhood; for Irishmen have fought, suffered, and died, through tco many centuries, in defence of those rights. And, thank God, Irishmen will always be found, in the darkest and dreariest nights that fall upon our country, to snatch up the torch from the slumbering fire, to hold it up aloft as a guiding light, and to hand it on, blazing afresh, to the succeeding generation."

Major MacBride's address on the Manchester Martyrs November, 1914.

Go Saoraidh Dia Éire.

Above: A memorial card for Major MacBride, issued on the first anniversary of his execution, including words from a speech he delivered at a Manchester Martyrs commemoration.

Left: Sean O'Sullivan's commemorative sketch of Major MacBride.

A memorial bust to John MacBride in his native Wesport. A plaque, which was unveiled by Éamon de Valera, also marks the location of his childhood home.

both the British government and Irish nationalists. The process of forming and arming a militia, which became known as the Ulster Volunteer Force (UVF), began in 1912, and the UVF was formally launched in January 1913. As an armed, paramilitary response to the planned legislation, it could not be ignored. In *Irish Freedom,* P. S. O'Hegarty warmly welcomed this arming, hoping it would lead to similar developments in the south:

> May you get arms, plenty of them, good and cheap, and may you get men to use them, and may they make as good use of them as did your forefathers who took up arms a hundred and thirty years ago .... History has a fashion of repeating itself, and we welcome with a shout this revival of public arming in Ulster.[379]

In the south, two armed bodies also emerged in 1913 – the Irish Citizen Army (ICA) and the Irish Volunteers. The Irish Citizen Army was established as a result of the Dublin Lockout, a period of real class tension in the city. Liverpool syndicalist Jim Larkin, who was concerned with establishing the right to membership of his Irish Transport and General Workers' Union (ITGWU) in the city, clashed with veteran entrepreneur and businessman William Martin Murphy, who refused to recognise the union. Murphy was himself something of an Irish nationalist, a passionate Home Ruler and a former Member of Parliament who had even refused a knighthood. For nationalists and republicans, the 1913 Lockout raised awkward questions on the issue of class. MacBride's own views on the dispute are unknown, though Maud Gonne was a passionate supporter of the cause of Larkin's union. Arthur Griffith poured scorn on the radical, writing:

> In Dublin the wives of some men that Larkin has led out on strike are begging on the streets. The consequences of 'Larkinism' are workless fathers, mourning mothers, hungry children and broken homes. Not the capitalist but the policy of Larkin has raised the price of food until the poorest of Dublin are in a state of semi-famine.[380]

During the dispute there were violent confrontations between the police and locked-out workers, and in response to this the Irish Citizen Army was born. While the ICA essentially emerged from a labour dispute, it had a nationalist focus in its ideological aims and objects. Men and women were encouraged to join the organisation that 'pledges its members to work for, organise for, drill for and fight for an independent Ireland', and the body proclaimed its willingness to work 'in harmony with the Labour and true National Movements'.[381]

Among the founding members of the Irish Citizen Army was Captain Jack White DSO (Distinguished Service Order), an Antrim-born British army veteran of the Boer War.

His father was John MacBride's old foe, Field Marshal Sir George White VC (Victoria Cross) who had been decorated with just about every honour the British Army could bestow, not least for his defence of Ladysmith during the Boer War. His son Jack had come on a particularly remarkable political journey since the Boer War, claiming that the writings of Leo Tolstoy, the Russian novelist who would become one of the most significant theorists of Anarchist ideology, were central to his transformation. Jack White put forward money for uniforms for this new body and he drilled the new proletarian army regularly in Croydon Park, Dublin – all a far cry from his days in the Boer War.

The second armed body to emerge in the south of Ireland was the Irish Volunteers. It was set-up as a direct response to the unveiling of the Ulster Volunteer Force. The IRB were centrally involved in the development of this new movement and Bulmer Hobson would later claim:

> In the middle of July, 1913, I told the Dublin Centres Board of the IRB, of which I was chairman – I was then a member of the Supreme Council – that in my opinion the time was rapidly approaching when it would be possible to start an Irish Volunteer organisation. As a preparation, I suggested, and it was decided, that members of the IRB in Dublin should commence drilling immediately.[382]

The Irish Volunteers were formally launched on 25

November 1913, at a packed meeting in the Rotunda Hospital in Dublin. Hobson further recalled:

> In addition to the 4,000 people inside the hall a crowd of about 3,000 were unable to gain admission. The path from Cavendish Row down to the entrance of the hall was a steep slope and we were much afraid that the pressure of people would smash in the doors which had been closed.

The Chief-of-Staff of this new body was Professor Eoin MacNeill, an academic of Early and Medieval Irish History at University College Dublin. MacNeill hailed from Glenarm in Antrim, and was a contemporary of John MacBride's at St Malachy's in Belfast. MacNeill was a co-founder of the Gaelic League, and in an article for the organisation's newspaper, *An Claidheamh Soluis,* he had called for the raising of an armed volunteer body. Crucially, MacNeill was not a member of the IRB, and he would remain largely oblivious to the role the secret society was playing in shaping the organisation he believed he controlled.

In Westport, John MacBride's brother Joseph was head of the local IRB circle and also the leading figure in the emerging Volunteers there. Edward Moane recalled:

> The IRB in fact started them in Westport. MacBride was in charge of the Volunteers at this time, and we had a strength of approximately one hundred and twenty. We had no arms of course, except for a few small calibre rifles and a few old

> Fenian guns, and we could mobilise a small number of shot guns. We never received any arms from the then headquarters of the Volunteers.[383]

In addition to the Volunteers, Na Fianna Éireann, the republican youth organisation, was also active in Westport. Established in 1909, with Bulmer Hobson and Countess Markievicz among its founding figures, the body was essentially a republican youth movement, which aimed to politicise and train young republican activists. Pages of *Irish Freedom* were devoted to details of Na Fianna news and drills. Thomas Ketterick recalled years later of Na Fianna in Westport that while this small body of lads lacked arms, they did have one single weapon: an old revolver which belonged to Major John MacBride, and which had been used in the Boer War. This was presented to them by Dr Anthony MacBride and was a source of much pride.[384]

MacBride appears to have been enthusiastic about the formation of the Irish Volunteers, though he never formally joined the organisation. He wrote to John Devoy that 'the Volunteer Movement will be a tremendous force in national life over here, if properly handled. The country people are at last commencing to kick against the Home Rule bluffers.'[385] That MacBride did not formally join the organisation is unusual, given his high-profile public presence, but it is important to note that the new organisation grew with rapidity right across the island. By March 1914, the Volunteers numbered some 20,000 men, while by June of the same year the body could count on 100,000 recruits.

Even John MacBride, who had forewarned of constitutional nationalists gaining positions of influence in the Volunteers, could not have anticipated what was to come in June 1914, as the year continued to be one of much excitement and tension. The leadership of the Irish Volunteers reluctantly consented to allow constitutional nationalist John Redmond of the Irish Parliamentary Party to nominate twenty-five people to the Volunteer Executive. Seán T. O'Kelly remembered:

> MacNeill, Casement and Hobson at an early stage came to the decision that it would be necessary to agree to the acceptance of a certain number of representatives of the Irish Parliamentary Party being co-opted on the Governing Body of the Volunteers. They expressed this view to their colleagues on the Volunteer Executive, and a number of the leaders were greatly disturbed at the thought of permitting any member of the Irish Parliamentary Party to join the Executive Committee of the Volunteers.[386]

Hobson later recalled that while he greatly resented Redmond's approach: 'I realised equally that if his request, which was in fact an ultimatum, were not acceded to, it would lead to a disastrous and, indeed, a fatal split in the Volunteers and in the country as a whole.'[387]

The issue of allowing Redmond and his party to gain influence on the Governing Body of the Volunteers created real tension within the IRB, whose agents were already seeking to influence the new body internally. Bulmer Hobson was court-martialled for his role in the affair and he resigned his seat on the Supreme Council. Hobson would claim years later that Tom Clarke and Seán MacDiarmada, who opposed the move, 'were both deeply sincere men, completely devoted to the national cause; but were both narrow partisans, inclined to distrust anybody who was not a member of our small organisation.'[388]

A plan, pre-dating the co-option of followers of Redmond into the body, came to fruition the following month, when the Irish Volunteers succeeded in landing significant quantities of arms and ammunition at Howth and Kilcoole. The gun-running plan was largely instigated by Roger Casement, who Bulmer Hobson claimed 'on his own initiative went to London in the early part of 1914 and got together a few friends who between them advanced £1,500.'[389] It was a very public response to ongoing events in Ireland as in April the UVF had succeeded in landing about 25,000 rifles at Larne, Donaghdee and Bangor. The financing of the gun-running for the Irish Volunteers came from individuals including Alice Stopford Green, Erskine Childers and Mary Spring Rice. Significantly, all came from Protestant Anglo-Irish backgrounds, and the plan was decided upon at a meeting in Grosvenor Road in London, home to Alice Stopford Green, the daughter of the Church of Ireland Archdeacon of Meath. It was upon the Childers' yacht, the *Asgard* that hundreds of Mauser rifles were landed in Dublin.

Roger Casement, the chief instigator, was a great admirer of Major MacBride. Having lunched with him in September 1913 and listened to MacBride's war stories of South Africa, he wrote to Mrs Alice Stopford Green that: 'MacBride is an Ulster Scot – a Scotch Irishman. He comes from Ballycastle – from Glenshesk – my own glen, and I know the family. Another blow this to the myth.'[390] Casement was undoubtedly attacking the old 'Ulster Scot equals Unionist' myth and taking a degree of pride in finding another man of Ulster blood who sought to break the connection with England. At the time of MacBride's exploits in South Africa, Casement was a member of the British Colonial Service, but the Boer War represented a significant turning point in his own political development, and in the emergence of his anti-imperialist sentiments.

Tensions were running high in Ireland as the opposing factors armed themselves. Home Rule seemed tantalisingly close and appeared an imminent and unstoppable reality by the summer of 1914. The *Leinster Express* reported on 25 July that the Special Reserve of the Third Battalion of the Royal Dublin Fusiliers were marching in the streets proclaiming 'We will have Home Rule at any cost!' and singing

'A Nation Once Again' amidst scenes of jubilation.[391] Ireland's position within the British Empire, however, would be shaped not only by domestic factors but also by international ones. The outbreak of the First World War, and more specifically Britain's declaration of war against Imperial Germany in August, created an entirely new situation. The Government of Ireland Act 1914, or the Home Rule Act, had been passed by parliament, but after the outbreak of war it was formally postponed for a minimum of twelve months.

For the Volunteer movement in Ireland, the war required a response. Ulster unionist leaders urged the men of the Ulster Volunteer Force to enlist. In the south, the Irish Volunteers did not enjoy the same ideological cohesion, and a split was imminent. Hard-line republican voices could never encourage Irishmen to enlist in the British armed forces, but moderate nationalist opinion, in the right circumstances, could do just that. On 20 September at Woodenbridge in Wicklow, John Redmond delivered a defining speech which would lead to a devastating split in the Irish Volunteers. He stated:

> The interests of Ireland, of the whole of Ireland, are at stake in this war. This war is undertaken in defence of the highest interests of religion and morality and right, and it would be a disgrace forever to our country, a reproach to her manhood, and a denial of the lessons of her history if young Ireland confined their efforts to remaining at home to defend the shores of Ireland from an unlikely invasion, and shrink-

> ing from the duty of proving on the field of battle the gallantry and courage which have distinguished their race all through its history.[392]

As Redmond had essentially urged the Volunteers to enlist in the Irish regiments of the British Armed Forces for the duration of the war, this led to an immediate response from the Provisional Committee of the Irish Volunteers, and the issuing of a statement signed by Eoin MacNeill, Thomas MacDonagh, Patrick Pearse, Liam Mellows and Bulmer Hobson among others. The statement made it clear that:

> Mr Redmond, addressing a body of Irish Volunteers on last Sunday, has now announced for the Irish Volunteers a policy and programme fundamentally at variance with their own published and accepted aims and objects, but with which his nominees are, of course, identified. He has declared it to be the duty of the Irish Volunteers to take foreign service under a Government which is not Irish.[393]

Yet, this response fell largely on deaf ears, as the vast majority of the Volunteers sided with Redmond. The split was devastating to the emerging Volunteer movement and it was by no means an even division. The historian J.J. Lee has estimated that 'perhaps only 13,000 of the 188,000 Volunteers joined MacNeill's Irish Volunteers, however, Redmond's majority now becoming known as the National Volunteers.'[394]

One place in which the ranks of the Irish Volunteers remained steadfast was Westport, were there was active participation from the MacBride family. Edward Moane of the Westport Irish Volunteers remembered that it was in the aftermath of this split that John MacBride visited the town:

> When John Redmond split the Volunteers by his famous Woodenbridge speech, in which he offered the Volunteers to the British government, Major MacBride came down to Westport and reviewed the Volunteers there and addressed them. The vast majority of our men remained loyal to the Irish Volunteer organisation and only the useless availed of this opportunity to get out. No branch of the Redmond or National Volunteers was ever formed in Westport.[395]

While the Irish Volunteers were greatly weakened by the loss of much of their membership, senior figures within the movement had already had meetings with other organisations who wished to utilise the war, to bring the old mantra that 'England's Difficulty is Ireland's Opportunity' to the fore once again. On 9 September 1914, eleven days before John Redmond's Woodenbridge speech, a secret conference was held in the library of the Gaelic League at 25 Parnell Square. This meeting brought together the IRB and others, such as the labour leader Connolly, who were all convinced of the necessity of armed action. John MacBride attended this meeting, and the fact that he was invited indicates he was still seen as a figure of importance. Tom Clarke, Seán MacDiarmada, Éamonn Ceannt, James Connolly, Joseph Plunkett, Patrick Pearse and Thomas MacDonagh were also present – the seven men who would all later put their names to the 1916 Proclamation. Also in attendance were Seán T. O'Kelly, William O'Brien and Arthur Griffith. The group had discussed whether armed insurrection during the war was something that should be strived for, and a decision to stage a rebellion was reached. O'Kelly stated that the meeting had brought together 'all shades of advanced nationalist political thought in Ireland', men to whom the Rising was 'a coldly and deliberately planned affair', with this meeting its foundation stone.[396] William O'Brien, one of only two participants present who would not ultimately take part in the rebellion, recalled that 'Connolly advocated making definite preparations for organising an insurrection, and, in connection therewith, getting in touch with Germany with a view to military support.'[397]

The Irish Neutrality League (INL) came out of this meeting and announced its arrival in October 1914, with the issuing of its first circular to the public. It was described by William O'Brien as 'a short-lived organisation' which consisted of 'leaders without members'. Essentially, the body was formed with the intention of drumming up anti-recruitment sentiment around the country. Major John MacBride actively spoke on Irish Neutrality League platforms, telling one meeting in Dublin that any Irishman who joined the British Army 'deserved to be shot in this world and damned in the next.' A pamphlet issued by the Irish Neutrality League made it clear that 'England's quarrel with Germany cannot involve Ireland', and that the body aimed to define 'Ireland's present attitude towards the Anglo-German War as one of neutrality.'[398]

The extent to which the Irish Neutrality League advocated 'neutrality' is highly questionable. MacBride was involved in the League's intention to publicly preach neutrality while behind-the-scenes plans were afoot to seek German intervention and support for insurrection on Irish soil. Just like the 'anti-war' movement that emerged during the Boer War had been driven largely by anti-British sentiment, the INL was similarly driven. Patrick Maume has noted that 'the identity of those advocating neutrality, and the absence of any means of enforcing it, left even sympathetic observers convinced that 'neutrality' simply meant hostility to Britain.'[399]

The war led to the enactment of the controversial Defence of the Realm Act, or DORA as it was popularly known. Passed only days after Britain's entry into the First World War, the act provided the authorities with far-reaching powers to maintain law and order and silence political dissent. With the outbreak of war, the level of surveillance on individuals like MacBride was intensified, and his name frequently appears in the almost daily 'movement of extremists' reports from the

Dublin Metropolitan Police. For example the presence of Major MacBride, along with the feminist campaigner Hanna Sheehy-Skeffington, James Whelan and other known political activists at the trial of P. S. O'Hegarty, one-time editor of *Irish Freedom*, was noted by the DMP.[400]

Constitutional nationalists had heralded 1914 as the year when Home Rule, the long denied and much sought constitutional 'solution' to the Irish question, finally seemed to be on the verge of becoming a reality. Yet the outbreak of war, and the suspension of the enacting of the Home Rule Bill, must have given hope to militant separatists like MacBride. To him, and those like him, England's difficulty was once more Ireland's opportunity.

Chapter 9

• • • • •

MacBride's Easter Week

While MacBride had attended the meeting in the Gaelic League's library in September 1914 and was clearly involved in early discussions on the possibility of staging an insurrection during the First World War, he appears to have fallen out of the planning structure after this point. MacBride was close to the new and militant IRB leadership, but crucially he was outside the leadership structure of the Irish Volunteers as he never officially became a member, and his brief period on the Supreme Council of the IRB was over, ensuring that he knew as little as the rank and file about what was to come.

In 1915, a Military Committee of the IRB was formed by Thomas Clarke and Seán MacDiarmada, with the explicit aim of planning a forthcoming insurrection. Patrick Pearse, Éamonn Ceannt and Joseph Plunkett also participated in this body, with James Connolly joining them in January 1916, and Thomas MacDonagh later still. Connolly had started hinting about the possibility of an insurrection in his militant socialist newspaper *The Workers' Republic* soon after the meeting in September 1914 and articles on insurrectionary tactics and historical examples of street warfare on the international stage were regularly printed throughout 1915.

Another clear sign of what was to come was provided at the funeral of Jeremiah O'Donovan Rossa in August 1915. A veteran Fenian, O'Donovan Rossa was among the five exiled men, including John Devoy, who had sailed to the United States on the *Cuba* in 1871. The death of 'Dynamite' O'Donovan Rossa, as he was known to sections of the press at the height of his infamy, created a perfect moment for a nationalist spectacle. Thomas Clarke later remarked to his wife that, 'If Rossa had planned to die at the most opportune time for serving his country, he could not have done better.'[401]

O'Donovan Rossa died in Staten Island hospital, New York and his remains arrived in Dublin on 26 July 1915. His body lay in state, first at the Pro-Cathedral and later in City Hall. John MacBride served on the O'Donovan Rossa Funeral Committee, a large body that drew from all sections of the separatist family, and he was photographed alongside his fellow members, who included Éamon de Valera, Thomas MacDonagh and Edward Daly. What is truly striking about the image of the Committee is the sheer number of the men and women featured who would take part in the Easter Rising on the streets of the capital less than a year later.

Every aspect of the funeral on 1 August 1915 was carefully managed. O'Donovan Rossa's coffin was provided with a guard of honour from the First Battalion of the Irish Volunteers, under the command of Edward Daly. A huge procession followed the hearse as it moved from City Hall to Glasnevin Cemetery, and the sight of tens of thousands lining the streets and marching behind the coffin troubled the authorities greatly. Sir Matthew Nathan, serving as Under Secretary for Ireland in Dublin Castle, felt compelled to write: 'I have an uncomfortable feeling that the Nationalists [meaning constitutional figures like Redmond] are losing ground to the Sinn Féiners and that this demonstration is hastening the movement.'[402] The funeral stood in stark contrast to that of MacBride's great friend and ally, John O'Leary in 1907.

At Glasnevin Cemetery, MacBride stood just behind Patrick Pearse, who was to deliver the oration. Before preparing his speech, Pearse had asked Tom Clarke what the tone should be. Clarke advised him to 'Make it as hot as hell, throw discretion to the winds'.[403] Pearse took this to heart, informing the gathered crowds that:

> They think that they have pacified Ireland. They think that they have purchased half of us and intimidated the other half. They think that they have foreseen everything, think that they have provided against everything; but the fools,

> the fools, the fools! – they have left us our Fenian dead, and while Ireland holds these graves, Ireland unfree shall never be at peace.

While Pearse's speech has become iconic, what occurred next was also important. A volley of shots rang out over the historic cemetery and Séan T. O'Kelly remembered feeling an immense pride and that he was part of an historic occasion as the salute was fired:

> This must have been one of the first if not the very first occasion on which this military demonstration took place in our lifetime and this too in its way made a deep impression not alone on all who were present but on all who read the report afterwards. The I.R.B. and the Irish Volunteers were very proud of having been able to accomplish this military demonstration despite the orders of the British against the carrying of arms.[404]

O'Donovan Rossa's funeral was covered extensively in the media throughout Ireland and focussed the public's attention back on the struggle for independence. It provided a degree of respectability to the radical separatists, who had succeeded in bringing large numbers onto the streets, and the enormity of the event led to a renewed confidence in the movement.

Over the following months, however, there was further contention within the Irish Volunteer leadership. An ideological rift developed between those who believed that imminent insurrection was the correct strategy and those, including Eoin MacNeill and Bulmer Hobson, who saw premature rebellion as potentially destructive and totally irrational. The majority of the Volunteers believed that armed confrontation should come only if the British State took direct action to disarm the movement. MacNeill and Hobson, and indeed the rank and file of the Irish Volunteers, were not aware that imminent insurrection was being planned by a small Military Council of the Irish Republican Brotherhood, and while Hobson was himself an IRB man there were now essentially secret societies within secret societies.

The clandestine planners in the IRB's Military Council had decided that MacNeill would need to be usurped before the uprising. Weeks before the outbreak of the Easter Rising, all senior officers of the Irish Volunteers who were not at that point members of the IRB, were approached, with many sworn into the organisation. They were then informed that they were no longer to accept orders from MacNeill, but rather to only follow orders signed by Patrick Pearse.[405] Unbeknownst to MacNeill and those around him, his authority and leadership were being diminished by the IRB men in the midst of the Volunteers, who were plotting the rebellion.

The Military Council also knew it was essential to produce evidence which would compel MacNeill, his supporters and also the rank and file to back an insurrectionary position. The opportunity to put these wheels in motion was provided by Eugene Smith. He was an employee of Dublin Castle who leaked internal intelligence to Volunteer leaders in April 1916. Smith recalled:

> Before the Rising I was an official in the Castle and in that capacity a certain document came into my hands. It was a long Communication from Major General Friend, General Officer Commanding the Forces in Ireland and addressed to the Chief Secretary in London. I believed at the time and still believe that it was sent in reply to a query as to what military precautions would be necessary with a view to the enforcement of conscription in Ireland. The document was not in code or cypher.[406]

This Castle documentation appeared to suggest that the authorities, on the orders of the Castle were willing to suppress not alone the Volunteers, but a range of nationalist organisations, including the Gaelic League and the Sinn Féin party. It also suggested the arrest of leading nationalist figures, including Eoin MacNeill. It is most likely that having acquired this documentation, members of the Military Council amended it, giving it a more alarmist tone to try to force the hand of MacNeill and his supporters. The 'Castle Document', as it became known, was read before Dublin Corporation on Wednesday, 19 April. Often dismissed as a forgery, it would instead appear to have been an amended and exaggerated document that still had some basis in real intelligence. Certainly, it did alarm MacNeill. He ordered the Irish Volunteers to be prepared to resist any attempt by the authorities to 'suppress or disarm' the movement.

The following day, events took a drastic turn, when Bulmer Hobson, who also favoured a defensive position, learned of the plot for insurrection. Hobson was so alarmed that he woke MacNeill from his sleep in the early hours of the morning and the two rushed to Scoil Éanna, where they demanded an immediate meeting with Patrick Pearse. MacNeill was crushed to learn that his authority in the Volunteers had been greatly diminished, and that an organisation he believed himself to control was now being directed by outside forces. He then discovered that Pearse had already issued mobilisation orders for a provisional date set for Easter Sunday. MacNeill vowed to do all in his power to prevent insurrection swearing that he would countermand the existing orders. Pearse remained resolute, and the scene was set for a confrontation between the two sides.

The next day, Good Friday, 21 April 1916, Bulmer Hobson was kidnapped by members of the IRB, and taken to a house on Cabra Road, which was the home of IRB activist Martin Conlon. Hobson was seized as he was regarded as the direct obstacle to insurrection, with Thomas MacDonagh commenting 'if we could separate MacNeill from his influence, all would be well.'[407] Hobson would claim later that in the situation, his response was that: 'I laughed and said "you are a lot of damn fools." There was nothing I could do, so I sat back and accepted the situation. I felt I had done my best to stop the Rising.'[408] Hobson was not to be released until the insurrection had begun, thus preventing him from stopping the event.

A series of frantic meetings followed between MacNeill and Thomas MacDonagh and MacNeill was informed of the imminent arrival of German arms in Kerry, again procured by Roger Casement. There was no way they could have known at that point that Casement's mission had proven a disastrous failure; owing to what Angus Mitchell has rightly termed 'a combination of misunderstanding, bad luck, careless preparation and incompetence'.[409] Casement had been arrested, the German *Aud* intercepted, and its cargo scuttled by its captain. Within hours, the news of this disaster filtered through to Dublin and it was met with grave disappointment by those planning the insurrection. The Military Council, however, believed the rebellion should proceed.

For MacNeill this disaster, coupled with emerging doubts about the validity of the 'Castle Document', led to him issuing a countermanding order, negating the orders previously issued by Pearse. The *Sunday Independent* of 23 April informed Volunteers that despite earlier orders, 'no parades, marches or other movements of the Irish Volunteers will take place.' MacNeill's order ensured that in the aftermath of the

Rising many republicans would lay a degree of blame at his feet. Margaret Skinnider, an active member of the Irish Citizen Army, and the only female volunteer injured during the Rising, was adamant however that 'It was his love for the Volunteers, the love of a man instinctively pacifist, that made him give that order. Oh, the satire of history!'[410]

A crisis meeting of the Military Council took place at Liberty Hall, early on Easter Sunday. It was decided that while the insurrection should proceed, it would now begin on Easter Monday, 24 April 1916.

The manner in which John MacBride came to participate in the Rising has been disputed. Maire O'Brolchain, Vice-President of Maud Gonne's Inghinidhe na hÉireann, recounted to the Bureau of Military History that she believed MacBride was informed of the uprising at the home of former IRB leader Fred Allan, where he was staying. From the recollections of Fred Allan's wife, Clara, O'Brolchain believed that:

> On Easter Monday she [Mrs Allan] saw from the front window a boy come up to the hall door. Shortly afterwards, MacBride told her that he was going out and did not know when he would be back. She saw him go out the gate and noticed a bulge in the pocket of his overcoat. Later she remembered the bulge when she knew that he was with Thomas MacDonagh in Jacob's factory.[411]

MacBride himself would later testify at his court martial that he left Allan's home at Glenageary and went into the city to meet his brother, Dr Anthony MacBride. Anthony was to be married that week, and John was due to meet him for lunch. MacBride stated that: 'In waiting round town I went up as far as Stephen's Green and there I saw a band of Irish Volunteers. I knew some of the members personally and the Commander told me that an Irish Republic was virtually proclaimed. … although I had no previous connection with the Irish Volunteers, I considered it my duty to join them.'[412]

Men of the Second Battalion of the Irish Volunteers had gathered at St Stephen's Green, just before noon. They were under the orders of Thomas MacDonagh, with Michael O'Hanrahan as his second-in-command. MacDonagh intended the Battalion to seize Jacob's biscuit factory, which was located on what is now the site of the National Archives of Ireland. As the men had arrived at their meeting point in dribs and drabs, one of them, Tom Slater, remembered the appearance of a familiar face:

> Between 11 and 11.30 the Volunteers started to arrive in good numbers until the number reached about 100. About 11.45 a gentleman came down from the city and stood looking on. He was at once recognised as Major MacBride. He was not in uniform … Tom MacDonagh was only too delighted to have a man of his experience with him and told him so.[413]

By noon on Easter Monday, 150 men or so of the Second Battalion had gathered in response to Pearse's mobilisation order. The low turnout was the result of the confusion caused by Eoin MacNeill's counter-order the previous day. It was a disappointing figure from MacDonagh's perspective and greatly hampered his plans. He had intended that a body of his men would also seize Trinity College Dublin, as it was located in a position of strategic importance, but this was no longer an option.

Vincent Byrne, a member of the Second Battalion, recalled the great confusion that existed around that week. He remembered that on Tuesday he had been informed that there would be a parade on Easter Sunday. He commented:

> On Easter Sunday I read the countermanding order in the *Independent*. Consequently, I did not parade as originally instructed. On Easter Sunday evening Davy Golden, who was the squad leader, called to my house and told me not to leave the city the next day [Easter Monday] as they expected there would be mobilisations at Stephen's Green on Monday morning.[414]

Another member of the garrison, Padráig O'Kelly, recalled that when he heard the Easter Sunday mobilisation had been called off, and received no new mobilisation order, 'I went to Fairyhouse Races on Easter Monday and there heard of trouble in Dublin.'[415] Across the city, men like O'Kelly would arrive late and confused at garrisons, as they only heard about the rebellion as it was unfolding.

At noon, across the River Liffey, rebel forces, drawn from a variety of organisations, seized the General Post Office (GPO) on O'Connell Street. A Proclamation of Independence was subsequently read out by Patrick Pearse, before a copy was placed at the base of the Nelson Pillar, the Doric column erected to the memory of British Admiral Horatio Nelson. Castlebar man Ernie O'Malley recalled seeing the proclamation on the ground there, noting that 'some looked at it with serious faces, others laughed and sniggered.'[416] Pearse and Connolly were joined by Thomas Clarke, Joseph Plunkett and Seán MacDiarmada, with the result that five of the seven men who had signed the proclamation were located at the GPO.

As the men were mobilising at St Stephen's Green, the authorities were already aware that something of note was occurring. Seosamh de Brún remembered: 'I noticed Detective Johnny Barton of the G Division, an interested spectator. Johnny was a well-known figure to Gaels.'[417] Barton would later be shot dead on the streets of the capital during the War of Independence. The G Men, working out of Great Brunswick Street Dublin Metropolitan Police station, were a constant threat to the republican movement, and indeed to other radical movements, relentlessly monitoring the movements of known radicals.

As the Volunteers marched off towards Jacob's Factory on Bishop Street, they were led by Thomas MacDonagh, his brother, John, and by John MacBride. Michael O'Hanrahan was, on paper, second-in-command to Thomas MacDonagh, but he was largely usurped on this position with the arrival of MacBride. O'Hanrahan had joined the Irish Volunteers at their inception, and was employed as a volunteer quartermaster in their Dawson Street offices.

John MacDonagh would recall the outright hostility the women in the area they travelled through displayed towards the marching men. These working-class wives were dependent on the financial assistance gained by their husbands risking life and limb in the trenches of Europe. Two of the leading employers in the district, Jacob's and the Guinness brewery, had both supported the war effort, with Guinness paying half-wages to the families of Guinness employees who enlisted in the armed forces, and guaranteeing jobs upon their return. MacDonagh remembered that the women 'became hysterical in their abuse of us', and that the 'mildest of their remarks' was that the men should go and fight the Germans rather than fight at home during the war.[418]

Why did the Volunteers occupy Jacob's? As Shane Kenna has noted, the building was five stories high at its tallest point and housed two large towers, which meant it could provide panoramic view of the city, and provide strategically important sniper positions.[419] Its proximity to Dublin Castle, and its proximity to the nearby occupied St Stephen's Green, was also an important factor in the decision to seize it. It occupied an important position on the route to the city and Dublin Castle, and, crucially – it was well stocked with food. Positioned near to both Portobello and Richmond Barracks, by establishing outposts at this position, the garrison also had the ability to create immense difficulty for the armed forces attempting to enter the city.

Having arrived at Jacob's, the Volunteers proceeded to break a number of windows so that they could gain access to the building. In the melee, John MacDonagh remembered that 'one man's shotgun went off', and while it didn't kill anyone, it proved a lucky escape for MacBride, who MacDonagh claimed 'picked a few pellets out of his moustache saying that shotguns should be treated carefully.'[420]

On entering the building, the Volunteers encountered the staff of the factory who were small in number owing to it being a bank holiday. These included a watchman, Henry Fitzgerald, and the caretaker, Thomas Orr. Orr attempted to call the chairman of the company, George Jacob. The rebels succeeded in preventing this by cutting the telephone and telegraph wires. MacDonagh allowed the staff to leave the premises, though Thomas Orr and Henry Fitzgerald refused to go, believing it their job to stay at the factory.[421]

Occupying a biscuit factory brought obvious advantages for the men in the garrison, and Vincent Byrne recalled that biscuit tins could be useful in a revolutionary situation:

> I had a great time eating plenty of cocoa chocolate and biscuits galore. The next thing I remember was that we threw a lot of empty tins out through the windows which were spread out over the roadway, so that if any of the enemy came along in the dead of night, he would, hit the tins and we would know that there was somebody on the move.[422]

The Irish Volunteers did not feast on biscuits alone as the garrison commandeered food and supplies from the nearby area. Seamus Pounch, a Fianna member, remembered that he 'commandeered lard from Cavey's, Wexford St. and potatoes from Quinlisk's Stores, Cuffe St., and several trays of loaf tread. As my armed men could not meet a sudden attack and carry in supplies acquired, I conscripted civilian help for this purpose and marched the convoy to Jacob's'.[423] Pounch remembered that MacBride was amused by Pounch's use of the conscripts, and that they were duly rewarded with two loaves a piece. A few years after the rebellion, Seamus Pounch returned to Quinlisk's Stores to pay for the potatoes![424]

News of the outbreak of the rebellion in Dublin caused confusion in rural Ireland. In Westport Joseph MacBride would claim that the Volunteers there were mustered twice in light of events, however 'we had one or two rifles, but that is all.'[425] While the Westport men lacked orders, it was primarily the absence of weapons that prevented rebellion there, and Joseph insisted that 'we would not have waited for instructions if we had rifles and stuff. We had nothing to go on with.'[426]

If the rebellion was to serve as a spark which would ignite a nationwide blaze, the under-armed nature of the Volunteers was just one factor which prevented this scenario from becoming a reality. Closer to home, MacBride's old Boer War comrade Thomas Byrne marched into Dublin from Kildare, after a small band of Irish Volunteers met in Maynooth. They marched all the way to the city, stopping at Glasnevin Cemetery to rest. One of the men who marched from Maynooth was Patrick Colgan, and he remembered that: 'We explored the Cemetery, reading the names on the tombstones. I found the grave where a relative of mine was buried.'[427] When Byrne ordered the men onwards, they continued their march towards the General Post Office.

At Jacob's, a headquarters for MacDonagh, O'Hanrahan and MacBride was established in the clerks' room. A medical unit was also established in the factory by members of Cumann na mBan, supervised by chemist Patrick Cahill. In addition to the Volunteers themselves, there were a number of prisoners held at the factory. Thomas Pugh of the Irish Volunteers recalled inspecting barricades at Clanbrassil Street and New Street on the first day of the rebellion, and taking several 'police and plainclothes men prisoners' in the process. He recalled that 'we brought our prisoners back to Jacob's when it getting dusk in the evening', and that 'the women around the Coombe were in a terrible state, they were like French revolution furies and were throwing their arms round the police, hugging and kissing them, much to the disgust of the police.'[428] Six captured policemen, and the two Dublin Metropolitan Police detectives, would spend the week of the uprising peeling potatoes in the factory, no doubt a far preferable occupation than being shot on the streets.

Curiously, while the Irish Volunteers had taken up positions in buildings on Camden Street, Wexford Street, Fumbally Lane and at other strategic locations in the vicinity of the factory, these outposts were abandoned by the evening of April 24, and the men returned to the Jacob's factory, perhaps owing to the intense hostility they encountered in the area. At the gates of the factory, they encountered an increasingly antagonistic crowd of locals.

William James Stapleton would later recall that for the men and women occupying the factory, the issue of moving the mob was one of paramount importance, as there was even an attempt to burn the gates:

> No sooner had we barricaded the entrance when the mob tried to burst the gate in. They kicked and barged it with some heavy implements, but seeing that that was of little effect they tried to set fire to it with old sacking which had been soaked in paraffin and pushed under the door and ignited. However, this was not of much use either as we

pushed it back out again and it only smouldered.[429]

Stapleton recalled that following this, 'Major McBride and Commandant Tom MacDonagh, who were on their rounds of inspection, came on the scene.' MacDonagh ordered Stapleton to: 'remove the shot from my shotgun cartridges and fire a couple of blanks through the iron grid at the top of the gates in the direction of the mob in the hope of frightening them off. I did this and they dispersed after a short time.'[430]

Hostile mobs and individuals remained a problem for the garrison, particularly on the first day and night of the occupation. This was an unsurprising feature of the occupation, given that almost 400 Jacob's employees alone had enlisted in the British Army during the First World War.

Padráig O'Kelly of the Irish Volunteers only heard about the rebellion through word of mouth and made his way to the General Post Office. Patrick Pearse then informed him that the men of his Battalion had seized Jacob's. As he walked back across the city towards St Stephen's Green, he was struck by the scenes of sheer confusion he witnessed, and the sight of people standing around in bemusement. At Jacob's, he recalled seeing a woman, who seemed drunk, throwing paraffin oil onto the factory gates and attempting to set them alight: 'A shot was fired over her head and she decamped … in my experience, the Rising was not popular amongst Dublin citizens generally during the actual course of the fighting.'[431]

Having gained entrance to the building, O'Kelly recalled:

The rank and file of the Volunteers in Jacob's ware practically all of the middle and working-class – clerks, shop-assistants, tradesmen, labourers – the great common people of Ireland. In Jacob's I met many G.A.A. players whom I knew.[432]

Volunteer Martin Walton was also struck by the hostility of the mob outside the factory and witnessed a woman being fired on by the garrison. He recalled: 'that was my baptism of fire, and I remember my knees nearly going from under me. I would have sold my mother and father and the Pope just to get out of that bloody place.'[433]

The men of the Jacob's garrison included, amongst others, Peadar Kearney who had penned the lyrics of 'The Soldier's Song'. It was sung with gusto by men at various rebel positions across Dublin during Easter Week. Kearney was Brendan Behan's uncle, and Behan later recalled his immense pride that 'the same blood ran in our veins.'[434] Phil Shanahan was there too, a Tipperary native whose public house in the heart of the Monto, Dublin's red light district, became a popular rendezvous point for republicans during the War of Independence.

Seosamh de Brún recalled that the soldiers of the Second Battalion presented 'a strangely incongruous appearance. Some were dressed in full, uniform, the green showing pale beneath its mist of flour in striking contrast with the civilian garb of others' and he recalled 'the assorted types of rifles, the devastating double-barrelled shot-gun, the crack Winchester repeater, and latest pattern Lee Enfield British service magazine rifle and bayonet, or the most powerful of all, the Howth rifle fitted with long curved French bayonet'.[435] De Brún remembered also the stirring speeches of both MacDonagh and MacBride, recalling that: 'the encouraging words of those two splendid personalities had a buoyant effect on the men, the seriousness of the situation was forgotten in the spirit of adventure. Cheers and cries of 'Long live the Republic' rang throughout the building'.[436]

The garrison at the Jacob's factory would grow to a total of 178 men. Some of the rebels found themselves there because they couldn't reach the GPO or other positions as it was too late by the time they heard about the rebellion; other insurgents had taken part in the fighting elsewhere and retreated to the Jacob's factory garrison when their own position was overrun. Willie Oman, a member of the Irish Citizen Army, arrived at the Jacob's factory after he'd managed to escape following the fall of the ICA's garrison at City Hall early in the rebellion. Wisely, he had hidden his ICA uniform under his overcoat, and spent the night sleeping in his grandmother's house at Blackpitts, before approaching the Jacob's garrison the following day:

> On Tuesday morning, a friend of the family informed us that there would be no difficulty in my approaching Jacob's

> as the British military had not come near it yet. Having had a good feed and a wash and brush-up, I set out for Jacob's. Fortunately for me, four or five Citizen Army men, who had retreated from Davy's public house at Portobello Bridge, were already in Jacob's and they identified me.[437]

The men Oman referred to had been holding a strategically important position beside the La Touche Bridge in Portobello. They had initially been tasked with obstructing soldiers from leaving the nearby Portobello Barracks and making sure the British forces didn't enter the city from there. However, when Davy's pub fell, and the Citizen Army men retreated into Jacob's, it left a clear path into the city for the British forces, allowing them to bypass the Jacob's factory entirely.

As British reinforcements flooded into the city to contain the Rising, the garrison at the Jacob's factory was cut-off from much of the fighting. Brigadier-General Lowe was co-ordinating British efforts to suppress the uprising. Lowe, like many of his British Army contemporaries, had served in the Second Boer War, leading the Seventh Dragoon Guards. At the time of the outbreak of the rebellion, he was stationed at The Curragh, County Kildare. He arrived at Kingsbridge Station, now Heuston Station, at 3.45am on Tuesday morning. Lowe's policy seems to have been to isolate the Jacob's garrison, using snipers and deploying armoured cars around the factory at night. Undoubtedly the aim was to give the men inside the impression that direct conflict was an ever-approaching reality. For Peadar Kearney, 'the ear-splitting crash of all sorts of arms gave the impression that the building was being attacked from front and rear.'[438]

MacDonagh and MacBride deployed snipers to the towers of the factory, who caused considerable difficulty for British forces, yet there was no direct assault on Jacob's.

MacBride's presence in the factory, as a veteran of armed combat who had fought the British in South Africa, helped to steady the nerves of many Volunteers. Thomas MacDonagh, a member of the Military Council which had orchestrated the insurrection, was primarily an academic and not a soldier. Of MacBride, John MacDonagh would recall:

> Inside Jacob's, MacBride's influence was useful in steadying our men. One day, an excited Volunteer, Dick Cotter, entered the headquarters room, where I was sitting with MacBride, and announced that thousands of British troops were advancing up the street. MacBride coolly replied, "That's alright!" Thinking MacBride did not realise the importance of his message, Cotter persisted. MacBride again said, "That's alright", and, turning to me as if continuing our conversation said, "So I played my king and won the game".[439]

British efforts were focused on breaking other rebel positions, such as the General Post Office, leaving Jacob's eerily quiet, and the women of Cumann na mBan, who had established a medical centre in the building, had little work to do. There were moments of humour in the garrison, which broke the monotony. John MacDonagh remembered that some of the Volunteers discovered an old-fashioned gramophone in the factory, which played 'God Save the King'. They proceeded to play it as MacDonagh and MacBride made their inspections of the building, to get a rise from the men.[440]

An unusual victim of the limited fighting around the Jacob's factory was the nearby Marsh's Library, the oldest public library in the capital. The bullets from a British Army machine-gun stationed in the nearby St Patrick's Park, 'inadvertently' fired on the library at some point during the rebellion and inflicted permanent damage on a number of books, which can still be viewed in the library today. The keeper of the library Jason McElligott has recorded that 'each book has a relatively compact entry hole of 1.5cm on its spine, but the exit hole at the back is five to six times larger.'[441] The books had been deposited in the library by Elias Bouhereau, a Huguenot refugee who brought them with him as he fled religious persecution in France. The books had already survived so much, but did not come through Easter week intact.

The death of a member of the garrison, John O'Grady, brought the reality of the rebellion home to many of the men. On Thursday April 27 a messenger arrived from

Éamon de Valera's Third Battalion. They were engaged in heavy fighting at Boland's Mills and required immediate assistance. MacDonagh authorised a small group of men to go and create a diversion in the district. Volunteer Seamus Pounch remembered that: 'he [O'Grady] was shot from a house in Leeson St. by troops. His party were sent out from Jacob's to reconnoitre. He was brought back by his comrades, but he could not be saved; he died after he was attended to by the Adelaide Hospital.'[442]

O'Grady and the men with him had made it as far as Fitzwilliam Street and had briefly engaged with British armed forces, and it was on the return journey to Jacob's that he was shot and wounded. While O'Grady managed to cycle back to the garrison, he had to be supported by riders on either side of his bicycle. John O'Grady's brother, Charles, also took part in the Rising, spending much of the week at the site of Roe's Distillery in the Liberties. O'Grady was the only active member of the Jacob's garrison to die in the rebellion.

Largely unbeknownst to the men inside Jacob's, who found themselves disconnected from what was occurring beyond the walls of the factory, British authorities were suffocating the uprising, with the deployment of heavy artillery and a force of almost 20,000 men on the ground. At 2.30am on Friday, 28 April, General Sir John Maxwell arrived in Dublin. In correspondence with Field Marshal Lord French, Maxwell outlined his belief that: 'the fighting qualities so far displayed by rebels give evidence of better training and discipline than they have been credited with.'[443]

Of General Maxwell, Brian Barton has noted:

> At root, Maxwell bore no real affection for Ireland and fully shared the prejudices of the English officer class. He thought Dublin 'cold and cheerless', its 'poverty and improvidence appalling'. As for its people, 'the majority', he stated 'seem to be on the verge of madness which finds its outlet in poetry and emotional traits'.[444]

The bombardment of the General Post Office, and the use of eighteen pounder guns in its vicinity, meant that the rebel headquarters was ultimately an untenable position. Other rebel held garrisons came under severe fire and there was intense fighting in the built-up urban area around the Four Courts, across the river from Jacob's. The General Post Office on O'Connell Street was abandoned on Friday, because of the flames which were subsuming the building, flames that were evident from Jacob's. The GPO garrison retreated to Moore Street, leaving the burning building behind them, destined to become a symbol of the insurrection. The uprising, like the GPO itself, was in danger of imminent collapse.

A meeting of five members of the Provisional Irish Government occurred at 16 Moore Street on the Saturday morning and the decision to surrender, to prevent further loss of civilian life, was reached.

Elizabeth O'Farrell, a member of the GPO garrison who had provided medical assistance to injured rebels, left the Moore Street building and proceeded under a white flag to Lowe's position, to tell him that Pearse was willing to negotiate terms of surrender. Despite the best attempts of the rebels to negotiate terms with General Lowe, it became clear that only an unconditional surrender would be accepted. Ultimately, faced with no other option beyond fighting to the death, an unconditional surrender was accepted by those in Moore Street as the only available conclusion.

News of this surrender arrived at Jacob's via Elizabeth O'Farrell, who had been tasked with informing the men and women in the various garrisons that the rebellion was over. Father Aloysius and Father Augustine of the Capuchin Friary then arrived at the factory to act as intermediaries to negotiate with the garrison and to encourage the men to surrender. They brought with them a letter signed by Pearse and Connolly, which ordered the rebels to down arms and made it clear the insurrection had been ended to prevent the loss of further civilian lives.

Father Aloysius would later claim that 'we met Major MacBride who said that he would oppose any attempt at surrender.'[445] MacDonagh outlined to the priests that 'as Pearse and Connolly were under arrest they were not free men and the letter written by them in custody could have no weight.'[446]

In the aftermath of the Moore Street surrender, and the

arrival of Elizabeth O'Farrell, MacDonagh agreed to meet with General Lowe at the nearby St. Patrick's Park, though he insisted on travelling to the meeting accompanied by another member of the garrison, perhaps fearful of a trap. Father Augustine recalled:

> MacBride volunteered to accompany him, but remembering the fine part he had played in the Boer War, I said it was better not. A volunteer was then called, and the four of us proceeded on foot.'[447]

MacDonagh later returned to the factory having been informed in no uncertain terms by General Lowe that if he had not heard from the leaders of the garrison by 3pm, the British army would commence their attack upon the premises.

Evidently, MacDonagh's report on the meeting made MacBride change his mind. The Major's influence over the men was important in convincing some of those who were most hostile to surrender that it was in their best interests and in the best interests of their people. As Joseph Furlong recalled:

> On Sunday morning I saw MacDonagh and MacBride go out. After a long spell we were told to parade down in one of the lower rooms and there MacDonagh and MacBride told us that we were to surrender and the fight was over. They told us that Pearse had surrendered and that the G.P.O.

> and Liberty Hall were destroyed and all O'Connell Street was in ruins .... Some of the men kicked against surrendering and wanted to continue the fight, but MacBride asked them did they think he would surrender if he thought there was any chance of success, adding, that we must now save the lives of our people. This had the effect he wanted, and we all agreed.[448]

The Rising had turned out to be a remarkably different war for MacBride when compared with his exploits in South Africa. John MacDonagh recalled MacBride saying to him that 'the next time he fought, he would fight in the open and not be caught like a rat in a trap.'[449] That statement also indicated that at this point MacBride had some hope of keeping his life.

Other Volunteers who were present also recalled similar statements from MacBride. He was trying to encourage them that a future fight must be out in the open, though it would appear from some of their recollections that MacBride knew what fate awaited him personally. MacBride ably assisted some of the men who donned civilian clothes and fled the factory while there was still time. He later recalled, 'I could have escaped from Jacob's factory before the surrender had I so desired but I considered it a dishonourable thing to do.'[450]

Before leaving the factory to meet the 3pm deadline, MacBride showed a member of Jacob's staff where bombs and grenades were being stored, as they posed a great risk if handled incorrectly. Peter Cushen, an employee of Jacob's, remembered that when soldiers came rushing into the factory they were more concerned with removing the rebel flag from the roof of the premises than with ensuring the safety of the building.[451]

Curiously, John MacDonagh noted in his statement to the Bureau of Military History that as the rebels were surrendering their arms, it was noticed that 'Major MacBride had a beautiful rifle that had been presented to him in commemoration of his Boar campaign. It was suitably inscribed and a Dublin Fusilier, thinking no doubt he would get a stripe for his pains, who read that inscription, told his officer that MacBride had fought against the British in the Boer War.'[452] Given the manner in which MacBride most likely found himself participating in the events of that Easter week of 1916, it seems unlikely that this rifle would have been on his person in the factory.

Regardless of what weapon the Major had carried in the fight, he joined the defeated rebels on the short march to their surrender point at Saint Patrick's Park. Once again, the rebels were met by outright hostility, jeering and cries of treachery from the working-class inhabitants of Dublin. This was not a cry of political treachery – but a very personal one, in communities where a sizeable percentage of the local men were fighting in Europe. Rose McNamara of Cumann na mBan remembered that on the march from the park to

Richmond Barracks, MacBride told her and her comrades, 'Sing away, girls, You'll be alright. You'll be out tomorrow.' When McNamara asked what he anticipated of himself and the rebel leaders, a dejected MacBride told her 'Ah no. We won't be out. We'll be shot.'[453]

When the rebellion was over, and the death toll was accounted for, it was clear the fighting had brought misery, hardship and death into the lives of ordinary Dubliners. The British forces' use of heavy artillery in the city centre meant that the tactics of the First World War were employed in an urban, heavily-populated environment, with devastating consequences. Francis Johnston's beautiful General Post Office had been destroyed, as were other fine Dublin buildings, but architecture counts for little when human lives are lost too. It has been estimated that forty children lost their lives in the insurrection, including young rebel participants like Charles Darcy of the Irish Citizen Army, while others were innocent members of the public. It was something General Maxwell would later speak candidly about:

> These rebels wore no uniform, and the man who was shooting at a soldier one minute might, for all he knew, be walking quietly beside him in the street at another .... They [British soldiers] saw their comrades killed beside them by hidden and treacherous assailants, and it is even possible that under the horrors of this peculiar attack some of them 'saw red'. That is the evitable consequence of a rebellion of this

kind.[454]

News of Major John MacBride's involvement in events in Dublin attracted significant media attention, much of it well beyond Ireland and Britain. Indeed, Maud Gonne first heard of the rebellion through the press, writing to W. B. Yeats that 'tragic dignity has returned to Ireland', though she was still unaware of her estranged husband's execution at that point.[455] What was the response to the insurrection in South Africa? On Saturday, 29 April, as Dublin was still subsumed by flames, a telegram arrived for John Redmond from General Louis Botha, the famed Boer commander. Botha expressed his 'heartfelt sympathy' for the parliamentary leader, telling him of his regret 'that a small section in Ireland are jeopardising the great cause.'[456]

Chapter 10

• • • • •

'Changed, Changed Utterly'

On the morning of Monday, 1 May 1916, at the Richmond Barracks, Inchicore, members of the Irish Volunteers and the Irish Citizen Army, along with assorted other participants in the insurrection, were standing in the gymnasium in silence as Dublin Metropolitan Police detectives observed them. The G-men then started moving through the ranks, removing known leaders from the mass of men. Naturally, John MacBride was immediately identified. W. T. Cosgrave, also selected by the detectives, remembered that they were then escorted to another area of the barracks, 'and left standing under the guard of escort until 9pm.'[457]

The prisoners' quarters were locked at 8pm, and Cosgrave recalled that, with no beds and no bedclothes, the prisoners discussed their feelings among themselves well into the night. MacBride informed Cosgrave that: 'his life-long prayer had been answered. He said three Hail Mary's every day that he should not die until he had fought the British in Ireland.'[458]

W. T. Cosgrave's recollections of MacBride at the Richmond Barracks Inchicore provide us with a real insight into the Major's mindset at the very end of the struggle. Despite having told the women of Cumann na mBan that he expected to be shot, Cosgrave gives the impression that at this stage MacBride believed otherwise:

> MacBride evidently thought he was facing a term of imprisonment, as he expressed to me his anxiety that his position as an official of the Dublin Corporation would be there for him on his release and for those of the Volunteers who were officials or employees of the Municipality.[459]

MacBride's composure impressed the men, indeed to Cosgrave 'he was as cool and collected, we heard, during Easter Week as if he were walking to Church'.[460]

Gerald Doyle, a member of the Irish Volunteers, recounted an incident that underlines the specific interest the British had in MacBride:

> We were marched out to the big square and, while lined up, three officers came over to where McBride was standing. One of them had a camera and the first two leading soldiers stood out while the officer started to take photos of MacBride standing in front with his hands in his pockets and the dust-coat over his arm. I believe that one of the officers had met Major McBride during the Boer War and recognised him.[461]

The court martial appearance of John MacBride, Prisoner Number 34, took place on 4 May 1916. The charge put before MacBride was that he:

> Did an act to wit did take part in an armed rebellion and in the waging of war against His Majesty the King, such an act being of such a nature as to be calculated to be prejudicial to the Defence of the Realm and being done with the intention and for the purpose of assisting the enemy.[462]

Before him on the Bench were Brigadier General C. H. Blackader, Lieutenant Colonel G. German and Lieutenant Colonel W. J. Kent. MacBride pleaded not guilty. Three witnesses were brought forward to testify in relation to MacBride's involvement in the rebellion. In his defence, MacBride called on Clara Allan, his landlady and the wife of Fred Allan. She told the court-martial that she had known MacBride for twenty-five years, and that she remembered him leaving the house dressed in civilian clothes. She stated too that, 'I remember receiving a letter from the accused's brother Dr. MacBride saying that he was coming up from Castlebar and asking the accused to meet him at the Wicklow Hotel'.[463]

In his defence, MacBride stated that 'although I had no previous connection with the Irish Volunteers I considered it my duty to join them. I knew there was no chance of success, and I never advised nor influenced any other person to join.'[464]

Following his court-martial appearance, MacBride encountered Sean T. O'Kelly in the barrack square. He told him: 'Nothing will save me Seán. This is the end. Remember this is the second time I have sinned against them.'[465]

Victor Collins, MacBride's friend in Paris, would later write to John Devoy about the trial. He said that he heard from barrister Charles Wyse Power, who had been present in the Richmond Barracks, that Brigadier-General Blackader had stated:

> All the men behaved well, but the one who stands out as the most soldierly was John MacBride. He, on entering, stood to attention facing us and in his eyes I could read: 'You are soldiers. I am one. You have won. I have lost. Do your worst.'[466]

MacBride was taken from the Richmond Barracks to the nearby Kilmainham Gaol, where he was informed that he would be executed by firing squad at dawn the next morning.[467] In a moment of semi-private discussion with Mrs Allan on the eve of his execution, he would ask her to 'mind the flag', a reference to the flag of the Irish Brigade that he loved so dearly.

Maire O'Brolchain, in her Witness Statement to the Bureau of Military History, would later claim that MacBride asked Mrs Allan to send on the wedding ring he still had safe for his brother Anthony, as he was supposed to have been best man at his wedding days earlier. Anthony was married on 26 April, with a brother of the bride standing in for John as best man. Of the flag he wanted Mrs Allan to mind, O'Brolchain remembered:

> MacBride's proudest possession, according to Mrs. Allen, was the Inghinidhe flag presented to him in 1900, when he was Major in the Transvaal Irish Brigade. He took great care – shaking it free from its wrappings, at intervals – always saying, when Mrs. Allen wondered at his enthusiasm, 'I must mind the flag. It will wave over a free Ireland yet.'[468]

Given John MacBride's vow to see this flag fly 'over a free Ireland', the fact that he did not have it on his person during the rebellion may be, as Donal P. McCracken has argued, the most compelling evidence that 'MacBride did not come into the centre of Dublin with the intention of fighting.'[469] Thanks to Mrs Allan, the beloved flag and MacBride's other souvenirs of the Boer War survived:

> Mrs. Allan did mind the flag and the 'sight' of the captured cannon and the MacBride papers so successfully that they were never found during the raids. The flag was rolled round her during the first raid, the sight and papers hidden in an outhouse afterwards for a few years the flag was stitched into a feather bed. She gave the flag and 'sight' eventually to Joe MacBride of Westport and his widow after his death presented them to the Museum.[470]

Father Augustine of the Capuchin Friary would remember being called for in the early hours of 5 May 1916: 'On reaching the prison I was immediately shown to a cell and on its being opened I gripped the hand of Major MacBride. He was quiet and natural as ever.' MacBride then 'emptied his pockets of whatever silver and coppers he had, and asked me to give it to the poor. Finally, placing his Rosary tenderly in my hand, he uttered a little sentence that thrilled me: 'And give that to my Mother.''[471]

Major John MacBride faced his firing squad at dawn that morning. At the time, it was reported that MacBride told the men facing him 'do not let what you have to do ever disturb your rest.' He reportedly requested not to be blindfolded, telling the men: 'I've been looking down rifle-barrels all my life. Fire when I bow my head.'[472] As per regulations, however, MacBride was blindfolded before the squad opened fire.

From the Jacob's garrison, both Thomas MacDonagh and Michael O'Hanrahan had faced the same fate before him. Father Augustine recalled the execution of the Major:

> Six kneel now on one knee and behind them six stand. He faces them about 50 feet from the guns, two or three feet from the wall. The two soldiers withdrew to the left near the Governor and the Doctor, and I, oblivious of all but him, stand close at his right in prayer. The officer approaches, takes me gently by the arm and leads me to a position below himself at the right. He speaks a word, the

> prisoner stiffens and expands his chest. Then quickly a silent signal, a loud volley, and the body collapses in a heap.[473]

MacBride's execution was reported in newspapers throughout Ireland, as public opinion was beginning to turn with each execution. Owing to his involvement in the Boer War, Major MacBride's execution in particular attracted a degree of international media attention. Tom Kettle, the Irish Home Rule nationalist, poet and former MP, would later mock MacBride's statement that he had looked down rifle-barrels all his life. Kettle said this was a lie, as MacBride 'had been looking down the necks of porter bottles all his life.'[474] Kettle, who had enlisted in the Royal Dublin Fusiliers, was himself killed on 9 September 1916, fighting at Ginchy on the Somme.

Katharine Tynan, a well-known writer living in Mayo at the time of the insurrection, claimed that 'Mayo is given to minding her own business .... The little war up in Dublin left Mayo as unmoved as the Great War – in our part of it.'[475] When news of MacBride's death reached Westport, however, Honoria MacBride was devastated, but proud and defiant, stating: 'I am proud to have reared a son to die for Ireland.'[476]

Some decades after the insurrection, a reference was made in an American publication to a flag 'made of a flour bag and flown in 1916 from the shop of Honoria MacBride, an Irish patriot in Westport, County Mayo.'[477] If Honoria did make such a public statement of support for the uprising in Dublin, it was certainly a brave one. In the streets of Westport, a small demonstration of a few dozen men, which included Joseph MacBride, marched through the town in opposition to Major MacBride's execution.[478]

For the British administration in Ireland, understanding the events leading up to the insurrection was important. A Commission was established to examine the 'Sinn Féin Rising' a few weeks after the events of Easter week. The response in Westport to MacBride's death was raised and a recruitment officer stated:

> In his native town of Westport we found it is like a dead horse to get a man for the Army or Navy. In Ballina, which is only forty miles from Westport, things were quite different.[479]

Joseph MacBride was among the local nationalist activists imprisoned in the widespread sweeps that followed the uprising. Men who had been active in the Volunteers but had not participated in the insurrection or who were deemed sympathetic to militant republicanism found themselves interned, along with those who had participated in the Rising. Joseph would later become the first Sinn Féin TD for Mayo in 1918, before supporting the Anglo-Irish Treaty and becoming a TD for the Cumann na nGaedheal party.

The mass arrests which followed the insurrection had a demoralising effect on the nationalist cause. Westport republican Sean Gibbons recalled:

> 1916, after the Rising, seemed to be a year of despair to a great extent, and I suppose all the localities participated in the general hopelessness, but gradually a surge upwards began again and, when the releases came at the end of 1916, Westport, or at least national Westport, began to smile again and activities in republican circles went rapidly ahead.[480]

There are conflicting stories of how young Seán MacBride heard of the death of his father. One relates that it occurred while he was attending school in St Louis de Gonzague. At a time when many young boys like him across the continent were losing their fathers and brothers to the slaughter of the First World War, there was a certain poignancy to the manner in which the twelve-year-old Seán heard the news. At a weekly ceremony in the school, the rector read out the list of the pupils' fallen relations and on that week in early May Major MacBride's name was included:

> The name of my father was read out and the rector made a very eloquent speech, and indeed I always felt gratitude towards him then, saying that my father had been executed by the British, who were the allies of the French, but who had occupied Ireland and treated Ireland as a colony, and that the Irish people were fighting for their liberation.[481]

Maud Gonne, however, claimed to have told Seán of his

father's death, telling him: 'Your father has died for his country — he did not behave well to us — but now we can think of him with honour.'[482] Certainly, for Gonne, news of MacBride's death changed her perception of the man. Writing to her New York solicitor John Quinn, she told him:

> My husband is among those executed. He and MacDonagh gave themselves up from Jacob's biscuit factory to save the civil population of that crowded district from indiscriminate shelling by the English. He has died for Ireland and his son will bear an honoured name. I remember nothing else.[483]

William Butler Yeats would write to Lady Gregory on 11 May 1916, before the conclusion of the executions, 'I am trying to write a poem on the men executed – "terrible beauty has been born again."'[484] His poem, 'Easter 1916', would first appear in print four years later in the *New Statesman*.[485] In it, he referred to MacBride as a 'drunken, vainglorious lout', indicating the hurt he still felt at the loss of Maud Gonne to the Major years earlier but redemption came in the following lines:

> Yet I number him in the song;
> He, too, has resigned his part
> In the casual comedy;
> He, too, has been changed in his turn,

Transformed utterly:
A terrible beauty is born.

Later in 1916, Yeats proposed to Gonne once more, though she again refused to marry him. Her focus was on returning to Ireland, and she once more became Maud Gonne MacBride, adopting the surname of her deceased husband. Having been repeatedly denied permission to enter the country by the authorities, she boarded the Holyhead ferry in disguise and returned to Ireland in 1918. Her credentials as an 'Easter Week Widow' were questioned by some, most notably Alice Milligan, who stated: 'as an Easter Week widow she is an absurdity and an insult to John MacBride's memory.'[486]

State intelligence noted that Gonne, 'in spite of her anti-English sentiments and her attachment to the Irish cause', had refrained from propaganda during the First World War and 'maintained a very reserved attitude.'[487] Yet, with news of the execution of John, Maud was once more transformed into a combative and militant nationalist activist. She would tell friends she wore black in mourning, not for her loss – but for the loss of Ireland. Owing to her political activism, Gonne would find herself behind bars, leaving young Seán without a mother while she was incarcerated in Holloway Prison, London for several months, during which time her health suffered. She shared a cell with Countess Markievicz, veteran of the rebellion, and Kathleen Clarke, widow of the executed Tom Clarke. She remained an active figure in Irish republican politics – and indeed broad radical left wing politics – in the decades that followed her return to Ireland's shores. Ireland's 'Joan of Arc' died in 1955 at her home in Clonskeagh, her beloved Roebuck House.

Seán MacBride would follow in the footsteps of his father, joining the republican movement during the War of Independence as a teenager, firstly becoming an activist in Na Fianna and later joining the ranks of the Irish Republican Army. As a student at University College Dublin, he hoisted a tricolour at half-mast over that institution, to mourn the execution of Kevin Barry. In 1922, he found himself an Anti-Treaty IRA man inside the occupied Four Courts, in the company of Ernie O'Malley, who had thought so highly of Major MacBride. Like his father, Seán believed in the tradition of physical force republicanism, and the Civil War saw him moving amongst men who had earlier fought in the insurrection of 1916.

Following the fall of the Four Courts garrison, Seán was imprisoned by the forces of the new Irish Free State. Ernest Blythe, a Minister in the Free State government, recalled Maud Gonne complaining to the cabinet, which included John MacBride's old friend Arthur Griffith, about this:

> There was some uproar amongst the prisoners in Mountjoy a few days after the Four Courts surrender and the guards

> were reported to have fired on them. A note arrived in to a Cabinet meeting from Maud Gonne, asking Griffith to go out and speak to her. Griffith refused to go, whereupon a second note came in saying 'They are firing on the prisoners in Mountjoy. They are firing on the son of your old friend John MacBride'. Griffith turned the note over and wrote on the other side of it, 'If your son behaves himself he will be in no danger', and sent it out to her.[488]

Major John MacBride was buried, along with the other men executed in Kilmainham Gaol, in a mass grave in Arbour Hill Prison, Dublin, on which quicklime was poured. MacBride's old enemy from the Boer War, General Sir John Maxwell, had decreed that the men's final resting place should be unmarked so that their graves did not become a rallying point for further insurrection.

The executions of the leaders of the uprising proved to be a watershed moment in Irish history. The republican activist Maire Comerford remembered that 'afterwards, there was no longer any such thing as practical politics.'[489] Today, a monument to the Irish Brigade stands in the Northern Cape, while a bust of John MacBride can be found on The Quay in his native Westport.

Certainly, MacBride's life was a complex one, driven by a sense of radical nationalism that would take him to the battlefield of Colenso and lead him to the Easter rebellion. As R. F. Foster has noted, it was not 'ideologues' like Pearse and MacDonagh with whom MacBride shared the most in common, but rather 'the IRB architects of the revolution who do not appear in [the Yeats poem] 'Easter 1916', Tom Clarke and Seán MacDermott.'[490] He embodied a physical force republican tradition of the nineteenth century, and was a Fenian at heart, first and foremost.

MacBride spent much of his later years speaking of the pantheon of Irish nationalist heroes – addressing gatherings on the Manchester Martyrs, Robert Emmet and the like. On 5 May 1916, he found his own place in that pantheon.

Notes

Introduction

Quoted in Elleke Boehmer, *Empire, the National, and the Postcolonial, 1890–1920: Resistance in Interaction (Oxford University Press, 2005), p26.*

2 Maud Gonne's correspondence with Irish American lawyer John Quinn, quoted in Nancy Cardozo, *Maud Gonne (New Amsterdam Books, 1990), p92.*

3 'Short history of the rebels on whom it has been necessary to inflict the supreme penalty' sent by General Sir John Maxwell to Herbert Asquith, 11 May 1916. Reprinted in Brian Barton, *The Secret Court Martial Records of the Easter Rising* (The History Press, 2010), p209.

Chapter 1:

4 National Library of Ireland (hereafter NLI) MS 29,817.

5 *Irish Press, 2 August 1963.*

6 *Connaught Telegraph, 18 May 1889.*

7 Éamon de Valera's 1963 Westport speech appeared in the 1990 edition of Westport history journal *Cathair Na Mart (Vol. 10. No. 1). Multiple articles on the MacBride family have appeared in this journal since its inception.*

8 *Connaught Telegraph, 8 February 1919.*

9 Donald E. Jordan, *Land and Popular Politics in Ireland: County Mayo from the Plantation to the Land War (Cambridge University Press, 1994), p203.*

10 James F. Lydon, *The Making of Ireland: From Ancient Times to the Present (Routledge, 1998), p315.*

11 Jordan, *Land and Popular Politics in Ireland*, p227.

12 Oliver Rafferty, *Catholicism in Ulster, 1603–1983: An Interpretive History (South Carolina Press, 1994), p147.*

13 Patrick McCartan, Bureau of Military History Witness Statements (hereafter BMH WS) 99.

14 NLI MS 29,817.

15 Desmond Ryan, *The Fenian Chief: A Biography of James Stephens,* (Hely Tom, 1967), p92.

16 Quoted in: Owen Hughes, 'Major John MacBride', *Cathair Na Mairt (Westport Historical Society, Vol. 6. No. 1.).*

17 NLI MS 29,817.

18 *The Chemist and Druggist, March 10 1900.*

19 Owen McGee, *The IRB: The Irish Republican Brotherhood from the Land League to Sinn Féin* (Four Courts Press, 2005), p85.

20 John O'Leary, *Recollections of Fenians and Fenianism* (Downey & Co, 1896), p243.

21 Marjorie Elizabeth Howe, *Colonial Crossings: Figures in Irish Literary History (Field Day Publications, 2006), p106.*

22 F. S. L. Lyons quoted in Fintan Cullen, *The Irish Face: Redefining the Irish Portrait* (National Portrait Gallery, 2004), p65.

23 John Devoy, *Recollections of an Irish Rebel* (Irish University Press, 1969 edition), p282.

24 Roy Foster, *W. B. Yeats: A Life, 1: The Apprentice Mage 1865–1914* (Oxford University Press, 1997), p43.

25 Ibid.

26 William Butler Yeats, *Autobiographies* (Gill & Macmillan, 1955 edition), p95.

27 W. F. Mandle, 'Parnell and Sport', *Studia Hibernica XXVIII (1994).*

28 Lydon, *The Making of Ireland*, p320.

29 W.F. Mandle, 'The I.R.B and the Beginnings of the Gaelic Athletic Association' in *Irish Historical Studies (Vol. 20, No. 80).*

30 Eoghan Corry, *An Illustrated History of the GAA* (Gill & Macmillan, 2005), p7.

31 Anthony Jordan, *Major John MacBride, 1865 –1916: MacDonagh and MacBride and Connolly and Pearse* (Westport Historical Society, 1991), p6.

32 Patrick Nally's entry by Owen McGee, *Dictionary of Irish Biography* (Royal Irish Academy 2009).

33 Owen McGee, *The IRB: The Irish Republican Brotherhood from the Land League to Sinn Féin* (Four Courts Press, 2005), p112.

34 Ibid.

35 Quoted in Joseph Valentine, *The Myth of Manliness in Irish National Culture, 1880 – 1922* (University of Illinois, 2011), p68.

36 McGee, *The IRB*, p235.

37 J. J. O' Kelly, BMH WS 384.

38 Augustine Ingoldsby, BMH WS 582.

39 Matthew Kelly, '…and William Rooney spoke in Irish.', *History Ireland (Vol.15, No.1)*

40 Caoimhe Nic Dháibhéid, '"This is a case in which Irish national considerations must be taken into account": the breakdown of the MacBride-Gonne marriage, 1904-1908', *Irish Historical Studies, vol. xxxvii, no. 146 (November 2010)*

41 Dr Mark Ryan, 'Report of presentation to Dr. Ryan at the Mansion House, Dublin, 3rd March 1936' in *Fenian Memories* (Gill & Son, 1945), p218.

42 *Los Angeles Herald*, 27 September 1895.

43 *Skibereen Eagle*, 26 October 1895.

44 Quoted in Anthony J. Jordan, 'Joseph MacBride 1860–1938', *Cathair na Mart (No. 30, 2012)*

45 NLI MS 29,817.

46 Ryan, *Fenian Memories*, p174.

47 Ibid, p175.

48 Ibid, p110.

49 J. J. O'Kelly, BMH WS 384.

Chapter 2

50 Gregory Fremont-Barnes, *The Boer War 1899–1902 (Essential Histories) (Osprey, 2003), p13.*

51 André du Toit and Hermann Giliomee (ed.), *Afrikaaner Political Thought: Analysis and Documents. Vol. 1 1780–1850 (University of California, 1983), p19.*

52 *The Nation*, 22 January 1881.

53 Quoted in Joseph H. Lehmann, *The First Boer War* (Jonathan Cape, 1972), p263.

54 H. Rider Haggard, *The Last Boer War (Kegan Paul, 1900). (Available at Project Gutenberg.)*

55 Geoffrey Wheatcroft, *The Randlords: The Men Who Made South Africa (Weidenfeld & Nicholson, 1993), p182.*

56 Letter from Cecil Rhodes to Alfred Beit, August 1895, reprinted in Thomas Pakenham, *The Boer War* (Abacus, 1991), p.1.

57 Ian Knight, *Men-at-Arms Series: The Boer War, 1899–1902 (Osprey Publishing, 2000), p3.*

58 Ibid.

59 Donal P. McCracken, *MacBride's Brigade: Irish Commandos in the Anglo-Boer War (Four Courts Press, 1999), p13.*

60 Arthur Conan Doyle, *The Great Boer War (ReadHowYouWant, 2008 edition), p34.*

61 Ibid.

62 Fermont-Barnes, *The Boer War 1899–1902, p.6.*

63 Donal P. McCracken, 'MacBride's Brigade in the Anglo-Boer War', *History Ireland (Vol. 8, Issue 1).*

64 *History and album of the Irish Race Convention which met in Dublin the first three days of September, 1896 (Sealy, Byers and Walker, 1896), p51.*

65 NLI, MS 22,817.

66 National Archives of Ireland, State Paper Office, Crime Branch Special (DMP), 5/13020, dated 14 January 1897.

67 *The United Irishman, 25 November 1899.*

68 *Freeman's Journal, 12 January 1907*

69 *County Down Grand Orange Lodge, Annual Report for the year ending 31 December 1903.*

70 Thomas Byrne, BMH WS 564.

71 *The Nation, 10 October 1896.*

72 Richard Walsh, BMH WS 400.

73 Padraic Colum, *Arthur Griffith (Browne & Nolan, 1959), p34.*

74 Maryna Fraser (ed.), *Johannesburg Pioneer Journals, 1888-1909 (Van Riebeeck Society, 1986), p41.*

75 NLI, MS 22,817.

76 NLI, MS 29,817.

77 John MacBride's series of articles for the *Freeman's Journal, 13 October 1906–29 July 1907. Quote from MacBride's first article, of 13 October 1906. While the articles are accessible via the 'Irish Newspaper Archive' service, this author recommends consulting Anthony J. Jordan's edited collection Boer War to Easter Rising: The Writings of John MacBride (Westport Books, 2006), where the articles are reprinted in full, with helpful observations and notes. Hereafter these articles are referenced as Freeman's Journal series.*

78 *Irish Examiner, 30 August 1898.*

79 Dr Senia Paseta, '*1798 in 1898: The Politics of Commemoration' in The Irish Review (Cork University Press, No. 22, Summer 1998).*

80 Peter Collins, *Who Fears to Speak of '98?: Commemoration and the Continuing Impact of the United Irishmen (Ulster Historical Foundation, 2004), p39.*

81 *Irish Examiner, 21 March 1898.*

82 Maud Gonne MacBride, *A Servant of the Queen (Colin Smythe, 1994 edition), p256.*

83 *Western People, 15 January 1898.*

84 *Western People, 7 May 1898.*

85 Ibid.

86 Ryan, *Fenian Memories, p188.*

87 Ibid.

88 Catherine Morris, *Alice Milligan and the Irish Cultural Revival (Four Courts Press, 2013), p191.*

89 Ibid. p176.

90 David Mackay Wilson, *Behind the Scenes in the Transvaal (Cassell & Company, 1901), p119.*

91 Ryan, *Fenian Memories, p187.*

92 *Freeman's Journal, 18 July 1898.*

93 Donal P. McCracken, 'Irish Settlement and Identity in South Africa before 1910' in *Irish Historical Studies (Vol. 28, No. 110, November 1992).*

94 *The United Irishman, 4 March 1899.*

95 Alexander Norman Jeffares and Anna MacBride White (eds.), *The Gonne-Yeats Letters, 1893–1938 (W.W. Norton, 1994 edition), p478.*

96 Stanislaus Joyce, *My Brother's Keeper: James Joyce's Early Years (Da Capo Press, 2003 edition), p169.*

Chapter 3

97 Seamus Robinson, BMH WS 1721.

98 Donal P. McCracken, *Forgotten Protest: Ireland and the Anglo-Boer War (Ulster Historical Foundation, 2003 edition) p42.*

99 David Lynch, *Radical Politics in Modern Ireland: The Irish Socialist Republican Party 1896–1904 (Irish Academic Press, 2008), p78.*

100 *The Irish Times, 27 October 1899.*

101 *The Irish Times, 20 October 1899.*

102 Kevin O'Shiel, BMH WS 1770.

103 Karen Steele, *Maud Gonne: Irish Nationalist Writings 1895–1946 (Irish Academic Press, 2004), p161.*

104 Ibid, p162.

105 Maire O'Brolchain, BMH WS 321.

106 Helena Molony, BMH WS 391.

107 *The Irish Times, 10 November 1900.*

108 M. J. Kelly, *The Fenian Ideal and Irish Nationalism, 1882 in–1916 (Boydell Press, 2006), p153.*

109 Michael Davitt, *The Boer Fight for Freedom (Funk & Wagnalls, 1902), p319.*

110 *Freeman's Journal, 5 January 1907.*

111 John MacBride's *Freeman's Journal series. See: Anthony J. Jordan, Boer War to Easter Rising: The Writings of John MacBride (Westport Books, 2006) for edited collection.*

112 Thomas Byrne, BMH WS 569.

113 Ibid.

114 *Freeman's Journal series.*

115 Michael Davitt, *The Boer Fight for Freedom, (Funk & Wagnallis Company, 1902) p319.*

116 Colonel J.Y. F. Blake, *A West Pointer with the Boers (Angel Guardian Press, 1903), p46.*

117 Ibid, p.51.

118 Donal P. McCracken, *MacBride's Brigade in the Anglo-Boer War in History Ireland (Vol. 8 No. 1).*

119 *Freeman's Journal series.*

120 Ibid.

121 McCracken, *MacBride's Brigade, p42.*

122 *Freeman's Journal series.*

123 Ibid.

124 Blake, *A West Pointer with the Boers, p64–65.*

125 Christopher Murray, *Sean O'Casey: Writer at Work: A Biography (Gill & Macmillan, 2004), p52.*

126 Blake, *A West Pointer with the Boers, p64–65.*

127 *Freeman's Journal series.*

128 *Freeman's Journal series.*

129 Thomas Pakenham, *The Boer War, p152.*

130 *Freeman's Journal series.*

131 Blake, *A West Pointer with the Boers, p79.*

132 Donal P. McCracken (ed.), *The Irish in South Africa 1759 –1910 (University of Durban-Westville, 1992), p57.*

133 *Freeman's Journal series.*

134H. H. S Pearse, *Four Months Besieged: The Battle of Ladysmith (MacMillan & Co., 1900). (Available via Project Gutenberg.)*

135 Winston Churchill, *London to Ladysmith via Pretoria (Longmans, Green and Co., 1900). (Available via Project Gutenberg.)*

136 Christian Rudolf De Wet, *Three Years' War (Archibald Constable & Co, 1902). (Available via Project Gutenberg.)*

137 *Freeman's Journal series.*

138 Ibid.

139 Ibid.

140 Ibid.

141 Ibid.

142 Edward Spiers (ed.), *Letters from Ladysmith: Eyewitness Accounts from the South African War (Jonathan Ball Publishers, 2010), p72.*

143 Blake, *A West Pointer with the Boers, p102.*

144 Roy Digby Thomas, *Two Generals: Buller and Botha in the Boer War (AuthorHouse UK, 2012) p86.*

145 Ibid.

146 *Freeman's Journal series.*

147 Ibid.

148 Majors C. F. Romer and A. E. Mainwaring, *The second battalion Royal Dublin Fusiliers in the South African War: with a description of the operations in the Aden hinterland (A. L. Humphreys, 1908), p40.*

149 *The Irish Times, 23 December 1899.*

150 *Freeman's Journal series.*

151 *Freeman's Journal series.*

152 Ibid.

153 Robert Kee, *The Green Flag: A History of Irish Nationalism (Penguin, 2000), p444.*

154 Ibid, p455.

155 Davitt, *The Boer Fight for Freedom, p12.*

156 *The United Irishman, 17 February 1900.*

157 *Freeman's Journal, 18 July 1900.*

158 John Redmond delivered this speech in Westminster on 7 February 1900.

159 *Western People, 14 September 1901.*

160 Neal Garnham, *Association Football and Society in Pre-Partition Ireland (Ulster Historical Foundation, 2004), p139.*

161 NLI MS 26,757, Letter from John M. Coghlan in New York to John MacBride in the Transvaal, 10 February 1900.

162 Gonne MacBride, *A Servant of the Queen, p59.*

163 *New York Tribune, 4 February 1900.*

164 *Kentucky Irish American, 25 November 1899.*

165 *The Intermountain Catholic, 3 March 1900.*

166 *Freeman's Journal series.*

167 Thomas Bartlett and Keith Jeffery (eds.), *A Military History of Ireland (Cambridge University Press, 1996), p353.*

168 *Freeman's Journal series.*

169 McCracken, *Ireland's Forgotten Protest, p127.*

170 Alfred M. Golin, *No Longer an Island: Britain and the Wright Brothers, 1902 –1909 (Stanford University Press, 1984), p80.*

171 Bartlett and Jeffery (eds.), *A Military History of Ireland, p380.*

172 *Freeman's Journal series.*

173 Ibid.

174 Quoted in Jordan, *Major John MacBride 1865–1916, p45.*

175 Pakenham, *The Boer War, p572.*

176 Paula M. Krabs, *Gender, Race, and the Writing of Empire: Public Discourse and the Boer War (Cambridge University Press, 1999), p38.*

177 Gomolemo Mokae, *Robert McBride: a Coloured Life (Vista University, 2004) p221.*

178 *Irish Independent, 18 March 1998.*

179 James Connolly, 'Socialism and Nationalism' in *The Shan Van Vocht, January 1897.*

180 NLI MS 29,817.

Chapter 4

181 Gonne MacBride, *A Servant of the Queen, p308.*

182 Margaret Ward, *Maud Gonne: Ireland's Joan of Arc (Pandora, 1990), p2.*

183 Karen Steele, *Maud Gonne's Irish Nationalist Writings: 1895–1946 (Irish Academic Press, 2004), pxx.*

184 Gonne MacBride, *A Servant of the Queen, p32.*

185 1950 interview with Maud Gonne by M.J McManus of the *Irish Press, quoted in Caoimhe Nic Dháibhéid, Seán MacBride: A Republican Life 1904–1946 (Liverpool University Press, 2011) p5.*

186 Gonne MacBride, *A Servant of the Queen, p42.*

187 Ibid, p45.

188 Maud Gonne MacBride, BMH WS 317.

189 Ward, *Maud Gonne,* p15.

190 Gonne MacBride, *A Servant of the Queen*, p65.

191 Ibid.

192 W. B. Yeats, *Autobiographies*, p123.

193 Ella Young, *Flowering Dusk: Things Remembered Accurately and Inaccurately (Longmans, Green and Company, 1945)*

194 R. F. Foster, W. B. Yeats: A Life, Volume 1: *The Apprentice Mage: 1865–1914, (Oxford University Press, 1998)* p101.

195 Brian Atkins, *The Thought of W. B. Yeats (Peter Lang, 2010), p43.*

196 Foster, *The Apprentice Mage*, p116.

197 Ibid, p203.

198 Ibid, p202.

199 Ward, *Maud Gonne*, p56.

200 *The Shan Van Vocht*, 7 February 1896.

201 Gonne MacBride, *A Servant of the Queen*, p310.

202 *Irish Examiner*, 16 November 1900.

203 Ibid.

204 *Southern Star, 8 December 1900.*

205 Quoted in McCracken, *MacBride's Brigade*, p150.

206 Ibid.

207 Gonne MacBride, *A Servant of the Queen*, p341.

208 Dublin Castle Special Branch Files, CO904/208/258.

209 William O'Brien and Desmond Ryan (eds.), *Devoy's Post Bag, 1871-1928 (Fallon, 1948), p347.*

210 Patrick Maume, *Dictionary of Irish Biography, 'John Devoy' entry.*

211 John Devoy, *Recollections of an Irish Rebel* (Chase D.Young, 1929), p4.

Chapter 5

212 *Kentucky Irish American, 8 December 1900*

213 NLI MS 29,817.

214 O'Brien and Ryan (eds.), *Devoy's Post Bag, p350.*

215 Cardozo, *Maud Gonne*, p204.

216 Ward, *Maud Gonne, p69.*

217 Ibid.

218 Gonne MaBride, *A Servant of the Queen, p311.*

219 Gonne MacBride, *A Servant of the Queen, p312.*

220 Ibid.

221 *Irish Examiner, 20 June 1892.*

222 Helen Litton, *16 Lives: Thomas Clarke (O'Brien Press, 2014), p76.*

223 NLI MS 26,761.

224 NLI MS 29,817.

225 Gonne MacBride, *A Servant of the Queen, p312.*

226 Ibid, p313.

227 *San Francisco Call, 23 June 1901.*

228 Ward, *Maud Gonne, p 70.*

229 Gonne MacBride, *A Servant of the Queen, p319.*

230 Ibid, p352.

231 Dublin Castle Special Branch Files, CO904/208/258.

232 *Connaught Telegraph, 23 November 1901.*

233 Yeats, *Autobiographies, p450.*

234 Stephen Gwynn, quoted in Okifumi Komesu and Masaru Sekine (eds.) *Irish Writers and Politics (Barnes and Nobles Books, 1990), p177.*

235 Margaret Ward, *In Their Own Voice: Women and Irish Nationalism (Attic Press, 1995), p24.*

236 Dublin Castle Intelligence File, CO904/208/258.

237 Gonne MacBride, *A Servant of the Queen, p343.*

238 O'Brien and Ryan (eds.), *Devoy's Post Bag, p350.*

239 Gonne MacBride, *A Servant of the Queen, p344.*

240 NLI MS 29,817.

241 Anthony J. Jordan, *The Yeats-Gonne-MacBride Triangle (Westport Books, 2000), p33.*

242 Ibid.

243 NLI MS 29,817.

244 Quoted in *Ulster Herald, 21 February 1903.*

245 Gonne MacBride, *A Servant of the Queen, p348.*

246 Nancy Cardozo, *Maud Gonne: Lucky Eyes and a High Heart (New Amsterdam, 1990), p228.*

247 Gonne MacBride, *A Servant of the Queen, p348.*

248 Ibid, p349.

249 Ibid.

250 Ibid.

251MacBride White and Jeffares (eds.), *The Gonne-Yeats Letters, p158.*

252 Ibid, p166.

253 Ibid., p157.

254 Sinéad McCoole, *Easter Widows: Seven Irish Women who Lived in the Shadow of the 1916 Rising. (Transworld Ireland, 2014), p48.*

255 Ibid. p49.

256 *United Irishman report of the wedding, reprinted in Ulster Herald, 7 March 1903.*

257 Ibid.

258 David A Ross, *Critical Companion to William Butler Yeats, A Literary Reference to his Life and Work (Facts on File, 2009), p170.*

Chapter 6

259 Ward, *Maud Gonne, p82.*

260 Gonne MacBride, *A Servant of twhe Queen, p78.*

261 Anna MacBride White and A. Norman Jeffares, *The Gonne-Yeats Letters, p168.*

262 Ibid.

263 NLI MS 29,819.

264 Ward, *Maud Gonne, p80.*

265 Jordan, *Major John MacBride, 1865–1916, p62.*

266 Quoted in Jordan, *Boer War to Easter Rising: The Writings of John MacBride.*

267 Foster, *The Apprentice Mage, p331.*

268 Senia Pašeta, *Irish Nationalist Women, 1900–1918 (Cambridge University Press, 2013), p49.*

269 Maud Gonne MacBride, BMH WS 317.

270 *Ballinrobe Chronicle, 28 May 1903.*

271 *Nenagh News, 7 May 1904.*

272 Maud Gonne MacBride, BMH WS 317.

273 *San Francisco Call, 26 May 1904.*

274 *Fermanagh Herald, 14 May 1904.*

275 NLI MS 29,817

276 Ibid.

277 NLI MS 29,819

278 Ibid.

279 Ibid.

280 Ibid.

281 Ibid.

282 Correspondence with John O'Leary, within NLI MS 29,819.

283 Anna MacBride White and A. Norman Jeffares, *The Gonne-Yeats Letters, p179.*

284 Maud Gonne MacBride, BMH WS 317.

285 NLI MS 29,817.

286 1905 notebook.

287 Dr Caoimhe Nic Dháibhéid, '"This is a case in which Irish national considerations must be taken into account": the breakdown of the MacBride-Gonne marriage, 1904-1908', *Irish Historical Studies (Vol. xxxvii, no. 146, November 2010).*

288 Ibid.

289 Ibid.

290 NLI MS 29,819

291 MacBride White and Jeffares, *The Gonne-Yeats Letters, p183.*

292 Foster, *The Apprentice Mage, p332.*

293 Dr Caoimhe Nic Dháibhéid, '"This is a case in which Irish national considerations must be taken into account": the breakdown of the MacBride-Gonne marriage, 1904 –1908' in *Irish Historical Studies* (Vol. xxxvii, no 146, November 2010).

294 NLI MS 29,823

295 MacBride White and Jeffares, *The Gonne-Yeats Letters, p150.*

296 NLI MS 29,825.

297 NLI MS 29,817.

298 Ibid.

299 Ibid.

300 Ibid.

301 Augustine Ingoldsby BMH WS 582.

302 Nic Dháibhéid, '"This is a case in which Irish national considerations must be taken into account": the breakdown of the MacBride-Gonne marriage, 1904-1908'.

303 NLI MS 29,816.

304 NLI MS 29,819.

305 NLI MS 29,819.

306 MacBride White and Jeffares, *The Gonne-Yeats Letters,* p232.

307 NLI MS 29,817.

308 Quoted in Elizabeth Keane, *Seán MacBride, A Life: From IRA Revolutionary to International Statesman* (Gill & Macmillan, 2007), p15.

309 NLI MS 28,517.

310 *Connaught Telegraph, 27 August 1904.*

311 NLI MS 28,517.

312 Jordan, *The Yeats–Gonne–MacBride Triangle, p5.*

313 Nic Dháibhéid, '"This is a case in which Irish national considerations must be taken into account": the breakdown of the MacBride-Gonne marriage, 1904-1908.'

314 Jordan, *The Yeats-Gonne-MacBride Triangle, p11.*

315 See John MacBride entry at www.ricorso.net for detail of the controversy on the issue of MacBride and Eileen Wilson. The entry includes references to public debate.

316 Paul Durcan, *Paul Durcan's Diary* (New Island, 2003), p136.

317 Dennis McCullough, BMH WS 915

318 Ibid.

Chapter 7

319 Dublin Castle Special Branch Files, CO904/208/258.

320 Ibid.

321 Ibid.

322 Ibid.

323 Ibid.

324 Henry C. Phibbs BMH WS 848.

325 CO904/208/258

326 Joost Augusteijn, *From Public Defiance to Guerrilla Warfare: The Experience of Ordinary Volunteers in the Irish War of Independence 1916-21* (Irish Academic Press, 1996), p32.

327 Manifesto and constitution of the Dungannon Club, Belfast, August 1905: NLI MS 13,166(4)

328 George Lyons, BMH WS 104.

329 *Connaught Telegraph, 21 December 1907*

330 Owen McGee, 'Frederick James Allan (1861 –1937), Fenian & civil servant' in *History Ireland (Issue 1 (Spring 2002) Vol. 10)*

331 CO904/208/258

332 Ernie O'Malley, *On Another Man's Wound: A Personal History of Ireland's War of Independence (Roberts Rinehart Publishers, 1999 edition), p51.*

333 *Connaught Telegraph, 18 August 1906*

334 *Irish Examiner*, 18 December 1906.

335 *The Times, 18 March 1907.*

336 M. P. Sinha, *W.B. Yeats: His Poetry and Politics (Atlantic Publishers, 2003), p77.*

337 *Freeman's Journal*, 20 August 1907.

338 MacBride White and Jeffares (eds.), *The Gonne-Yeats Letters, p181.*

339 *Irish Independent, 19 October 1908.*

340 Sean T. O'Kelly, BMH WS 1765.

341 Patrick McCartan, BMH WS 99.

342 R. F. Foster, *The Irish Story: Telling Tales and Making It Up in Ireland (Oxford University Press, 2001), p63.*

343 Gearoid Ua h-Uallachán, BMH WS 336.

344 CO904/208/258.

345 The Union Defence League pamphlet, 'Convicted: The Goal of Nationalism Disclosed by Irish Home Rulers' digested by Cedar Lounge Revolution blog.

346 Jordan, *Major John MacBride, 1865–1916, p95.*

347 *Freeman's Journal, 18 March 1911.*

348 Helena Molony, BMH WS 391.

349 Seán MacBride, *That Day's Struggle: A Memoir 1904–1951 (Curragh Press, 2005), p16.*

350 Ibid, p17.

351 Nic Dháibhéid, *Seán MacBride, p12.*

352 Samuel Levenson, *Maud Gonne (Reader's Digest Press, 1976), p290.*

353 MacBride White and Jeffares (eds.), *The Gonne-Yeats Letters, p292.*

354 CO904/208/258.

355 *Irish Freedom, November 1910.*

356 Quoted in Kee, *The Green Flag.*

357 Michael Laffan, *The Resurrection of Ireland: The Sinn Féin Party 1916–1923 (Cambridge University Press, 2004 edition), p224.*

358 *Irish Freedom*, October 1911.

359 *Irish Freedom*, March 1911.

360 Bulmer Hobson, BMH WS 30.

361 Ibid.

362 Quoted in McGee, *The IRB*, p321.

363 *Irish Independent, 10 July 1905.*

364 Brian Barton, *The Secret Court Martial Records of the 1916 Easter Rising (The History Press, 2010), p211.*

365 Frederick Engels and Karl Marx, *Collected Works, Volume 42 (Lawrence & Wishart, 1987), p47.*

366 *Donegal News, 2 December 1911.*

367 *KIllarney Echo and South Kerry Chronicle, 30 November 1912.*

368 *The National Student*, December 1915.

369 Shane Kenna, *16 Lives: Thomas MacDonagh (O'Brien Press, 2014), p73.*

370 NLI MS. 26755

371 O'Malley, *On Another Man's Wound, p32.*

372 Éire, 26 May 1923. Republished on 'The Irish Revolution' blog (www.theirishrevolution.wordpress.com).

373 Sean T. O'Kelly, BMH WS 1765.

Chapter 8

374 *Western People, 6 April 1912.*

375 Desmond Fitzgerald, *Desmond's Rising: Memoirs, 1913 to Easter 1916 (Liberties Press, 2006), p20.*

376 O'Brien and Ryan (eds.), *Devoy's Post Bag, pp396-7.*

377 J. J. Lee, *Ireland, 1912-1985: Politics and Society (Cambridge University Press, 2001 edition), p6.*

378 *United Irishman cutting contained within NLI MS 28,917.*

379 *Irish Freedom, December 1910.*

380 *The Irish Times,* 10 September 2013.

381 Advertisement for the Irish Citizen Army, NLI MS 15,673.

382 F. X. Martin (ed.) *The Irish Volunteers 1913–1915: Recollections and Documents (Irish Academic Press, 2013 edition), p37.*

383 Edward Moane, BMH WS 896.

384 Thomas Ketterick, BMH WS 872.

385 Quoted in Cardozo, *Maud Gonne, p290.*

386 Sean T. O'Kelly, BMH WS 1765

387 Martin (ed.) *The Irish Volunteers 1913 –1915, p58.*

388 Bulmer Hobson, *Ireland Yesterday and Tomorrow (Anvil Books, 1968), p52.*

389 Martin (ed.) *The Irish Volunteers 1913 –1915, p45.*

390 Letter from Roger Casement to Alice Stopford Green, September 1913. My thanks to Angus Mitchell, author of *16 Lives: Roger Casement (O'Brien Press, 2013) for providing this source.*

391 *Leinster Express, 25 July 1914.*

392 Martin (ed.) *The Irish Volunteers 1913–1915, p159.*

393 Ibid, p166.

394 Lee, J.J., *Ireland, 1912 –1985, p22.*

395 Edward Moane, BMH WS 896.

396 *An Phoblacht, 30 April 1926.*

397 Edward MacLysaght and William O'Brien, *Forth the Banners Go: Reminiscences of William O'Brien (Three Candles, 1969) p270.*

398 Ibid, p271.

399 Christopher M. Kennedy, *Genesis of the Rising, 1912-1916: A Transformation of Nationalist Opinion (Peter Lang Publishing, 2010) p84.*

400 'Movement of Extremists' report from 8 June 1915, NAI, CSO/JD/2/7

Chapter 9

401 Helen Litton, *16 Lives: Thomas Clarke (O'Brien Press, 2014), p129.*

402 León Ó Broin, *Dublin Castle and the 1916 Rising: The Story of Sir Matthew Nathan* (Helicon, 1966), p53.

403 Ibid, p130.

404 Sean T. O'Kelly, BMH WS 1765.

405 Litton, *16 Lives: Thomas Clarke, p151.*

406 Eugene Smith, BMH WS 334.

407 Shane Kenna, *16 Lives: Thomas MacDonagh (O'Brien Press, 2014), p194.*

408 Dr Marnie Hay, 'Kidnapped: Bulmer Hobson, the IRB and the 1916 Easter Rising' *in Canadian Journal of Irish Studies (Vol 35, No 1, Spring 2009), pp53–60.*

409 Angus Mitchell, *16 Lives: Roger Casement (O'Brien Press, 2013), p264.*

410 Margaret Skinnider, *Doing My Bit for Ireland (Sinn Féin Centenaries Committee, 2014 edition), p110.*

411 Maire O'Brolchain, BMH WS 321.

412 *Trial of John MacBride, Public Records Office (hereafter PRO) WO71/350.*

413 Thomas Slater, BMH WS 263.

414 Vincent Byrne, BMH WS 423.

415 Padráig O'Kelly, BMH WS 376.

416 Donal Fallon, *The Pillar: The Life and Afterlife of the Nelson Pillar (Dublin, 2014), p55.*

417 Seosamh de Brún, BMH WS 312.

418 John MacDonagh, BMH WS 532.

419 Kenna, *16 Lives: Thomas MacDonagh, p206.*

420 John MacDonagh, BMH WS 532.

421 Kenna, *Thomas MacDonagh: 16 Lives, p208.*

422 Vincent Byrne, BMH WS 423.

423 Seamus Pounch, BMH WS 267.

424 Ibid.

425 Joseph MacBride, Military Pension application, MSP34REF3464

426 Ibid.

427 Patrick Colgan, BMH WS 850.

428 Thomas Pugh, BMH WS 397.

429 William James Stapleton, BMH WS 822.

430 Ibid.

431 Padráig O'Kelly, BMH WS 376.

432 Ibid.

433 Kenneth Griffith and Timothy O'Grady, *Curious Journey: An Oral History of Ireland's Unfinished Revolution (Mercier Press, 1998 edition), p59.*

434 Michael O'Sullivan, *Brendan Behan: A Life (Roberts Rinehart, 1999), p89.*

435 Seosamh de Brún, BMH WS 312

436 Ibid.

437 William Oman, BMH WS 421.

438 Kearney, Peadar, 'Personal Narrative of Easter Week' in Seamus de Burca, *The Soldier's Song: The Story of Peadar Ó Cearnaígh (P. J. Bourke, 1958) p. 119.*

439 John MacDonagh, BMH WS 532.

440 Ibid.

441 Jason McElligott, 'In the line of fire' in *History Ireland* (Issue 3, Volume 20, May/June 2012)

442 Seamus Pounch, BMH WS 267,

443 Barton, *The Secret Court Martial Records of the 1916 Easter Rising, p. 55*

444 Ibid, p61.

445 Father Aloysius, BMH WS 200.

446 Ibid.

447 Father Augustine, BMH WS 920.

448 Joseph Furlong, BMH WS 335.

449 John MacDonagh, BMH WS 532.

450 Trial of John MacBride, PRO WO71/350

451 May Moran, *Executed for Ireland: The Peter Moran* Story (Mercier Press, 2010), p34.

452 John MacDonagh, BMH WS 532.

453 Rose McNamara, BMH WS 482.

454 Quoted in David Fitzpatrick (ed.), *Terror in Ireland: 1916–1923* (Lilliput Press, 2012), p52.

455 Declan Kiberd, *Inventing Ireland: The Literature of the Modern Nation (Vintage, 1995), p 216.*

456 *The Straits Times, 5 May 1916.*

Chapter 10:

457 W. T. Cosgrave, BMH WS 268.

458 Ibid.

459 Ibid.

460 Ibid.

461 Gerald Doyle, BMH WS 1511.

462 PRO WO71/350

463 Trial of John MacBride, PRO WO71/350.

464 Ibid.

465 Sean T. O'Kelly, BMH WS 1765.

466 Piaras F. Mac Lochlainn, *Last Words: Letters and Statements of the Leaders Executed After*

the Rising at Easter 1916 (Stationery Office, 1990), p100.

467 Trial of John MacBride, PRO WO71/350.

468 Maire O'Brolchain, BMH WS 321.

469 McCracken, *MacBride's Brigade, p164.*

470 Maire O'Brolchain, BMH WS 321.

471 Father Augustine, BMH WS 920.

472 *Irish Independent, 27 May 1916.*

473 Father Augustine, BMH WS 920.

474 Kettle quoted in Keane, *Seán MacBride, A Life*, p26.

475 Mick O'Farrell (ed.), *1916: What The People Saw (*Mercier, 2013), p77.

476 *Irish Press, 2 August 1963.*

477 *The New Yorker* (Vol. 27, No.3)

478 Jordan, *From Boer War to Easter Rising, p4.*

479 *Skibbereen Eagle, 3 June 1916.*

480 Sean Gibbons, BMH WS 927.

481 MacBride, *That Day's Struggle, p13.*

482 Keane, *Sean MacBride: A Life, p27.*

483 Ibid.

484 David A. Ross, *Critical Companion to William Butler Yeats, p88.*

485 *New Statesman* 23 October 1920.

486 Morris, *Alice Milligan and the Irish Cultural Revolution, p75.*

487 September 1915 police report on Gonne contained within CO 904/208/259.

488 Ernest Blythe, BMH WS 939.

489 Griffith and O'Grady, *Curious Journey, p82.*

490 R. F. Foster, Vivid Faces (Penguin, 2014)

Bibliography

Original Sources

Bureau of Military History Witness Statements, Cathal Brugha Barracks Dublin

Dublin Corporation Minute Books, Dublin City Library and Archives

Frederick J. Allan Papers, National Library of Ireland

John O'Leary Papers, National Library of Ireland

Joseph McGarrity Papers, National Library of Ireland

Public Records Office, Northern Ireland (PRONI)

Sinn Féin and Republican Suspects 1899–1921, Dublin Castle Special Branch Files (Colonial Office Record Series, Eneclann, 2006)

Online Sources

1901/1911 Census of Ireland returns: www.census.nationalarchives.ie

Dictionary of Irish Biography, Royal Irish Academy

James Connolly Internet Archive, hosted by www.marxists.org

Project Gutenberg

Newspapers, Journals and Periodicals

An Phoblacht

Ballinrobe Chronicle

Canadian Journal of Irish Studies

Cathair na Mart

Connaught Telegraph

Donegal News

Éire-Ireland

Fermanagh Herald

Freeman's Journal

History Ireland

Irish Examiner

Irish Freedom

Irish Historical Studies

Irish Independent

Irish Press Kentucky Irish American

Killarney Echo and South Kerry Chronicle

Los Angeles Herald

Nenagh News

New York Tribune

Saothar

Skibereen Eagle

Southern Star

Studia Hibernica

The Chemist and Druggist

The Gaelic American

The Intermountain Catholic,

The Irish Review

The Irish Times

The Nation

The National Student

The Shan Van Vocht

The Straits Times

The Times

The Workers' Republic

Ulster Herald

United Irishman

Western People

Books and Articles

Atkins, Brian, *The Thought of W. B. Yeats*, Peter Lang (2010).

Augusteijn, Joost, *From Public Defiance to Guerrilla Warfare: The Experience of Ordinary Volunteers in the Irish War of Independence 1916–21*, Irish Academic Press (1996).

Bartlett, Thomas and Jeffery, Keith (eds.), *A Military History of Ireland*, Cambridge University Press (1996).

Barton, Brian, *The Secret Court Martial Records of the Easter Rising*, The History Press (2010).

Blake, John, *A West Pointer with the Boers*, Angel Guardian Press (1903).

Boehmer, Elleke, *Empire, the National, and the Postcolonial, 1890–1920: Resistance in Interaction*, Oxford University (2002).

Cardozo, Nancy, *Maud Gonne*, New Amsterdam Books (1998).

Collins, Peter, *Who Fears to Speak of '98?: Commemoration and the Continuing Impact of the United Irishmen,* Ulster Historical Foundation (2004).

Colum, Padraic, *Arthur Griffith*, Browne & Nolan (1959).

Corry, Eoghan, *An Illustrated History of the GAA*, Gill & Macmillan (2005).

Cullen, Fintan, *The Irish Face: Redefining the Irish Portrait*, National Portrait Gallery (2004).

Davitt, Michael *The Boer Fight for Freedom*, Funk & Wagnalls (1902).

De Búrca, *Seamus, The Soldier's Song: The Story of Peadar Ó Cearnaígh*, P. J. Bourke (1958).

Devoy, John, *Recollections of an Irish Rebel*, Irish University Press (1969 edition).

Digby Thomas, Roy, *Two Generals: Buller and Botha in the Boer War*, AuthorHouseUK (2012).

Engels, Frederick and Marx, Karl, *Collected Works, Volume 42*, Lawrence & Wishart (1987)

Fallon, Donal, *The Pillar: The Life and Afterlife of the Nelson Pillar*, New Island Books (2014).

Fitzgerald, Desmond, *Desmond's Rising: Memoirs, 1913 to Easter 1916*, Liberties Press (2006).

Fitzpatrick, David (ed.), *Terror in Ireland: 1916–1923*, Lilliput Press (2012).

Foster, R. F., *The Irish Story: Telling Tales and Making It Up in Ireland*, Oxford University Press (2001).

Foster, R. F., *Vivid Faces: The Revolutionary Generation in Ireland, 1890–1923*, Penguin (2014).

Foster, R. F., *W. B. Yeats: A Life, 1: The Apprentice Mage 1865–1914,* Oxford University Press (1997).

Fraser, Maryna (ed.), *Johannesburg Pioneer Journals, 1888 –1909,* Van Riebeeck Society (1986).

Fremont-Barnes, Gregory, *The Boer War 1899–1902*, Osprey (2003).

Garnham, Neal, *Association Football and Society in Pre-Partition Ireland,* Ulster Historical Foundation (2004).

Griffith, Kenneth and O'Grady, Timothy, *Curious Journey: An Oral History of Ireland's Unfinished Revolution*, Mercier Press (1998 edition).

Golin, Alfred M., *No Longer an Island: Britain and the Wright Brothers, 1902–1909*, Stanford University Press (1984).

Hobson, Bulmer, *Ireland Yesterday and Tomorrow*, Anvil Books (1968).

Howe, Marjorie Elizabeth, *Colonial Crossings: Figures in Irish Literary History*, Field Day Publications (2006).

Jeffares, Alexander Norman and MacBride White, Anna (eds.), *The Gonne-Yeats Letters, 1893–1938*, W.W. Norton (1994 edition).

Jordan, Anthony J., *Boer War to Easter Rising: The Writings of John MacBride*, Westport Books (2006).

Jordan, Anthony J., *Major John MacBride, 1865–1916: MacDonagh and MacBride and Connolly and Pearse*, Westport Historical Society (1991).

Jordan, Anthony J., *The Yeats-Gonne-MacBride Triangle*, Westport Books (2000).

Jordan, Donald E., *Land and Popular Politics in Ireland: County Mayo from the Plantation to the Land War*, Cambridge University Press (1994).

Joyce, Stanislaus, *My Brother's Keeper: James Joyce's Early Years*, Da Capo Press (2003 edition).

Keane, Elizabeth, *Seán MacBride, A Life: From IRA Revolutionary to International Statesman*, Gill & Macmillan (2007).

Kee, Robert, *The Green Flag: A History of Irish Nationalism*, Penguin (2000).

Kelly, M. J., *The Fenian Ideal and Irish Nationalism, 1882–1916*, Boydell Press (2006).

Kenna, Shane, *16 Lives: Thomas MacDonagh*, O'Brien Press (2014).

Kennedy, Christopher M., *Genesis of the Rising, 1912–1916: A Transformation of Nationalist Opinion*, Peter Lang (2010).

Kiberd, Declan, *Inventing Ireland: The Language of a Modern Nation*, Vintage (1995).

Knight, Ian, *Men-at-Arms Series: The Boer War, 1899–1902*, Osprey Publishing (2000).

Krabs, Paula M., *Gender, Race, and the Writing of Empire: Public Discourse and the Boer War*, Cambridge University Press (1999).

Laffan, Michael, *The Resurrection of Ireland: The Sinn Féin Party 1916–1923*, Cambridge University Press (2004 edition).

Lee, J. J., *Ireland, 1912–1985: Politics and Society*, Cambridge University Press (2001 edition).

Lehmann, Joseph H., *The First Boer War*, Jonathan Cape (1972).

Levenson, Samuel, *Maud Gonne*, Reader's Digest Press (1976).

Litton, Helen, *16 Lives: Thomas Clarke*, O'Brien Press (2014).

Lydon, James F. *The Making of Ireland: From Ancient Times to the Present*, Routledge (1998).

Lynch, David, *Radical Politics in Modern Ireland: The Irish Socialist Republican Party 1896–1904*, Irish Academic Press (2008).

MacBride, Maud Gonne, *A Servant of the Queen*, Colin Smythe, (1994 edition).

MacBride, Seán, *That Day's Struggle: A Memoir 1904–1951*, Currach Press (2005 edition).

MacLochlainn, Piaras F., *Last Words: Letters and Statements of the Leaders Executed After the Rising at Easter 1916*, Stationery Office (1990).

MacLysaght, Edward and O'Brien, William, *Forth the Banners Go: Reminiscences of William O'Brien*, Three Candles (1969).

Mackay Wilson, David, *Behind the Scenes in the Transvaal,* Cassell & Company (1901).

Mainwaring, A. E. and Romer, C. F., *The second battalion Royal Dublin Fusiliers in the South African War: with a description of the operations in the Aden hinterland,* A. L Humphries (1908).

Martin, F. X., (ed.) *The Irish Volunteers 1913–1915: Recollections and Documents*, Irish Academic Press (2013).

McCoole, Sinéad, *Easter Widows: Seven Irish Women who Lived in the Shadow of the 1916 Rising.*, Transworld Ireland (2014).

McCracken, Donal P., *Forgotten Protest: Ireland and the Anglo-Boer War,* Ulster Historical Foundation (2003 edition).

McCracken, Donal P., *MacBride's Brigade: Irish Commandos in the Anglo-Boer War,* Four Courts Press (1999).

McGee, Owen, *The IRB: The Irish Republican Brotherhood from the Land League to Sinn Féin,* Four Courts Press (2005).

Mitchell, Angus, *16 Lives: Roger Casement*, O'Brien Press (2013).

Mokae, Gomolemo, *Robert McBride: a Coloured Life,* Vista University (2004).

Moran, May, *Executed for Ireland: The Peter Moran* Story, Mercier Press (2010).

Morris, Catherine, *Alice Milligan and the Irish Cultural Revival,* Four Courts Press (2013).

Murray, *Christopher, Sean O'Casey: Writer at Work: A Biography,* Gill & Macmillan (2004).

Nic Dháibhéid, Caoimhe, *Seán MacBride: A Republican Life 1904–1946,* Liverpool University Press (2011).

O'Brien, William and Ryan, Desmond (eds.), *Devoy's Post Bag, 1871–1928,* Fallon (1948).

O'Leary, John, *Recollections of Fenians and Fenianism,* Downey & Co (1896).

O'Malley, Ernie, *On Another Man's Wound: A Personal History of Ireland's War of Independence,* Roberts Rinehart Publishers (1999 edition).

O'Sullivan, Michael, *Brendan Behan: A Life,* Roberts Rinehart (1999).

Pakenham, Thomas, *The Boer War,* Abacus (1991).

Pašeta, Senia, *Irish Nationalist Women, 1900–1918,* Cambridge University Press (2013).

Rafferty, Oliver, *Catholicism in Ulster, 1603–1983: An Interpretive History,* South Carolina Press (1994).

Ross, David A., *Critical Companion to William Butler Yeats, A Literary Reference to his Life and Work,* Facts on File (2009).

Ryan, Desmond, *The Fenian Chief: A Biography of James Stephens,* Hely Tom (1967).

Ryan, Mark, *Fenian Memories*, Gill & Son (1945).

Sinha, M. P., *W. B. Yeats: His Poetry and Politics,* Atlantic Publishers (2003).

Skinnider, Margaret, *Doing My Bit for Ireland,* Sinn Féin Centenaries Committee (2014 edition).

Spiers, Edward (ed.), *Letters from Ladysmith: Eyewitness Accounts from the South African War*, Jonathan Ball Publishers (2010).

Steele, Karen, *Maud Gonne: Irish Nationalist Writings 1895–1946*, Irish Academic Press (2004).

Valentine, Joseph, *The Myth of Manliness in Irish National Culture, 1880–1922*, University of Illinois (2011)

Ward, Margaret, *In Their Own Voice: Women and Irish Nationalism*, Attic Press (1995).

Ward, Margaret, *Maud Gonne: Ireland's Joan of Arc*, Pandora (1990).

Wheatcroft, Geoffrey, *The Randlords: The Men Who Made South Africa*, Weidenfeld & Nicholson (1993).

Yeats, William Butler, *Autobiographies*, Gill & Macmillan (1955 edition).

Young, Ella, *Flowering Dusk: Things Remembered Accurately and Inaccurately*, Longmans, Green and Company (1945).

Index

D

E

F

G

H

I

16 LIVES

The Easter Rising of 1916 was an attempt by armed revolutionaries to overthrow British rule in Ireland. A small group of Irishmen and Irishwomen seized key buildings in Dublin and fought a pitched battle with British soldiers for one week. The execution of sixteen men awakened a generation to the cause of Irish freedom.

16 Lives will record the full story of those executed leaders …

16LIVES
John O'Callaghan

16LIVES
Mary Gallagher

16LIVES
EDWARD DALY

16LIVES
JAMES CONNOLLY
Lorcan Collins

16LIVES

16LIVES
MICHAEL MALLIN

16LIVES
ROGER CASEMENT
Angus Mitchell

16LIVES
SEÁN HEUSTON

16LIVES
SEÁN MACDIARMADA
Brian Feeney

16LIVES
THOMAS CLARKE
Helen Litton

16LIVES
THOMAS MACDONAGH
Shane Kenna

16LIVES